FEAR: CRITICAL GEOPOLITICS
AND EVERYDAY LIFE

Re-materialising Cultural Geography

Dr Mark Boyle, Department of Geography, University of Strathclyde, UK, and Professor Donald Mitchell, Maxwell School, Syracuse University, USA

Nearly 25 years have elapsed since Peter Jackson's seminal call to integrate cultural geography back into the heart of social geography. During this time, a wealth of research has been published which has improved our understanding of how culture both plays a part in, and in turn, is shaped by social relations based on class, gender, race, ethicity, nationality, disability, age, sexuality and so on. In spite of the achievements of this mountain of scholarship, the task of grounding culture in its proper social contexts remains in its infancy. This series therefore seeks to promote the continued significance of exploring the dialectical relations which exist between culture, social relations and space and place. Its overall aim is to make a contribution to the consolidation, development and promotion of the ongoing project of re-materialising cultural geography.

Fear: Critical Geopolitics and Everyday Life

Edited by

RACHEL PAIN
Durham University, UK

SUSAN J. SMITH
Durham University, UK

LONDON AND NEW YORK

First published 2008 by Ashgate Publishing

Published 2016 by Routledge
2 Park Square, Milton Park, Abingdon, Oxfordshire OX14 4RN
711 Third Avenue, New York, NY 10017, USA

First issued in paperback 2016

Routledge is an imprint of the Taylor & Francis Group, an informa business

British Library Cataloguing in Publication Data
Fear : critical geopolitics and everyday life. -
 (Re-materialising cultural geography)
 1. Fear - Social aspects 2. Social psychology
 I. Pain, Rachel II. Smith, Susan, 1956-
 302.1'7

Library of Congress Cataloging-in-Publication Data
Fear : critical geopolitics and everyday life / edited by Rachel Pain and Susan J. Smith.
 p. cm.
 Includes index.
 ISBN: 978-0-7546-4966-3
 1. Fear. 2. Social psychology. I. Pain, Rachel. II. Smith, Susan, 1956-

 BF575.F2F395 2008
 152.4'6--dc22

2007037045

ISBN 13: 978-1-138-27148-7 (pbk)
ISBN 13: 978-0-7546-4966-3 (hbk)

Contents

List of Figures, Maps, Plates and Tables

Figures

Map

Plates

Tables

Notes on Contributors

Nadia Abu Zahra is a DPhil student in Geography at St Antony's College and the Oxford University Centre for the Environment, UK. She has guest edited the journal *Practicing Anthropology*, contributed to an anthology against the war in Iraq by Clergy Against Nuclear Arms, and written on development, education, environmental issues, and human rights. She has a chapter in *War, Citizenship, Territory* and also in a book on state terrorism.

Catherine Louise Alexander is a Research Associate in Human Geography, University of Durham, UK. Catherine's research interests focus on youth identities, everyday hopes/fears and intergenerational geographies. Catherine is currently developing her profile as a social geographer and writing for publication in a variety of sources, whilst working part time on her PhD 'Rumour, Fear and Everyday Urban Lives'.

Kye Askins is a Lecturer in Human Geography at Northumbria University, UK, having completed her PhD research, from which her chapter is drawn, at the University of Durham. Alongside teaching (and being a parent) she is currently conducting longitudinal research exploring the 'place' and 'placing' of refugees and asylum seekers in Byker, Newcastle-upon-Tyne. She is a keen walker (see www.northumbria.ac.uk/mywalks) and enjoys visiting family and friends around the world, but is becoming increasingly concerned about her carbon footprint so intending to spend more and more time on public transport in England.

Deborah Cowen is Assistant Professor in the Department of Geography at the University of Toronto, Canada. She is the author of *Military Workfare: The Soldier and Social Citizenship in Canada* (University of Toronto Press, forthcoming), and is co-editor, with Emily Gilbert, of *War, Citizenship, Territory* (Routledge, forthcoming). She has published her work on war, citizenship, and cities in various edited collections and journals.

Emily Gilbert is Associate Professor in the Program in Canadian Studies and the Department of Geography at the University of Toronto, Canada. She is co-editor, with Eric Helleiner, of *Nation-States and Money: The Past, Present and Future of National Currencies* (Routledge, 1999) and, with Deborah Cowen, of *War, Citizenship, Territory* (Routledge, forthcoming). She has published on issues relating to territoriality, the economy, citizenship, and security.

Michael Haldrup is a Senior Lecturer, Department of Geography and International Development Studies, Roskilde University, Denmark. His research and publications are on place identity, everyday life and tourism. He co-authored *Performing Tourist Places* (Ashgate, 2004).

Peter E. Hopkins is a Lecturer in Social Geography, Newcastle University, UK. Peter is a social geographer with research interests focusing on urban geographies of race, ethnicity and religion, the geographies of Muslim identities, young people's geographies and qualitative methods. He is co-editor of *Geographies of Muslim Identities: Gender, Diaspora and Belonging* (Ashgate, 2007) and *Muslims in Britain: Race, Place and Identities* (Edinburgh University Press, 2008) and is preparing *Islam, Youth, Masculinity* (Edwin Mellen).

Kathrin Hörschelmann is a Lecturer in Human Geography, University of Durham, UK. Kathrin is a cultural geographer with research interests in globalisation and youth identity. She has published numerous articles in international journals, and is co-editor of *Spaces of Masculinities* (Routledge).

Henk van Houtum is an Associate Professor of Human Geography and Director of the Nijmegen Centre for Border Research, Radboud University Nijmegen, The Netherlands. Henk's current research is on the power and governance structures concerning borders, identities, migration and territory (see http://www.ru.nl/ncbr/hvh/). Henk is co-author of *Borders, Regions and People* (PION, 2000); *Routing Borders between Territories, Discourses and Practices* (Ashgate, 2003) and of *B/Ordering Space* (Ashgate, 2005) and is Editor of the *Journal of Borderlands Studies*.

Alan Ingram is a Lecturer in Geography, University College London, UK, is a political geographer with research interests in geopolitics, globalisation and security. He has written on post-Soviet Russian nationalism and geopolitical thought, and the new geopolitics of disease.

Cindi Katz is Professor of Geography at the Graduate Center of the City University of New York, USA. Her work concerns social reproduction and the production of space, place, and nature; children and the environment; and the consequences of global economic restructuring for everyday life. She recently completed two books on these themes: *Growing Up Global: Economic Restructuring and Children's Everyday Lives* (Minnesota UP, 2004) and *Life's Work*, co-edited with Sallie Marston and Katharyne Mitchell (Blackwell, 2004).

Lasse Koefoed is completing his PhD in Social and Cultural Geography, Roskilde University, Denmark. The major themes in his research are nationalism, globalization, post-colonialism, geopolitics, everyday life and narrative identity. He recently defended his PhD dissertation, 'Glokale Nationalismer' from the Department of Environmental, Social and Spatial Change.

Jo Little is Professor of Gender and Geography at the University of Exeter, UK. She is a rural geographer who has worked extensively on issues of gender and identity in rural communities. Her early work focused on women's employment in rural areas but more recently she has undertaken research on rural sexual identity and the performance of heterosexuality in the UK, New Zealand and Australia. Recent publications include *Gender and Rural Geography* (Prentice Hall, 2002) and *Critical Studies in Rural Gender Issues* (Ashgate, 2005).

Nick Megoran is a Lecturer in Geography at Newcastle University, UK. He studies the political geographies and geopolitics of post-Cold War inter-state relations. He is currently exploring this through research in two main areas. The first is the building of nation-states in modern Uzbekistan and Kyrgyzstan. The second is the role of religion (especially Christianity) in the so-called 'war on terror'.

Greg Noble is Associate Professor in Cultural Studies in the School of Humanities and Languages and a member of the Centre for Cultural Research at the University of Western Sydney, Australia. His research interests include: youth, ethnicity and identity; material culture and technology; and consumption, subjectivity and embodied practice. He has published widely on various topics and is co-author of *Cultures of Schooling* (Falmer, 1990), *Kebabs, Kids, Cops and Crime: Youth, Ethnicity and Crime* (Pluto, 2000) and *Bin Laden in the Suburbs: Criminalising the Arab Other* (Institute of Criminology, 2004).

Rachel Pain is a social geographer at the University of Durham, UK. Rachel's current participatory action research project with young people is examining everyday fears, migration and the 'war on terror', and is funded by a Philip Leverhulme Prize. She is co-author of *Introducing Social Geographies* (Arnold, 2001), co-editor of *Connecting People, Participation and Place: Participatory Action Research Approaches and Methods* (Routledge, 2007) and *Handbook of Social Geography* (Sage, 2008).

Roos Pijpers is an assistant professor at the Department of Human Geography and the Nijmegen Centre for Border Research, Radboud University Nijmegen, the Netherlands. She recently finished her dissertation, entitled 'Between Fear of Masses and Freedom of Movement: Migrant Flexwork in the Enlarged European Union' (PhD thesis, Nijmegen: Radboud University Nijmegen (2007)).

Scott Poynting is Professor of Sociology at School of Manchester Metropolitan University. His research focuses on the intersection of ethnicity, gender and class; education and inequality; racism; and the study of social movements. He is a co-author of *Cultures of Schooling* (Falmer, 1990), *Kebabs, Kids, Cops and Crime* (Pluto, 2000), *Bin Laden in the Suburbs* (Institute of Criminology, 2004) and *Ruling Class Men: Money, Sex, Power* (Peter Lang, 2006). He also co-edited *The Other Sydney* (2000) and *Outrageous: Moral Panics in Australia* (Australian Clearinghouse for Youth Studies, 2007).

Peter Shirlow is a Senior Lecturer in the School of Law at Queen's University Belfast. He is co-author (with Brendan Murtagh) of *Belfast: Segregation, Violence* *and the City* (Pluto Press, 2006). He has worked on the issue of violence and conflict transformation in Northern Ireland and has published work in various journals. He is presently working on the issue of criminalisation and former political prisoners and the transformation of republican and loyalist paramilitary groups.

Kirsten Simonsen is Professor in Social and Cultural Geography, Roskilde University, Denmark. Kirsten's research is based in a practice approach to human geography and comprises works on everyday life, urban culture, the body and conceptions of space and place. She has published numerous journal articles and recent books in English are edited volumes *Voices from the North* (with J. Öhman) and *Space Odysseys* (with J.O. Bærenholdt) (both Ashgate)

Susan J. Smith is Professor of Geography at Durham University, UK. Her work is centrally concerned with the problem of inequality and the pursuit of justice. Her research has focused on the affront of racism, the discriminatory nature of the health divide, the threat of crime, and the management of a wide range of social, financial and environmental risks. She was one of the first British social scientists to take fear and its effects seriously, and she has retained an active interest in this theme for nearly 20 years. Her books include *Crime, Space and Society* (Cambridge University Press, 1986), *The Politics of Race and Residence* (Polity Press, 1989), *Social Policy and Housing* (Macmillan, 1990), and *Children at Risk?* (Open University Press, 1995).

Sarah Wright is a Lecturer in Development Studies and Human Geography at the University of Newcastle, Australia where she teaches global poverty and critical development. She is a scholar/practitioner with many years experience working with community groups in the Philippines, Cuba, Australia and the United States. Her research interests are in critical development theory and practice, feminist theory, and social movements. Professionally, she has coordinated and conducted research for community and environmental groups including Greening Australia, the Mineral Policy Institute (Australia), MASIPAG (Farmer-Scientist Partnership for Development in the Philippines), and for the Food Gardener Education in Urban Havana Project (Cuba).

Acknowledgements

We would like to thank all those who attended the conference 'Fear: Critical Geopolitics and Everyday Life' in Durham, July 2005 for their contributions to the event which prompted this book. We are grateful to Valerie Rose and Carolyn Court at Ashgate for their support, and to Vic Jupp who provided invaluable editorial assistance. We acknowledge the support of an ESRC fellowship RES-051 27 0126 (Susan Smith), and a Philip Leverhulme Prize (Rachel Pain).

We are grateful to the following for granting permission:

Pion Limited, London, for permission to publish an abridged and updated version of 'The Critical Geopolitics of Danger in Uzbekistan and Kyrgyzstan' by Nick Megoran, first published in *Environment and Planning D: Society & Space*, 2005, 23, pp. 555–80.

Routledge, New York, for permission to publish an abridged version of 'Me and My Monkey: What's Hiding in the Security State' by Cindi Katz, first published as a chapter in Sorkin, M. (2007) *Indefensible Space: The Architecture of the National Insecurity State*.

Blackwell Publishing, Oxford, for permission to publish a reworked version of 'The European Union as a Gated Community: The Two-faced Border and Immigration Regime of the EU', by Henk Van Houtum and Roos Pijpers, first published in *Antipode*, 2007, 39, pp. 291–309.

Sarit Michaeli, B'tselem for an excerpt used in Chapter 13 from testimony 20030626 entitled: Zeita: Border Police officer forces man from 'Attil to commit sexual act with donkey, June 2003. Source: http://www.btselem.org/English/Testimonies/.

Machsom Watch for permission to reproduce Plates 13.1 and 13.6.

Neta Efroni for permission to reproduce Plates 13.2 and 13.3.

Horit Herman-Peled for permission to reproduce Plate 13.4.

Gustaf Hansson for permission to reproduce Plate 13.5.

The Asian Peasants Coalition for permission to reproduce Plate 16.1.

The Mosaic Partnership for permission to reproduce Plates 17.1–17.3.

Preface
Placing Terror Fears in Perspective

On 11 and 12 July 2005, we held a conference at Durham in the UK, at which some of the contributors to this book first presented their ideas. Like this book, the conference set out to examine fear, terrorism and security as just *one* pertinent set of issues of fear, amongst others, which needed critically evaluating and grounding. The aim throughout has been to place concerns about terror in perspective, rather than give them greater prominence – to buck the trend of what has become an increasingly appealing academic and popular discourse. Together, the range of contributions cover different fears in different places, highlight the unjust patterning and uneven visibility of people's fears, and place concerns about terror in perspective as one of many concerns in everyday life within twenty-first-century neoliberal geopolitical regimes.

The bombings on public transport in London on 7 July, four days before the conference began, shifted this emphasis somewhat. Our conference, which previously had seemed to the University public relations office less appealing than students' summer graduations, suddenly attracted intense interest from the national press and elsewhere. Rachel was interviewed about the fear which might result among the British population: 'I was asked to make predictions, not only about "how afraid will people now be?", but "how afraid *should* people be?" and "what should they really be afraid of?"' I felt a little coy: these are huge questions that demand an ability to prophesise on behalf of others. The issue of fear and the 'war on terror' brings issues of positioning to the fore: who could I, or anyone, speak for? Most importantly, whose fear are we talking about?"

Along similar lines, a wave of academic analysis has followed the World Trade Centre attacks in New York on 11 September 2001. While this event did present a turning point of sorts, it was not the dawn of a *new* era, either for the nexus of international relations and everyday life or for the spatial politics of fear. The historicised and ground-truthed accounts of fear which we present in this collection make the continuities clear. For the west, 11 September triggered a deepening of oppressive governance, an extension of regulation and curtailment of liberties, and an intensification of the racism and hate that certain groups already experienced in everyday life. For the other parts of the world too – places the US and Britain have since targeted with military interventions – the ramifications of terror can also be seen as having continuity with previous times. The aim of this book is to problematise and develop an agenda for understandings of fear through all of this, to examine geopolitical events through the prism of the emotional landscapes of everyday life, but ultimately to collapse the geopolitical and everyday as separate spheres of life. Analyses of post-11 September fears throw into sharp perspective the wider tendency to dualise the geopolitical and the everyday, scale them hierarchically, and lock them into a self-reproducing cycle of unease. We wanted to find a different way of understanding fear; one that would also provide a glimpse of its 'Other' – a geography of hope.

In developing this agenda, the book diverges considerably from terror fears alone. A small number of chapters take the 'war on terror' as their main focus; others examine some of its effects on marginalised groups; some draw parallels with other fears. Most focus on other fears entirely, and so together this collection demonstrates the variegated landscapes of fear which play out at the global and local levels simultaneously. Chapters are written from contexts including Palestine, Uzbekistan, the Philippines, Northern Ireland, Denmark, Australia, the UK and North America, and address fears connected to rural livelihoods, racism, crime, youth exclusion, health security, child safety, immigration and ethno-sectarianism. While emotions threaded through various terrorisms are here to stay (as they have been *there* for some time), they are often little more than a wrinkle in the emotional landscapes of everyday people and places. This collection begins to map a geography of fear which is much wider in scope than it was; it also shows that fear in the twenty-first century is diverse and multifaceted, situated and relational; and finally, and most importantly, it explains how these fears are contested, resisted, revised and in the end replaced by other ways of human being.

To my Dad, Arthur
It is, in the end, a book about hope!

(S.J.S.)

For my parents, with love and thanks

(R.P.)

Chapter 1

Fear: Critical Geopolitics and Everyday Life

Rachel Pain and Susan J. Smith

Introduction

Fear is on the up. It is the denouement of books diagnosing the ills of western society; the bread and butter of self-help manuals designed to effect a cure. Fear is written on the world, in lurid orange embossed letters, in sedate newspaper headers, embedded in memos, emblazoned on YouTube; it is written on the bodies that police dark corners, hide underground, that avoid, evade and evacuate multiple landscapes of risk. As the twenty-first century gathers momentum, fear is a motif for the human condition.

Fear cuts across the personal and societal, welfare and commerce, the emotive and the rational. Whether linked to scares about cot death, juvenile crime, internet porn, asylum, avian flu, or terrorism, the place of fear is as salient as material risk as a driver of political manoeuvring and a constraint on personal well-being. The turn to risk as a foundational state for civil society has saturated almost every aspect of our lives and times. Fear is deployed in the marketplace, as various threats are drawn into the development and advertising of new and old consumer goods – weapons; sports utility vehicles; child tracking devices; organic food. Moral panics about dangerous groups, places and behaviours inform policing and community safety policies, and within urban development unjust fortressing and surveillance strategies clash with rhetoric about inclusive and peopled cities (Gilling 1997; Garland 2001). Such exclusionary tensions and effects spill into everyday life, exacerbating social and spatial disparities, and contributing to the demonisation of those social groups who are at the sharp end of fear (Hopkins 2007; Shirlow and Pain 2003; Poynting et al. 2004).

There may have been a period in history when fear was restricted to real and imaginary risks in primarily local settings: but increasingly, risk and fear are experience, portrayed and discussed as globalised phenomena (Pain 2007), particularly since the onset of the 'war on terror'. There may be historical continuities in this 'new' geopolitics of fear; but it is more attention-grabbing now that it has ever been before, not least because it is so politically convenient. Bombarding the world with messages about new and renewed risks allows governments to capitalise on fears by governing through the beliefs, behaviours and assent of the 'neurotic citizen' (Isin 2004). Fear of terrorism and threats around the consequences of global population movements have, for example, been persuasive tools in the recent US and European national elections; and domestically, discourses of fear are now routinely utilised to legitimise more punitive justice, restrictions on workplace rights, and freedom of movement (Robin 2004).

What is perhaps most extraordinary is the extent to which the everyday – the feelings, experiences, practices and actions of people outside the realm of formal politics – has become so invisible in the flurry of interest in the globalised geopolitics of fear. Early work on fear of crime developed an empirical tradition which was almost exclusively 'bottom up', using local events and experiences to formulate theoretical and policy solutions to multifaceted lived experiences of risk. In contrast, empirical and conceptual work at the interfaces of geopolitical practice, public discourse and everyday life are relatively sparse. Instead there is an uneasy yet taken-for-granted assumption that fear-provoking incidents take place, and fear-inducing discourses are circulated, at one (global) scale/space, inducing people to become fearful at other (more local) sites. This received wisdom is, however, at odds with the recent 'emotional turn' in social and economic research which recognises the complexity, situatedness, sociality, embodied and – critically – constitutive qualities of emotional life. Fear does not pop out of the heavens and hover in the ether before blanketing itself across huge segments of cities and societies; it has to be lived and made. Its making may only in very small ways be about the 'large acts' of terror that are played, replayed, revisited and reconstituted on an almost daily basis in the press. And, as we shall see, it is just one of the emotional geographies at work in the world.

The aim of this book is to critique, disentangle and to an extent re-package the increasingly complex, too often taken-for-granted and rarely seriously unpacked engagement between geopolitics and everyday fears. It traces empirically, and accounts critically, for the inscription into lives, times and societies of everyday fears and practices as well as global discourses and events. How do global insecurities worm their way into everyday life? Where do they figure in local landscapes of risk? What do people do with them? What are the tangible threats to safety and well-being, outside of those fears of 'mainstream' society which grab the headlines, and what are the fears of those who are feared? And while fear may be part of the human condition, you only have to be alive to know it is not the only way of human being: so how does fear survive; can it be resisted; what processes of absorption, resistance or reformulation of fear are possible, and where do they come from? How are collective emotions mobilised to engage political action? How do these affect geopolitical relations and processes? Following these many threads into a network of politics, power, danger and damage, but encountering also hopes, dreams and the road to repair, the contributors to the book compare, contrast and, most importantly, strive to *connect* the themes of geopolitical and everyday fears in different national, cultural and local contexts.

The motivation for this new collection of essays is, then, our dissatisfaction with the way new accounts of the geopolitics of fear tend to fix the everyday in a hierarchical relationship with more global threats (and thus reproduce the problem they are identifying). While many of these accounts are critical of the state and its work, geopolitical events and processes are nonetheless positioned as leading and influencing what people feel in everyday life (Pain 2007). Our goal, and the impulse driving the chapters which follow, is to splice the two approaches together, to develop a spatial politics of fear that not only includes both, but finds ways to bring them together in one account (see Megoran 2005). This does, inevitably, build from the two strands to analysing fear which have been prominent in social science scholarship to date – the everyday and the geopolitical – but in the end it is an argument against their hitherto separated trajectories. Our point is that there are not two scales which inspire and address fear by variously *relating* to one another; rather there are assemblages of fear built, trained, embedded, woven, wired, nurtured and natured into the way specific times, places, and events work.

To develop this argument, we begin by setting out a problematic which, in our view, limits current understandings of fear. In this problematic, work on geopolitics of fear and work on fear in everyday life are disconnected. In the account that follows, we first address the conflicts and disunities that arise when viewing fear through these two alternate lenses. We then go on to set out a new way of envisioning fear. The argument we put forward, and go on to develop in the book, is that attending to the specific materialities, spatialities, experiences and practices of emotions in particular contexts is more enlightening than vague, utilitarian or hierarchically scaled conceptions of fear. We therefore conclude our overview by presenting an argument for rethinking the connectedness of global and everyday fears, through the lens and practice of moral and material geographies. The final paragraphs of the introduction scroll forwards to the chapters that follow, showing how, in their different ways, each helps to build on and advance this new agenda.

The Geopolitics of Fear is Everyday Life …

The literature as it stands contains both a 'top down' and a 'bottom' up take on fear: they look somewhat different, but in the end, we will argue, they are part of the same assemblage.

The first significant strand in the analysis of fear focuses upon everyday life. In this vein, research across the social sciences over more than three decades has emphasised the social and spatial constitution of the micropolitics of fear. Feminist scholars in sociology, criminology and human geography have been especially prominent here, seeking to draw out the way social politics become entwined with the particularities of place to produce emotional landscapes for marginalised groups (e.g. Day et al. 2003; Pain 2001; Smith 1989a; Stanko 1990; Valentine 1989). The emphasis in this literature has been on giving voice and credence to the fear-full experiences and practices of everyday life. Many scholars have therefore called for in-depth methodological approaches which allow for appreciation beyond the snapshot of doorstop survey. As a consequence, qualitative and ethnographic research, and, more recently, collaborative knowledge production, with fearful and feared communities, have become the norm (for example Loader et al. 1998;

Moser and McIlwaine 1999; Oslender 2007; Pain et al. 2007). Such research has therefore been a political project which involves exposing the partiality or irrelevance of the fears which tend to be publicised by the media or in safety guidance issued by the state. Instead, and alongside political activism, this body of research highlights two things.

First, there is strong relationship between marginality and fear, as the contours of anxiety within cities tend to follow topographies of inequality. Second, and more crucially still, this work points to an extensive catalogue of hidden harm in private and unpoliced spaces stemming from racist violence, domestic violence, child abuse, elder abuse, police brutality against the young, homeless and dispossessed, and latterly Islamophobia (see Section 3 in this volume). Exposing the fears of people who are sometimes more often constructed as fear-provoking in popular discourses has become a defining task in such work. The political bent, as well as the rootedness in experience, of many of these accounts resists presumption about the immutable passivity of fearful subjects, and highlights the many ways of nurturing resilience and resistance to fear.

The second key strand of research on fear concentrates on those political geographies of fear inspired by events which have global and national reach. In this literature fear is most often analysed as a tool of governance, legitimising national and international actions on terrorism, informing issues of national security, restricting immigration and so on. The focus of this literature is fear and the state, and so the emphasis is not so much upon the emotional or experiential aspects of fear for individuals or communities, but rather with the way fear inspires actions which regulate and manipulate everyday life (Robin 2004; Gregory and Pred 2007; Sparke 2007). The active agents here may be terrorists or insurgent groups, competing national regimes, or layers of domestic governance; the fears they inspire are communicated and mediated through the mass media, popular culture and policy-making. While this spiral of fear-making and fear-mongering is a longstanding area of interest, the conflict between the west and the middle east, and the rise of a terrorist threat against the west in the twenty-first century have meant a sharp rise in interest and expansion of analysis of these kinds of fear. Other concerns about 'global' risks such as disease or immigration have also heightened in recent years, and informed this rising sense of panic.

What is key here is not necessarily the newness of these 'world class' risks, but a gradual realisation of the globalisation of risk – an acknowledgement that perceived threats and dangers are much closer to the west than they used to be (and it is largely western *fears* that this literature is concerned with). Terrorism in response to American bombing in the Middle East, avian flu, the mass movement of people in response to humanitarian crises, the effects of pollution on climate change, all now mean that potential risk travels fast. Places are more intimately connected, and so too follows fear. Any illusion of security by distance has been shattered by the continuing compression of time-space. In this way, the attacks on the United States of 11 September 2001 acted to crystallise the emotional landscapes of the west which had been developing for some time. These fears, while we might think of them in some way as global, are inward-looking: terror and crisis affecting non-western countries does not provoke the same emotions in the west. One effect of the 'war on terror' has been to raise the prominence of the geopolitical almost beyond question, and submerge the everyday – what is actually going on with people's emotions has, by and large, been forgotten.

While these global and local bodies of work have tended to ignore each other, their subjects are clearly linked. Just as the accounts of everyday fear bind wider social and political structures into their explanations (for example, see Betsy Stanko's (1987, 134) insistence on 'what it means to be universally vulnerable, a subordinate, in a male-dominated society' in shaping women's fear), global fears are also inherently, already everyday in their manifestations (witness Corey Robin's (2004) account of the impacts on terror discourses on Muslim workers in the United States). Indeed there is a growing literature, particularly longstanding in feminist international relations, that embraces these dual engagements effectively, as we outline below. More broadly, the scaling of social and spatial phenomena – of which global/local and geopolitical/everyday are two examples – is now more widely recognised as an artificial, hierarchical and essentially political device. Marston et al.'s (2005) critique of the scalism implicit in the 'globe talk' of some political scientists has resonance here, where the global (as the large, structural, all-encompassing) is seen as a more pressing concern in analysis. It is not always acknowledged that grounding observations at this scale is one way of avoiding assumptions that are sometimes disturbing, and of developing notions of power as complex, dispersed and contested. But the geopolitical and the everyday are unequal partners on a slanted playing field, in academic as well as wider political domains. As Sharp (2007) describes, there is a continuing tendency for the insights of feminist theory and empirical work – and grounded accounts of the everyday, the embodied and the emotional – to be marginalised in the political sciences. In the same way, we suggest (see also Megoran 2005; and Megoran and Pain, in this volume), it is anomalous that longstanding critical scholarship on the fear of violence has, precisely *because* it is scholarship rooted in the practices of everyday life, barely been mentioned in recent interest in critical geopolitics of fear.

Before going on to set out a new way of envisioning fear, we want to elaborate on some of the disconnections that arise when viewing fear through these two alternate lenses. For us, it is not enough to identify the everyday and geopolitical components of fear as equal partners in producing or exchanging fear, like pieces of a jigsaw: there are problematics, discontinuities and disconnections that need to be addressed. Geopolitical and everyday accounts often do not map onto each other. Everyday accounts tend to suggest it is the same old longstanding local fears which are most prominent in people's lives, rather than fears about terrorism or new killer viruses: the new 'global' fears simply do not figure that highly in everyday lives (see Alexander in this volume), or else they have more indirect impacts, or affect marginalised groups rather than the wider population (see Hopkins and Smith, Noble and Poynting and Hörschelmann in this volume). So, while we go on argue that global fears are continually being materialised in a bid to ingrain them into everyday lives, everyday lives are often immersed in more pressing matters.

There is also a concern that analyses of fear as geopolitical sometimes inadvertently reproduce the very state metanarratives about fear they oppose, in failing to question who feels what (see Pain 2007, and in this volume). Further, geopolitical analysis sometimes ignores people and their power, or uses representations as a kind of proxy for people's feelings and actions; yet politics is also made up of actions and practices among ordinary people everyday. What of people's consciousness, criticality and resistance in the face of geopolitical discourses and events? Equally, there are limitations to approaches to fear that overemphasise the everyday and place the local merely as a blank canvas for empirical description of broader processes. Here too, agency becomes lost, and an inward-looking focus on experiences and practices becomes insulated from its political, social and cultural contexts at a time when fear is rapidly globalising.

Many of the contributors to this book address these disjunctures. They also identify a last crucial disconnection: namely that there seem few means of *connecting* the geopolitical and the everyday in convincing ways. We are quite ignorant of the movement of fear; how it circulates from global to local, or how it moves from discourses/events to the bodies and feelings of individuals.

A well-established feminist critique of critical geopolitics provides a starting point for a new kind of reconnection. In linking the global and the local/intimate, it offers a helpful structure for recognising the entanglement of fear as discursive/intended/manipulative with fear as it is made and played out in local lives. Feminists writing about global/everyday relations, such as Dowler and Sharp (2001), Hyndman (2003), Katz (2004) and Pratt and Rosner (2006) identify some principles for grounding our understanding. In proposing feminist interventions to geopolitical analysis, Dowler and Sharp (2001) make three suggestions which are very relevant to this discussion of fear.

First, they argue that we need to *embody* geopolitics, focusing on how particular bodies are used and represented, in evaluating discourses and in highlighting everyday experience. Feminist analyses have pointed to the ways women's bodies are caught up in international relations – as workers, victims, mothers – at everyday, and so unremarkable, levels (see Hyndman 2003). Secondly, Dowler and Sharp suggest we need to *locate* geopolitical analysis more clearly, to counter previous western (and predominantly white, middle class, male, adult) discourses. For us, this demands giving credence to the accounts of those who are (or who are labelled) fearful; making space for the voices of those at the sharp end of fear to challenge authoritative/expert accounts (see Askins, Pain, and Wright in this volume). Thirdly, we need to *ground* geopolitics and consider how international representations and processes work out in everyday life.

Various examples of recent feminist work make these connections and insist on a 'microscale' geopolitics of the everyday. A rich case in point is Katz's (2004) 'countertopography' of US and Sudanese childhoods in the context of global restructuring, in which she draws out the ways that processes at different scales, affecting what appear to be very different places, are connected. Such arguments apply as well to fear, as there are contiguous inter-relationships between global processes and local topographies of emotion. As Pratt and Rosner (2006) insist with their collection of feminist work on the intertwining of global and intimate relations, the disruption of grand narratives of global relations and the upending of hierarchies of space and scale are vital. Disturbing the scales of local and global altogether, rather than simply highlighting and reifying the local, is necessary if everyday practices and actions are not simply taken to 'confirm the force and inevitability of certain modes of global capitalist expansion' (Pratt and Rosner 2006, 16).

Building on some of these ideas, we go on to suggest two related conceptual mainstays for understanding fear as simultaneously everyday and geopolitical – remoralising and rematerialising fear. To develop these themes, we want to suggest a change of visual motif for the way global and local fears work. This shift is represented in Figure 1.1. The existing model for thinking about the geopolitics of fear, which we have outlined, can be visualised as in Figure 1.1a. Here the political and the everyday are represented as two distinct realms, fixed in a hierarchical relationship, with events at one scale directly *relating* to those at another, implying that global risks affect and shape the manifestation of local fear.

Figure 1.1b offers an alternative visual metaphor for the reconceptualisation of critical geopolitics and everyday life. It is a motif which removes the spatial hierarchy linking large-scale risks with localised anxieties. But it is not so much a 'flat ontology' of fear as a model for the structuring of fear into – and potentially out of – life itself.

Recognising this space of potential makes the concepts of Figure 1.1b more politically enabling and therefore more satisfactory intellectually than the literature to date. The figure is in the form of a double helix, borrowed of course from the structure of DNA, which contains the genetic instructions for life. It has two equivalent strands (geopolitics and everyday life) that wind into a single structure and form the building blocks of every assemblage of fear. The 'two strands' carry the same information and are bound together by numerous connectors (in DNA, hydrogen bonds pairing complementary bases). We could see these connections as events, encounters, movements, dialogues, actions, affects and things: the materials that connect and conjoin geopolitics and everyday life. But these engagements are fragile – in DNA, the hydrogen bonds unzip and rejoin; that is why, as a safeguard, the genetic information is duplicated on each strand. The breaks and discontinuities that occur – both randomly and in patterned ways – might represent the awkward, unfinished, disunited, conflicting nature of relations between the geopolitical and the everyday; but ultimately they are inter-reliant and complementary. Our argument is that it is these connections and disconnections which are not just new and interesting, but also politically enabling – it is in these connecting and dynamic spaces and things where the opportunities lie to resist, have dialogue, influence and act. So while there is an inevitability about the fearful human condition, this model holds out also a prospect of designing in other ways of human being. Fear and hope are two sides of a single coin; they cannot be uncoupled but one is often more visible than the other. A new visual motif for the way fear works and is materialised is one route to a more rounded experience of this janus-faced condition.

In the remainder of the chapter, we elaborate on how this newly envisioned relationship might be conceptualised. In particular, we suggest some ideas by which global fears might be grounded, and the scales of everyday and geopolitical at least partially dismantled.

> Fear is produced through national/global political events and actions

↓

> Fear is felt in everyday life

1.1a   A hierarchical view of fear

1.1b   The double helix. The parallel strands are geopolitics and everyday life, the connections the events, encounters, movements, dialogues, actions, affects and things that conjoin them

Figure 1.1   A visual motif for fear

What is 'Fear', Anyway?

A 'common sense' understanding of fear portrays it as an emotional response to a material threat. People are fearful of individuals, places, actions and events that have inflicted, or are very close to inflicting, physical or psychological harm on themselves or on the people and things they hold dear. This is akin to a 'medical model' of fear, which presumes that risks are objective, that they cause or pass on fear in the way a pathogen causes disease, and that the condition can be both prevented and cured by applying the appropriate formula. Avoiding, evading, or removing real risks is, for this model of life, a logical way to deal with such grounded and immediate fears.

Another way of understanding fear is to regard it as an emotional geography that has somehow acquired a life of its own; a condition that is only loosely related to material risks. Then the challenge becomes one of working out what inspires levels of fear that are disproportionate to real risks, and addressing them in the interests of arriving at a less anxious world. One of the most debated mechanisms this model draws into the amplification of fear is that of 'moral panic' in which media representations, criminal justice scapegoating, and policing crackdowns whip up a frenzy of societal outrage against criminalised people and places. One result is toughened sentencing; another is heightened fear (Hall et al. 1978)

Reputations have been made, revised and subdued by a longrunning debate around the 'old chestnut' of just what it is – reality, imagination or moral indignation – that inspires fear, and why. But it is a tired debate which does not take account of the way the world of fear has been changing, and in particular which sheds little light on the vexed question of how to apprehend simultaneously the global fears rewriting the landscape of international (and internal) relations, and the local lives whose fears have hitherto featured most prominently in conventional literatures around, for example, fear of crime, fear for children and fear of sexual predation. In an attempt to move understanding of fear forward through, within, and perhaps despite, the global/local paradox, we flesh out Figure 1.1b by suggesting two rather different ways into the geography of fear-full lives. We offer first a moral, and then a material take on what fear is and how it works.

Moral Geographies

First, we draw attention to what might be called the moral geographies of fear. Eschewing the narrow confines with which definitions of fear have been scientised or medicalised, this book is about fear as a condition constituted beyond the pathological or individual. Fear is a social or collective experience rather than an individual state. But it is more than this – it is also a morality play and a product of the power relations that shape the moral codes of everyday conduct as well as those of international affairs. Fear does not just involve a relationship between the individual and a variety of societal structures; it is embedded in a network of moral and political geographies.

We can illustrate this by fleshing out the operation of two linked practices: naming and privileging. The naming and privileging of certain styles of fear implies that one kind of (authoritarian) politics has a grip on the moral geography of anxiety. But wound into the spiral of authoritarian morality is an everyday morality which contains a more radical politics – a politics that can reshape and recast the landscape of fear, a way of going on that could and *should* be interrogated for what it tells us about the way people experience, handle and recast fear.

Naming Fear

How do we understand such a wide ranging term as 'fear', with its various nuances in meaning? The answer to this question is much more diverse than today's headlines might suggest. A glimpse into the debate over 'naming' is itself a stark reminder of the extent to which dominant discourses take for granted the privilege routinely afforded to some 'names' over others. So it is worth noting these three things.

First, some critics of 'the fear of crime' have argued that the concept has little meaning at all; that it is a tautological discourse whose circularity is broken when people who are asked about other emotional reactions to crime choose these over 'fear' (Ditton and Farrell 2000). Fear from this perspective is 'misnamed'; it captures a range of experiences about which rather little is known.

Second, at the same time, some of the earliest accounts of fear of assault put forward by feminist scholars and activists (for example Stanko 1987; Wise and Stanley 1987), while countering the dominant individuated image of 'fear' as a physical response to an immediate threat where the heart races, palms sweat and body shakes, also recast gendered fear as far more than isolated moments of affect. These fears were named to capture an ongoing malaise engendered by people's structured position in a hierarchy of power. The wealth of detailed evidence on which these ideas were based told of the ways in which harassment, discrimination and other everyday 'normalised' encounters feed into a generalised sense of insecurity. For these writers the peaks of fear may be created by the threat of sexual or domestic abuse, but the baseline never returns to zero; and the two were not extremes but fundamentally tied to women's (or other marginalised groups') social and political position.

Third, and intriguingly, later work has also questioned the apparent universalism of feminist analysis. Whose label is fear? Do we call it fear before we know it is fear, and is this disempowering – for example identifying women as eternal victims and denying them the possibility of challenging that status (Segal 1990)? Following a predominantly Anglo-American debate, Koskela's (1997) work in Finland raised new questions about the cultural specificity of this malaise of fear, as well as the possibilities of boldness and resistance (see also Pain (1995) on old age and fear).

Far more remains to be said about resistance and hope (see Wright in this volume). For the moment, we raise these questions. Does naming certain groups as fearful do them a disservice? Does it become difficult to escape these categorisations, which have also been convenient vehicles for further constraining participation in social life (Midwinter 1990; Stanko 1990; Valentine 1996)? For Muslims in North America and Europe during the 'war on terror', is there a danger that the allotment by critical researchers of 'fearful' in addition to 'feared' is not just a means of identifying oppression, but a way of further fixing marginality? And so on. In short, with naming fear comes a presumption about whose experience this is; a presumption about who could and should address fear and how. With the practice of naming comes the politics of privileging.

Privileging Fear

The question of who can and does name fear is answered partly by understanding whose voices, and whose labels, are privileged. Successive politicians have played to the 'fears' of middle class, white suburbanites, while validating and reinforcing them, and as explored elsewhere, some recent academic analyses do the same (Pain 2007). Terror fears, reflecting imaginary geographies of western countries as newly risky (Graham and Pred 2007; Katz 2007), are fears of the white, privileged and protected. Analyses of the privileged, such as Gleeson's (2003) account of suburban white Australia, are necessary, exposing exclusionary tensions and the living conditions of less privileged groups by default.

But it is often the quietest fears, holding apparently little political capital but having a more immediate materiality, which have the sharpest impacts (Shirlow and Pain 2003). While these impacts may not be headline seeking, they are moral practices which can have effects: which can jump from strand to strand in the assemblage of fear, potentially changing the way fearful lives are replicated for the future. A number of authors argue that there are, embedded in the conduct of everyday life – in ordinary people's hopes and fears, in the routines of human being, in the lay practices that make local geographies teem with life – normative themes that are too often overlooked by policy makers and academics alike (Sayer 2003; Smith 2005). In fact, lay practices can differ radically from political assumptions and predictions; they can – quietly, defiantly, routinely, inadvertently or in many other ways – help privilege different takes on fear, and shape different responses to it. If the world does work more in line with our connective model of fear assemblages (Figure 1.1b) rather than with the traditional hierarchical approach (Figure 1.1a), there is a moral prerogative to emphasise people's own accounts of the pattern of their emotional landscapes. Ordinary lives often hold the solution to some of the more intractable political problems.

Material Panic

Hitherto, the power relations of naming and privileging fear have been understood through the lens of moral panic. Understanding the way fear works has been about being able to see how isolated events of criminality and victimisation are drawn into a frenzy of demonisation and vulnerabilities, and thereby into a politics of repression. Moral panic is an appealing explanation for the way in which fear becomes detached from material risk and takes on a life of its own. But it presumes too much about the way people come to know about, and react, to risks and threat; it assigns too much power to a press whose content is as likely to be taken with a pinch of salt as it is to be believed. The notion of moral panic might be in line with the understanding of fear represented in Figure 1.1a, but our attempt to unsettle this model points to two other themes. Elaborating the assemblage model depicted in Figure 1.1b we suggest the practices of knowing and placing fear give it a materiality of its own. Fear is not an abstract moral panic; it is an increasingly ingrained material practice. The uneven materialisation of some versions of fear and fearfulness is what drive the politics of control that have so much currency today.

Knowing Fear

How do we know about fear? What frameworks of analysis apply, and what methods allow people to tell it? For a subject so complex, there has been heavy reliance on analysis of media representations and superficial surveys. Material risk is hard to know, as few of those most at risk from crime, abuse and harassment ever report their experiences, but it is downplayed or ignored in many accounts of fear of crime. However, a key theme for this book is the extent to which fear has a materiality of its own. Fears of all kinds are networked, hardwired and signposted into life in ways that variously alert, protect and control. Walk across any hotel lobby in a large US city today, and wait for the lift. There will be a sign warning you that there are carcinogens all around; you are there at your own risk. Walk through security in any UK airport: forget the metal objects that keep the electronic alarms beeping in the background, but remember to put toiletries into a clear plastic bag. That is a material reminder of one airport bomb scare; others will leave different traces. They too will be written onto the innocent bodies that move across borders, and will be carried with them as they travel through space and time (see Abu Zhara, and Van Houtum and Pijpers, in this volume). Fear has a creeping materiality that pervades, constitutes, and binds together the ostensibly separate spheres of geopolitical and everyday life (Figure 1.1). Even though 'real' risks are unknowable and may seem remote, the fear they inspire gains momentum at it is materialised at every turn and in every body.

Placing Fear

Imaginaries of fear have always been spatialised: located in certain places rather than others. The ways in which fear is materialised and embodied brings these spatialities to life. In mainstream accounts of fear, in the discipline of criminology and the public policies it services (see Figure 1.1a), imaginary geographies of fear have been encouraged by the focus on fear, crime and violence almost exclusively as problems of public space and strangers (Stanko 1987; Pain 2000). Fear is viewed as a problem of city centres, urban streets and parks, rather than homes, semi-private spaces and people who are acquaintances or relatives. If fear is reduced by reducing risks, then the fact that most attempts at resolving fear are situational and limited to public space is problematic (Gilling 1997).

Yet tackling 'the wrong kind of fear' is still high on the agenda. And this is because these fears acquire a materiality, a facticity, of their own. What may begin as immaterial fears become materialised, for example through the safety industry which supplies technologies of surveillance and defence, supposedly to keep fears at bay, but, as Katz in this volume argues, they create more largely unnecessary concern. Elsewhere Katz (2007) suggests that terror fears have become a normalised part of the material urban environment in the US, as the presence of armed soldiers guarding bridges and streets no longer merits attention. Again, how much protection these materialisations of fear provide is dubious; but they can instil as well as reflect fear, allowing remote global fears to creep into our subconscious minds and rountised actions alongside those everyday fears we already know about and experience. Another example, the growth in popularity and marketing of sports utility vehicles as supposedly capable of keeping our (though not other) families safe (Lauer 2005), underlines that the materialisation of fear does not just lead to a changing landscape for all, but reflects a sharply unequal distribution of fear, privilege and risk.

Bodies are drawn into this unequal materialisation of fear too: certain people are more or less feared in different places and times, partly depending on bodily markers, and this profoundly affects their own feelings of security, as Hopkins (2004, 2007) has described in relation to young Muslim men. While fear as part of everyday life in poorer, riskier countries is more seldom mentioned (though see Abu Zhara, Megoran, and Wright in this volume), Hyndman (2003) has drawn a powerful contrast between the portrayal of women's and children's bodies in the 11 September attacks and the attacks on Afghanistan which followed.

Recognising the materiality of fear means that there are tracks and traces between the different lives of those who seek to control fear and those whose lives are pervaded by it. It is possible to follow the materialisation of certain fears into local landscapes; and it is important to show how everyday practices might be inspired by this, might tolerate it, could ignore it, will certainly pose alternatives, and may well have other, more pressing, 'things' to contend with – other materialities which could and perhaps should be privileged over the dominant manifestation of fear

Summary

So the moral and material geographies of fear are simultaneously about the ordinary social geographies of everyday life and about the extraordinary (exceptional) geopolitics of the twenty-first century. We have argued that it is time to shift the emphasis from authoritative, remote, top-down models of fear to more nuanced and grounded approaches. But more than this, the book aims to highlight entwined nature of globalised fears and the processes underlying them; to work with the immediate local everyday fears that are already there;

and to stimulate further thought about their connections and relationships with the wider world.

While it is increasingly acknowledged that political violences and fears are expressed in everyday and intimate spaces (Gregory and Pred 2007: 6), for us the task goes well beyond simply expanding the spaces and scales under consideration when charting the way politics has its effects. Indeed we make the case for rupturing the very idea of these spaces and scales, because they tend to fix commanding notions about emotions, power, human agency and being. Instead, we have suggested a new motif to account for fear – a figure in which geopolitical and everyday processes, events and actions are interwined, building assemblages of fear that are trained, embedded, woven, wired, nurtured and natured into the way specific times, places, and events work. In particular we want to underline the fact that the everyday always and already speaks back, resists, and changes seemingly immutable forces. Reimagining, indeed remaking, the nexus of geopolitical and everyday fears in this way opens up the possibilities for change: in that sense it is an empowering and enabling model of fear potentially resistant to political attempts to manipulate people's emotions. At the same time, it holds out the prospect of 'scaling up' the materialities of fear: small acts and practices can make a difference; the materialities of local geographies can find their way into the circuits of high politics. While materialising fear is substantially a bid to get a particular version of global politics ingrained into the everyday; there is no reason why it cannot also be about the way particular versions of everyday life travel into the geopolitics of fear.

The Contents of the Book

Taken as a whole, the chapters which follow identify the ways in which fear may be manufactured and manipulated for political purposes, and chart the association of fear discourses with particular spaces, times and sets of geopolitical relations. They relate fear closely to political, economic and social marginalisation at different scales, and explore the more complex social identities of which fear becomes a part. They highlight the importance and sometimes unpredictability of lived experiences of fear: the many ways in which fear is made sense of, managed and reshaped in particular contexts. People's emotional reactions to risk of course go much further than fear, encompassing anxiety, anger, boldness, hope, and so on. People's capacity to resist and act on their fears, rather than passively experiencing them, and the role of emotions in galvanizing this action, resurface as strong themes throughout the book.

The contributors were not asked to contribute uniformly to the model of everyday geopolitics we have mapped out here; some focus more on everyday lives, and some more on geopolitical relations and events. All draw out the connections between the two, some in more depth than others. Moreover, there are contrasts, collisions and controversies between the perspectives and arguments put forward in individual chapters. These point to the fractures in the materials of fear that might in the end open a window into other styles of human being.

The book is split into five sections. The first, 'State Fears and Popular Fears', offers different takes on the relationship. Nick Megoran demonstrates that a fuller understanding of fear must locate it both in geopolitical discourse and popular culture. He describes how politicians and popular culture in Uzbekistan draw on an 'ever-present and all-pervading sense of territorialised danger'. He illustrates the importance of geography to how fear works out: fear discourses play out in different sites, and people's response to them is embodied, blurring the distinction between the political and the personal and underlining the uniqueness of each national context. Catherine Alexander offers a local, grounded account of how fear of young people, and young people's own fears, construct their citizenship in north east England. Working from a moral perspective that is closely attuned to young people's own perspectives, she identifies that many of their fears may be relatively mundane and deeply embedded in this particular local community, but at the same time closely connected to wider discourses about youth nationally. Deborah Cowen and Emily Gilbert focus on the crucial and underplayed ways in which geopolitics interplays with the private sphere. In examining how the US governs through fear, and governs as fear, they describe the centrality of the home and the familial as constructs in the ideological battles that have shaped domestic and foreign policy since 11 September. Cindi Katz explores one aspect of this relationship in more detail. Drawing parallels between parental hypervigilance and homeland security doctrines in twenty-first century US, she discusses how certain materialities – the technologies of fear – encourage us to focus on certain fears while avoiding attention to the more salient risks for children.

The second section, 'Fear of Nature and the Nature of Fear', comprises two chapters which explore ideas about 'natural' fear and fear of nature, in rather different ways. Alan Ingram shows how the re-emergence of infectious disease is being harnessed to a politics of international migration. The re-emergence of malaria, the re-internationalisation of TB, the spectre of new diseases from AIDs to Ebola, from SARS to MRSA, has whipped up a new style of panic and a new generation of politics. Ingram points to the awful irony that infectious disease are a major cause of human suffering and mortality (so should logically engender more fear and attract more attention than terrorism), but that recognising this is more likely to fuel a politics of conflict and control than a compassionate co-operation. Similar ambiguities in the way fear works, and in the networks of ideas, feelings and materials fear mobilises, are drawn out by Jo Little in her discussion of the way ideas and encounters with nature both buffer and mobilise fears of all kinds. Being in and of nature is a way of distancing certain people, places and ways of life from fearful things. It is in also, in some sense, a way of resisting, reworking and revising fear; about a way of human being that is not always inspired by and defined in relation to risk.

The four chapters in 'Encountering Fear and Otherness' offer different conceptual angles on the fears of the feared. All come to focus on the intensification of racist abuse in different western contexts, as terror fears overlay older insecurities and prejudices. Peter Hopkins and Susan Smith explore the recent recasting of relations of race and religion: how religion is becoming increasingly racialised and the politics of fear are rescaled. This, they argue, is causing more harm in everyday life and redefining and retrenching segregation in the west. Michael Haldrup, Lasse Koefoed and Kirsten Simonsen examine how racism and discrimination are enabled through the 'mooding' of Orientalist and hegemonic geopolitical discourses, which are resultingly '(re) produced and negotiated in banal, bodily and sensuous practices'. For Greg Noble and Scott Poynting too, it is not a generalised (and predominantly white) culture of fear we should be addressing, but specific material experiences of threat that are racialised. They identify how the 'little things' of uncivil behaviour from neighbours and police towards migrants to Australia 'disenfranchise them from full participation in spaces of local and national belonging'. Kathrin Hörschelmann also argues for the inclusion of everyday voices into our understanding of the geopolitics of fear. She challenges the common accusation that young people are disinterested in politics, or hold merely self-centred or insular fears. In fact, their concerns about the 'war on terror' include the safety of distant others in the countries the UK government has launched attacks on.

The fourth section, 'Regulating Fear', contains the most fully worked overview of how fear is powerfully inspired and manipulated in order to legitimise political strategies which, while ostensibly designed to tackle problems that might be real, do so in ways which have little effect on the lives of those at risk, yet do meet wider, unstated, political goals. See Smith (1989b) for a more general discussion of this style of politics. Henk van Houtum and Roos Pijpers elaborate this most explicitly, showing that what used to be thought of as 'Fortress Europe' operates more like a 'gated community'. Europe is not closed to immigration; it is closed to a certain type of immigrant, and the selectivity of this closure is policed by fear. Policing by fear is one of the most enduring themes in human life, especially at a time when political intent is not just represented in the bodies and actions of the police themselves and in the laws they enact, but in a host of linked materials: communications technologies, biometrics, and human documentation of all kinds. The material legitimation for a strategy of policing by fear is starkly set out by Nadia Abu Zhara in her moving account of the way the possession and dispossession of identity cards is routinely used to monitor the position, control the movement, and inhabit the personality of Palestinians in the West Bank and Gaza Strip. Finally in this section, Peter Shirlow focuses on the contested residential boundary between Catholics and Protestants in Belfast, Northern Ireland. It has been clear for decades that sharp patterns of social, spatial and behavioural separation in Belfast have to do with strategies of safekeeping: it is a defensive tactic as well as an expression of religious solidarity (Boal 1981). But times have changed for Northern Ireland, and it might be that this sets the scene for a less marked policing of boundaries along sectarian lines. Shirlow finds that an emerging mindset is not enough to unthread the fears that have materialised into the fabric of Protestant and Catholic neighbourhoods; the fears built into daily life have as much inertia as the landscape itself – they are part of the art and architecture of living, and changing these will take time.

In the last section, the three chapters discuss diverse fears, surrounding children in the west (Rachel Pain), farmers' livelihoods in the Philippines (Sarah Wright), and efforts to increase the access of black and minority ethnic groups to the

English countryside (Kye Askins). All relate everyday experiences of fear and insecurity to wider social and political discourses and events. They move beyond the analysis of fear, however, to emphasise how this particular emotion is bound up with others, and never passive. Rachel Pain emphasises resistance to global fear metanarratives, critiquing expert knowledge about fear for children's safety (e.g. 'paranoid parenting') that ignore children's own experiences and knowledge of risk. She argues that, in a similar way, expert accounts of terror fears are riddled with assumptions, and ignore people's subjective agency in assessing and dealing with fear. Sarah Wright emphasises hope, arguing that it always exists even in the most oppressive situations, particularly the global south, and is a radical response to fear that galvanizes and is generated through social action. Finally, Kye Askins emphasises social change, and maps out what she calls the possibilities for what she calls 'a transformative geopolitics'. We take up these three issues of resistance, hope and transformation in our Afterword.

Bibliography

Boal, F. (1981), 'Ethnic Residential Segregation, Ethnic Mixing and Resource Conflict: A study in Belfast, Northern Ireland', in C. Peach, V. Robinson and S.J. Smith (eds), *Ethnic Segregation in Cities* (London: Croom Helm), 235–51.

Day, K., Stump, C. and Carreon, D. (2003), 'Confrontation and Loss of Control: Masculinity and men's fear in public space', *Journal of Environmental Psychology* 23, 311–22.

Ditton, J. and Farrall, S. (2000), *The Fear of Crime* (Aldershot: Ashgate).

Dowler, L. and Sharp, J. (2001), 'A Feminist Geopolitics?', *Space and Polity* 5:3, 165–76.

Garland, D. (2001), *The Culture of Control: Crime and social order in contemporary society* (Chicago: University of Chicago Press).

Gilling, D. (1997), *Crime Prevention* (London: UCL Press).

Gleeson, B. (2003), 'What's Driving Suburban Australia? Fear in the Tank, Hope on the Horizon', *Dreams of Land: Griffith Review 2* Griffith University, Brisbane.

Gregory, D. and Pred A. (2007), *Violent Geographies: Fear, terror, and political violence* (New York: Routledge).

Griffin, S. (1986), *Rape: The politics of consciousness* (New York: Harper and Row).

Hall, S., Critcher, C., Jefferson, T., Clarke J. and Roberts, B. (1978), *Policing the Crisis: Mugging, the state, and law and order* (London: Macmillan).

Hopkins, P.E. (2004), 'Young Muslim Men in Scotland: Inclusions and exclusions', *Children's Geographies* 2:2, 257–72.

Hopkins, P.E. (2007), 'Global Events, National Politics, Local Lives: Young Muslim men in Scotland', *Environment and Planning A* 39:5, 1119–33.

Hyndman, J. (2003), 'Beyond Either/Or: A feminist analysis of September 11th', *ACME* 2:1, 1–13

Isin, E.F. (2004), 'The Neurotic Citizen', *Citizenship Studies* 8:3, 217–35.

Katz, C. (2004), *Growing Up Global: Economic restructuring and children's everyday lives* (Minneapolis, MN: University of Minnesota Press).

Katz, C. (2007), 'Banal Terrorism', in D. Gregory and A. Pred (eds), *Violent Geographies: Fear, terror, and political violence* (Routledge: New York).

Koskela, H. (1997), '"Bold Walk and Breakings": Women's spatial confidence versus fear of violence', *Gender, Place and Culture* 4:3, 301–19.

Lauer, J. (2005), 'Driven to Extremes: Fear of crime and the rise of the sport utility vehicle in the United States' *Crime, Media, Culture* 1:2, 149–68

Loader, I., Girling, E. and Sparks, R. (1998), 'Narratives of Decline: Youth, dis/order and community in an English "Middletown"', *British Journal of Criminology* 38:3, 388–403.

Marston, S., Jones, J. and Woodward, K. (2005), 'Human Geography without Scale' *Transactions of the Institute of British Geographers* 30, 416–32.

Megoran, N. (2005), 'The Critical Geopolitics of Danger in Uzbekistan and Kyrgyzstan' *Environment and Planning D: Society and Space*, 23, 555–80.

Midwinter, E. (1990), *The Old Order: Crime and older people* (London: Centre for Policy on Ageing).

Moser, C. and McIlwaine, C. (1999), 'Participatory Urban Appraisal and its Application for Research on Violence', *Environment and Urbanization* 11:2, 203–26.

Oslender, U. (2007), 'Spaces of Terror and Fear on Colombia's Pacific Coast: The armed conflict and forced displacement among black communities', in D. Gregory and A. Pred (eds), *Violent Geographies: Fear, terror, and political violence* (New York: Routledge), pp. 111–32.

Pain, R. (1995), 'Elderly Women and Fear of violent Crime: The least likely victims?', *British Journal of Criminology* 35:4, 584–98.

Pain, R. (2000), 'Place, Social Relations and the Fear of Crime: A review', *Progress in Human Geography* 24:3, 365–88.

Pain, R. (2001), 'Gender, Race, Age and Fear in the City', *Urban Studies* 38:5–6, 899–913.

Pain, R., Panelli, R., Kindon, S. and Little, J. (2007), 'Moments in Everyday/Distant Geopolitics: Young people's fears and hopes', unpublished paper.

Panelli, R., Little, J. and Kraack, A. (2004), 'A Community Issue? Rural Women's Feelings of Safety and Fear in New Zealand', *Gender Place and Culture* 11:3, 445–67.

Poynting, S., Noble, G., Tabar, P. and Collins, J. (2004), *Bin Laden in the Suburbs: Criminalising the Arab Other* (Sydney: Federation Press/Institute of Criminology).

Pratt, G. and Rosner, V. (2006), 'Introduction: The global and the intimate', *Women's Studies Quarterly* 34:1/2, 13–24.

Robin, C. (2004), *Fear: The history of a political idea* (Oxford: Oxford University Press).

Sayer, A. (2003), '(De)commodification, Consumer Culture and Moral Economy', *Environment and Planning D: Society and Space* 21: 341–57.

Segal, L. (1990), *Slow Motion: Changing masculinities, changing men* (London: Virago).

Sharp, J. (2007), 'Geography and Gender: Finding feminist political geographies', *Progress in Human Geography* 31:3, 381–8.

Shirlow, P. and Pain, R. (2003), 'Introduction: The geographies and politics of fear', *Capital and Class* 80, 1–12.

Smith, S.J. (1989a), 'Social Relations, Neighbourhood Structure, and the Fear of Crime in Britain' , in D. Evans and D. Herbert (eds), *The Geography of Crime* (London: Routledge).

Smith, S.J. (1989b), 'The Politics of Race and a New Segregationism', in J. Mohan (ed.), *The Political Geography of Contemporary Britain* (Basingstoke: Macmillan).

Smith, S.J. (2005), 'States, Markets and an Ethic of Care', *Political Geography* 24: 1–20.

Sparke, M. (2007), 'Geopolitical Fears, Geoeconomic Hopes, and the Responsibilities of Geography', *Annals of the Association of American Geographers* 97:2, 338–49.

Stanko, E.A. (1987), 'Typical Violence, Normal Precaution: Men, women and interpersonal violence in England, Wales, Scotland and the USA', in J. Hanmer and M. Maynard (eds), *Women, Violence and Social Control* (London: Macmillan).

Stanko, E. (1990), *Everyday Violence: Women's and men's experience of personal danger* (London: Pandora).

Valentine, G. (1989), 'The Geography of Women's Fear', *Area* 21:4, 385–90.

Valentine, G. (1996), 'Angels and Devils: Moral landscapes of childhood', *Environment and Planning D: Society and Space*, 14, 581–99.

Wise, S. and Stanley, L. (1987), *Georgie Porgie: Sexual harassment in everyday life* (London: Pandora Press).

SECTION 1

State Fears and Popular Fears

To begin, the four chapters from Nick Megoran, Catherine Alexander, Cindi Katz, and Deborah Cowen and Emily Gilbert meddle with the building blocks of a widely held scaffold for geopolitical analysis: the state and the popular. Critical scholars have been at pains to point out that geopolitical work is done through everyday popular texts, discourses, representations and practices, and they have mapped out a range of material sites through which this work is accomplished. In relation to fear, state/popular is a distinction which is at the heart of understandings of the geopolitics of fear: it turns attention to the way fears move from the state to become embedded within populations via popular culture, and it raises questions about how emotions, beliefs and actions might be manipulated in the process.

The four chapters here climb through this scaffold in very different ways, providing varied examples and some critique of it as a hierarchically-structured process of cause and effect. Nick Megoran offers an elegant account of the state/popular nexus in Uzbekistan, arguing that state-induced fear has a powerful hold over the population so that they accept state violence. He examines discourses of danger, which are strongly linked to nation-building and border concerns, across the sites of presidential speeches and books, news media and popular music and video.

Deborah Cowen and Emily Gilbert also examine the processes by which powerful political discourses become embedded in everyday life, reflecting security concerns in this case in the United States. Their original focus is on the domestic, recognising – as feminist scholars have emphasised – that this vital arena is intimately bound to politics, publics, and popular life, but reminding us that it is rarely considered as having a role in cementing geopolitical goals. In the republican government's ideological battle over terrorism, the use of domestic metaphors (such as 'homeland') and the appeal to domestic concerns about normative western family life strengthens discourses of 'us versus them'. Because such delineation is practically impossible, the net effect of this ultimately is to increase insecurity. Cowen and Gilbert argue powerfully that the 'war on terror' is a war to prevent and protect from fear, as well as a war on terrorism; but paradoxically, the Bush regime has also governed through terror.

Cindi Katz is also concerned with the effects of drawing everyday familial concerns into the wider project of national security. Shifting between the US-led 'war on terror' and what might seem much more mundane, domestic fears for children's safety (an intersection revisited in Section 5 of this volume by Pain), she discusses some worrying parallels. She argues that parental hypervigilance is reflected in and actioned through various materialities and technologies of fear as, in neoliberal capitalist economies, commerce closely follows (and hastens, and creates) these trends in societal concern. The resulting regulation through fear is based on scaremongering around unlikely events, based on a growing culture of distrust and blame, and is inward-looking and privilege-protecting. While the salient risks for children in neoliberal regimes (such as poverty, abuse, obesity) are ignored, 'home' and 'childhood' are remade through the security state and individual anxiety, further eroding children's rights and well-being.

One critique of the state/popular scaffold is its tendency to read off effects on society, human behaviour and feeling without interrogating the encounters and analyses of those who are involved. Catherine Alexander's contribution is all the more welcome, then, in placing the experiences and perspectives of groups of young people who are particularly marginalised as central to her analysis as well as to her methodological approach. She begins by stating that global fears appear relatively unimportant for these young people in their everyday lives in this part of north east England. She finds that everyday local and national discourses about youth, disorder and criminality have more immediate materiality and pertinence in shaping their emotional lives. Her concern is with the ways that these discourses, enacted in everyday life, construct and restrict citizenship for young people in this location.

The state/popular scaffold can also be problematic where it is cast as a one way process. Popular culture and everyday life are important and vibrant sites for resisting fear and the political discourses which are circulated through emotionally charged media. Alexander makes this clear with her young people's struggle, however limited, to retain a presence in spaces which are significant to them. Cowen and Gilbert document some of the explosive tensions and disagreements over current discourses about normative family life in the US. Some of Megoran's interviewees are cynical about government efforts to affect their emotions and allegiances. In some places more than others, such resistance can ill-afford to be too noisy, so there is a search for different means of expression, utilising new technologies such as blogs and sometimes finding audiences and engendering solidarity far outside the places they are generated.

Chapter 2

From Presidential Podiums to Pop Music: Everyday Discourses of Geopolitical Danger in Uzbekistan[1]

Nick Megoran

In June 2005, I visited the 'Sasyk' refugee camp in Kyrgyzstan's part of the Ferghana Valley (see Map 2.1). It was providing temporary shelter to some 400 men, women and children who had fled the violent quashing of an anti-government protest in the nearby Uzbekistani city of Andijon a month earlier. I interviewed some of the asylum seekers, who relayed harrowing accounts of events, claiming that unarmed civilians were targeted at close range by high calibre fire from military vehicles. Certainly, the asylum seekers downplayed the role of armed opponents of the regime in immediately precipitating the crisis by organising a jailbreak, murdering state officials, and seizing the local government administration.[2] Nonetheless, the vast majority of independent reports agree that most of those killed in the city were not armed and were not personally implicated in the anti-state violence (Human Rights Watch 2005).[3] In spite of this, it was striking how many Uzbeki citizens whom I spoke to approved of government actions against, as they saw it, 'terrorists'.[4] How can people who do not have a personal investment in the state take this line? This is of course a complicated question, but part of the answer lies in a sense of fear induced by the successful articulation of geopolitical discourses of danger.

This chapter is an attempt to explain why many people in Uzbekistan were so afraid of perceived threats to their country that they could readily countenance

1   This is an abridged and updated version of 'The Critical Geopolitics of Danger in Uzbekistan and Kyrgyzstan', first published in *Environment and Planning D: Society and Space*, 2005, 23, 555–80. Some of the material in this chapter is reproduced from that article by kind permission of Pion Limited, London.

2   For details see the book by the President of Uzbekistan himself (Karamov 2005).

3   For a perspective closer to that of the Uzbek government, see Akiner 2005.

4   This is an anecdotal observation and is by no means intended to claim that a certain proportion of the population unreservedly either supported or opposed the government response. Although research on this topic is practically extremely difficult, I suspect that the general public are increasingly more sceptical of government rhetoric. For more on this see Kendizor (2007).

the unprecedented state killing of large numbers of people. It suggests that the population of the Uzbek polity was animated by material, discursive and embodied practices that inculcated an extreme sense of fear through the articulation of an ever present and all-pervading sense of territorialised danger. A useful handle on this question can be grasped by drawing together work by political geographers on the production of discourses of danger by elites and in popular culture, and work by social geographers on the experience of fear in daily life.

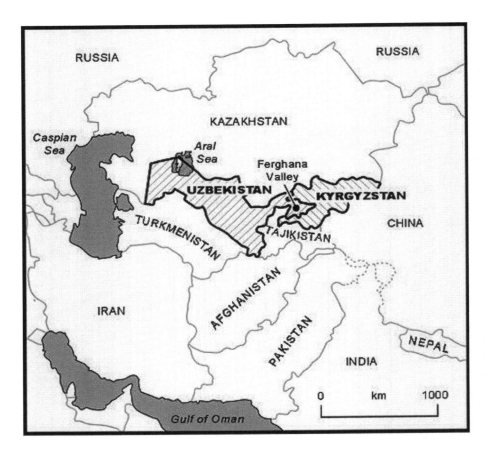

Map 2.1   Uzbekistan and Kyrgyzstan in Central Asia

Danger and Geopolitical Discourse

Danger is a core theme in international relations (IR) literature. In the paradigm of 'realism', students of IR have asked what dangers a state faces, and how these can be dealt with. This chapter, however, is located within an alternative theoretical paradigm, that of critical security studies and its geographical component, critical geopolitics. The main reference point of my work is David Campbell's provocative thesis about US identity, foreign policy and danger summed up in his insightful and influential book 'Writing Security'. He argues that foreign policy is not the external orientation of pre-established states with secure political identities, but rather a series of boundary-producing practices that are central to the constitution, production and maintenance of American political identity. Constituted through the logic of difference that constructs self in opposition to hostile other, he argues that, 'the texts that guided national security policy did more than simply offer strategic analyses of the 'reality' they confronted: they actively concerned themselves with the scripting of a particular American identity' (Campbell 1998, 31–2). This being so, the study of foreign policy becomes an investigation into how boundaries of self/other are discursively enacted and maintained through practices that depend upon identifying some 'danger' to the state.

However, critical security studies is not merely concerned with identity and the representation of danger as abstract notions. It emphasises that the successful specification of a threat allows a state to invoke extraordinary measures of control over its own population (Buzan et al. 1998, 207; Laustsen and Wæver 2000). As Rawnsley and Rawnsley argue, 'the threats from an external power are used more to secure *internal* benefits than *external security*' (Rawnsley and Rawnsley 2001, 10). Therefore, whereas realism takes the state as a given entity and asks 'how can it be secured?', critical security studies take 'discourses of insecurity' (Weldes et al. 1999) or 'representations of danger' and asks, 'what do they do, how do they work, and for whom?'

This theoretical framework is taken as the foundation for this chapter, although there are three ways in which it attempts to develop it.

Firstly, to avoid the danger of generalising, it is important to examine how the thesis works in other places than the North American and European contexts where it was devised. This approach has been profitably applied to a number of Asian contexts, including Sri Lanka (Krishna 1999) and Korea (Bleiker 2005) and here it will be used to extend work within this paradigm on Central Asia (Megoran 2004a; Thompson and Heathershw 2005).

Secondly, Campbell's thesis was narrowly focused on elite textual reproductions of discourses of danger. Sharp has argued that as these can commonly pass many 'ordinary' citizens by, their reproduction in the realm of popular culture also needs examining (Sharp 1996, 2000; Sharp et al. 2000). However, if discourses of danger are to be effective in inculcating fear, then it would be expected that they would be repeated in different sites. Rather than prioritising either elite or popular realms (as Campbell and Sharp do respectively), this chapter looks at the production and recycling of notions of danger in sites of both elite and popular discourses.

Thirdly, critical security studies has often obscured the lived experience of fear by those intended as the receivers of discourses of danger, the general public. Here, the work of social geographers using qualitative methods to understand how fear is experienced is important (Shirlow and Pain 2003). As I have argued elsewhere (Megoran 2004b, 2006), the crucial task, and that attempted by this book, is to understand the relationships between discourses of geopolitical danger *and* everyday lived experience – in a sense, to bring together the approaches represented by political and social geographers. Following some remarks about the current system of government in Uzbekistan, this chapter will consider three sites of the production and circulation of discourses of danger – presidential speeches and books, the news media, and popular music.

Authoritarianism in Uzbekistan

Uzbekistan is widely regarded as one of Asia's most authoritarian states. According to the UN and Amnesty International, torture is 'systematic'. Discriminatory arrests, incommunicado detention, harassment of relatives, show trials, severe prison sentences and public rallies to denounce 'enemies of the state' are all part of an ongoing campaign against anyone the government considers an actual or potential source of opposition. Human Rights Watch claimed there were 7,000 prisoners of conscience in Uzbekistani jails in 2003 (Human Rights Watch 2002). The Uzbek government itself defends its actions by arguing that a tough stance against 'Islamic extremists' and 'terrorists' is all that stands between the current system and Tajikistan-style 1990s instability or Afghanistan-style Taliban fundamentalism.

This campaign was predicated on and justified by the notion that the polity faced extreme danger. This sense of danger was inculcated in the population at large through its unremitting representation across a range of discursive sites. Three of these – the books of the president, the news media, and popular music – are examined here.

Discourses of Danger in Uzbekistan

Presidential

The first channel that inculcated a sense of extreme danger was the enforced study of the stream of books purportedly written by the president himself. Mass produced and sold at subsidised prices in bookshops and kiosks around the country, they form a compulsory course of study for all university students.

The importance of the social construction of danger for understanding Uzbekistan is highlighted by President Karimov's 1997 book *Uzbekistan on the Threshold of the Twenty-First Century* (Karimov 1997). Danger is at the heart of the President's analysis. Divided into two sections, part one is entitled 'Threats to Security' and is a dark litany of the 'problems, difficulties and trials' that Uzbekistan will face in attaining its historical destiny, including drugs and arms trafficking, religious extremism, terrorism, nuclear weapons manufacture, ecological dangers, nationalism, criminality and great power chauvinism. Although the 'ideology of national independence' is shaping citizens of high moral value and laying the foundations of a prosperous and happy state, this is threatened because 'Uzbekistan is encircled by countries burdened with ethnic, demographic, economic and other problems'. The President's book scripts a stark dualistic geography in the division of boundaries between a domain of freedom and a domain of danger, between an inside realm of community and an outside realm of anarchy. Danger was all around.

News Media[5]

Although widely available, the books and texts of President Karimov were only compulsory reading for students and a range of government employees and professionals. The same geopolitical visions were conveyed to a far wider audience through national news media, which essentially acted as government mouthpieces.

The news incessantly rehearsed two opposite images of place. Uzbekistan was framed as a site of prosperity, peace and happiness. The media constantly reported news about the latest achievements of Uzbek industry, health, art, sport, agriculture, architecture, intellectual and cultural life, and diplomacy. This image of happiness contrasted with the portrayal of neighbouring states as places of violence, poverty, unhappiness and greed. This has been a key justification both of the failure to introduce promised democratic reforms, and the decision to maintain tight control over the population.

But the official media did not merely picture two separate realms of happiness and sorrow; it continually suggested that the chaos and evil of its neighbours was threatening to engulf Uzbekistan, and the site where this conflict was being played out was the border. Media reports frequently cover the dramatic apprehension of dangerous people or illicit shipments into or out of the country. Throughout 1999 and 2000 the media carried repeated stories of terrorists / religious extremists / drug runners / smugglers apprehended as they engaged in, or prepared to perpetrate, some heinous crime. At the same time, the importance of the border defence forces were increased by institutional reforms. The particular grievances of political opponents of the regime were never discussed, nor was the poverty that forced many into smuggling as a way of survival – or, indeed, the murky connections between the security forces and smuggling (Megoran et al. 2005).

The binary geopolitical envisioning of Uzbekistan as a land of plenty and its neighbours as places of deprivation has thus been central to the legitimisation of authoritarian rule.

Popular Music

In recent years, geographers have increasingly recognised the importance of music as a medium for shaping cultural identities. Connel and Gibson insist that popular music is embedded in the creation and maintenance of nationhood, being an important cultural sphere where identities are affirmed, challenged and reconstructed (Connell and Gibson 2003).

---

5   For a fuller discussion of discourses of danger in the Uzbek news media, see Megoran 2005: especially 562–3.

In contemporary Uzbekistan the most influential form of popular culture is arguably music. As a result of both state sponsorship and the enormous appetite for music on the part of Uzbeks, the music scene in Uzbekistan is extremely vibrant. This reach has been exploited and deepened by the government to inculcate its project of national identity creation amongst young people. Structurally, the government has fashioned an environment that ensures maximum exposure of suitable music by creating a youth TV channel and obliging singers to perform songs that hymn the nation in order to obtain the precious licences to perform.[6]

The notion of the nation being under extreme danger is portrayed most clearly in the music of the group *Setora* (see Plate 2.1). A chic girl-band combining Uzbek rhythm with western rock and pop, they have been nicknamed 'the Spice Girls of Uzbekistan'. The video of one of their best-known song *Sen Borsan* ('You're there'), is a poignant depiction of the tragic end of a love affair between one of the young women (a university student) and her boyfriend (or husband?), a soldier. The video opens by cycling between scenes of a wicked-looking man restraining frightened children, the three young women in mourning, a military funeral, the handsome soldier on drill, and rose-tinted images of the lovers cavorting through a city and parks. This confusing medley is explained as the plot unfolds. The boyfriend is part of a unit of special forces that moves in on a derelict warehouse-industrial complex, where a helpless woman and children have been kidnapped by stereotypical 'Islamic terrorists', identified by malicious smiles, beards and Palestinian headscarves (Plate 2.2). The haunting music provides an atmospheric accompaniment to rising tension as rotating camera angles follow the soldiers as they close in on the terrorists, who are callously beating their petrified captives. These scenes are intermingled with further images of the happy young couple, playing in the snow or reading love letters in lectures, adding to the pathos when the inevitable tragedy occurs. The captives are eventually rescued and the terrorists overcome, but the hero dies in the firefight, gunned down by a terrorist at whom he does not return fire, apparently to avoid hitting a little girl held by a knife to her throat as a human shield. The video concludes with the girls singing beside his grave, remembering his handsome smile and the lost days of love, whilst another shot shows a liberated child roaming freely in the fresh air. At the same time as the release of *Sen Borsan*, Arslan reported the explosion of the phenomenon of army television programmes hosted by khaki-clad presenters sentimentalising military life (Arslan 2000).

This hit was followed by a song that gave historical depth to the idea of Uzbeks resisting the dangers of barbarism, *Ajdodlar Ruhi* ('Spirit of the Ancestors'). The video opens with the three women happening upon an unusual book in a library. Opening it up, a story comes alive. It is the tale of the invasion of what is

---

6   Kerstin Klenke, personal communication. For what may be the first detailed study of the politics of the production of contemporary Uzbek pop, see her forthcoming doctoral thesis. See also Klenke (2001). Cited with permission.

Plate 2.1   Uzbek music group *Setora*

**Plate 2.2   Dangerous terrorist: kidnapper of innocent children, from video of
Setora hit, *Sen Borsan***

now Uzbekistan by the Mongols.[7] The savage horsemen rudely interrupt scenes of pastoral bliss, sadistically massacring all present, with only three baby girls escaping with their lives. They grow up to become Amazon-type warriors, played by the three singers, who track down the Mongols and exact violent revenge in mortal combat, splattering the blood of their enemies all over the set (and here, parallels with Spice Girls videos become harder to sustain!).

The video concludes in modern-day Uzbekistan, with the three students paying homage at a new statue of Jamoluddin Manguberdi, who is claimed by President Karimov as a forerunner and model for modern Uzbekistan. After kneeling to lay flowers, the women look from the face of the statue through the crowd and see the handsome warrior Manguberdi who fought for them in the historical scenes, now standing amidst the people. As the music fades, text appears on the screen reminding the viewer that 'The homeland is as holy as a place of prayer' – the title of one of the President's books (Karimov 1995). Whilst Uzbekistan may still be threatened, the 'Spirit of the ancestors' endures, an abiding essence of Uzbekness calling the people to protect the beloved homeland from the evil foes that endanger it – and stressing the value of strong leadership.

Revill argues, against purely textual readings, that national music is far more than just a conveyor of the texts of patriotic ideology. Its sounds appear to speak to us directly, communicating through bodily involvement, 'the participatory imperative generated by its rhythmic and melodic qualities' (Revill 2000, 605; see also Anderson et al. 2005).

Uzbeks learn to dance as small children through communal rites of passage such as weddings, and people dance a lot – at discos, in schools and university dormitories, and parties of all kinds. In these contexts, the music of Setora and others is extraordinarily compulsive. An example is furnished by the words of one young Uzbek woman, exposed to an English-language intellectual milieu and fully aware of external criticisms of her state's national identity building project, who said to me at a party where Uzbek music was playing, 'Me and my friends know all this stuff is just propaganda: but when I hear it, I just can't stop myself dancing and feeling that I love Uzbekistan'.

These songs became diffused throughout Uzbek social life. 'Military-Patriotic Song festivals', where thousands of young Uzbeks wept with emotion at concerts as the patriotic songs were performed, were given wide coverage in the media (Megoran 2000). After becoming familiar with the video and live versions, it became impossible not to hear the haunting opening bars of *Sen Borsan* or the galloping stridency of *Adodlari Ruhi*, or to sing or dance along to the former, *without* remembering the threat of the bearded Islamic terrorist. In another example, a colleague of mine went to a 'Christmas–New Year' presentation in an Uzbek school. Children declaimed seasonal poems, and someone dressed up as *Qor Bobo,* a Father Christmas equivalent. The children performed both the Setora songs discussed above: in their version of *Sen Borsan,* little children with toy guns kidnapped poor old *Qor Bobo,* before being overcome by other children!

---

7   For a further discussion of this video, including the historical contradictions and ironies in it, see Martin 2001.

Thus through music, the Uzbek population – and particularly its youth – learned to dance to a geopolitical script that could be found in learned academic tones, the news media, the universities, and in discos and dining rooms across the state, binding the population together in a fearful experience of a nation in danger. This illustrates the contention of Ó Tuathail and Dalby that 'geopolitics saturates the everyday life of states', its sites of production being both multiple and pervasive (Ó Tuathail and Dalby 1998, 5). Furthermore, the unabated bombardment of public and private space with these discourses of danger enacted a notion of the correct historical identity of Uzbeks, and legitimised the role of the president as the moral guarantor of that order. It is no surprise, therefore, that so many people today should willingly accept the slaughter of their country-folk in the name of defeating an all-pervasive danger.

Conclusion

How is it that domestic populations will sometimes support severe curtailment of their civil liberties, and even harsh repression? This chapter has argued that part of the answer lies in the efficacy of the social circulation of discourses of danger. In the context of Uzbekistan, discursive constructions of danger were integral to the production and maintenance of the political identity of the state, and were intimately tied to the exercise of state power and the justification of political violence. Of course, this does not only apply to Uzbekistan. As Noam Chomsky has argued forcefully, the US government's exaggeration and misrepresentation of danger in the Cold War (Chomksy 1992) and the 'war on terror' (Chomsky 2004) underwrote the consolidation of hegemony through the manipulation of domestic politics and aggressive foreign policies.

The theoretical foundation of this study has been the approach of critical security studies (including critical geopolitics). I wish to conclude by suggesting three ways of developing this line of theorisation.

Firstly, it is important to test such theories in multiple contexts. My work argues here that Campbell's thesis works well for Uzbekistan, but elsewhere I have argued that it was less applicable to Kyrgyzstan at the same time (Megoran 2005). As the anthropologist Mary Douglas has reminded us, not all societies operate the same mechanisms of demonisation and exclusion (Douglas 1992), and we must be wary of re-inscribing them as inevitable conditions of social formation. It is important to carefully disaggregate the concept of danger in order to highlight its working in specific historical and geographical circumstances (Gold and Revill 2003) or, as Shirlow and Pain have argued, be sensitive to the fact that there is a *geography* as well as a politics of fear.

Secondly, scholars could profit by examining the reproduction of discourses of danger across a number of sites, and transcending the high politics / popular culture dualism that tends to characterise geographical work in this field.

Thirdly, paying attention to the 'reception' of discourse, by qualitative methods such as ethnography, focus-groups and performative studies of youth culture, to trace how fear is experienced by embodied individuals in everyday life, as they watch the television, dance, etc.

It is my belief that the interaction and collaboration of political and social geographers, enabling data collection using multiple techniques and analysis over multiple sites at different scales, would be a promising and exciting way to facilitate a more nuanced understanding of the role of geopolitics in everyday life. As the manipulation of danger to codify numerous power struggles as localised manifestations of a global 'war on terror' wreaks violence across the globe, this is an urgent and necessary task.

Bibliography

Akiner, S. (2005), *Violence in Andijan, 13 May 2005: An independent assessment* (Central Asia: Caucasus Institute Silk Road Studies Programme).

Anderson, B., Morton, F. and Revill, G. (2005), 'Practices of Music and Sound', *Social and Cultural Geography* 6, 639–44.

Arslan, C. (2000), 'Military Music Videos as Uzbek Pop Propaganda', *Central Asia-Caucasus Analyst* 5 July 2000, <http://www.cacianalyst.org>, accessed June 2003.

Bleiker, R. (2005), *Divided Korea: Toward a culture of reconciliation* (London: University of Minnesota Press).

Buzan, B., Wæver, O. and Wilde, J.D. (1998), *Security: A new framework for analysis* (London: Lynne Rienner).

Campbell, D. (1998), *Writing Security: United States foreign policy and the politics of identity* (Manchester: Manchester University Press).

Chomksy, N. (1992), *Deterring Democracy* (London: Vintage).

Chomsky, N. (2004), *Hegemony or Survival: America's Quest for global dominance* (London: Penguin).

Connell, J. and Gibson, C. (2003), *Sound Tracks: Popular music, identity and place* (London: Routledge).

Douglas, M. (1992), *Risk and Blame: Essays in Cultural Theory* (London: Routledge).

Gold J. and Revill, G. (2003), 'Exploring Landscapes of Fear: Marginality, spectacle and surveillance', *Capital and Class* 80, 27–50.

Human Rights Watch (2002), 'Religious Persecution of Independent Muslims in Uzbekistan from September 2001 to July 2002', <http://www.hrw.org> (home page), accessed June 2005.

Human Rights Watch (2005), '"Bullets were Falling like Rain": The Andijon Massacre, May 13, 2005', <www.hrw.org> (home page), accessed June 2005.

Karimov, I. (1995), *Vatan – Sajdagoh kabi Muqaddasdir (The Homeland is a Sacred as a Place of Prayer)* (Tashkent: O'zbekiston).

Karimov, I. (1997), *Uzbekistan on the Threshold of the Twenty-First Century* (Richmond: Curzon).

Karimov, I. (2005), *O'zbek Halqi Hech Qachon, Hech Kimga Qaram Bo'lmaidi (The Uzbek Nation Will Never be Dependent upon Anyone)* (Tashkent: O'zbekiston).

Kendizor, S. (2007), 'Poetry of Witness: Uzbek identity and the response to Andijon', *Central Asian Survey*, 26, 3, 317–34

Klenke, K. (2001), 'Eurasian Grooves: Popular music, identity, and politics in Uzbekistan', unpublished paper presented at *Ethnomusicological Research Seminar*, Goldsmiths College, London.

Krishna, S. (1999), *Postcolonial Insecurities: India, Sri Lanka, and the question of nationhood* (London: University of Minnesota Press).

Laustsen, C.B. and Wæver, O. (2000), 'In Defence of Religion: Sacred referent objects for securitization', *Millennium: Journal of International Studies* 29, 705–39.

Megoran, N. (2000), 'Batken Remembered: Militarism and pop concerts', *Eurasianet* 11/21/00, <http://www.eurasianet.org>, accessed June 2005.

Megoran, N. (2004a), 'The Critical Geopolitics of the Uzbekistan-Kyrgyzstan Ferghana Valley Boundary Dispute, 1999–2000', *Political Geography* 23, 731–64.

Megoran, N. (2004b), 'Review of P. Shirlow and R. Pain *The Geographies and Politics of Fear*', *Progress in Human Geography* 28, 413–14.

Megoran, N. (2005), 'The Critical Geopolitics of Danger in Uzbekistan and Kyrgyzstan', *Environment and Planning D: Society and Space* 23, 555–80.

Megoran, N. (2006), 'For Ethnography in Political Geography: Experiencing and re-imagining Ferghana Valley boundary closures', *Political Geography* 25, 622–40.

Megoran, N., Raballand, G. and Bouyjou, J. (2005), 'Performance, Representation, and the Economics of Border Control in Uzbekistan', *Geopolitics* 10, 712–42.

Ó Tuathail, G. and Dalby, S. (eds) (1998), *Rethinking Geopolitics* (London: Routledge).

Rawnsley, G. and Rawnsley, M.-Y. (2001), *Critical Security, Democratisation and Television in Taiwan* (Aldershot: Ashgate).

Revill, G. (2000), 'Music and the Politics of Sound: Nationalism, citizenship and auditory space', *Environment and Planning D: Society and Space* 18, 597–613.

Sharp, J. (1996), 'Hegemony, popular culture and geopolitics: the *Reader's Digest* and the construction of danger', *Political Geography* 15, 557–570.

Sharp, J. (2000), *Condensing the Cold War: Reader's Digest and American Identity* (London: University of Minnesota Press).

Sharp, J., Routledge, P., Philo, C. and Paddison, R. (2000), 'Entanglements of Power: Geographies of domination/resistance', 1–42 (London: Routledge).

Shirlow, P. and Pain, R. (2003), 'The Geographies and Politics of Fear', *Capital and Class* 80, 15–26.

Thompson, C. and Heathershaw, J. (eds) (2005), 'Discourses of Danger in Central Asia', *Central Asian Survey* 24, 1–96.

Weldes, J., Laffey, M., Gusterson, H. and Duvall, R. (1999), 'Introduction: Constructing insecurity', in J. Weldes, M. Laffey, H. Gusterson and R. Duvall (eds), *Cultures of Insecurity: States, communities and the production of danger*, Vol. 14 (London: University of Minnesota Press).

Chapter 3

'Growing Pains'? Fear, Exclusion and Citizenship in a Disadvantaged UK Neighbourhood

Catherine Louise Alexander

Introduction

Historically, fear of crime has been understood as a national problem, and in the current political climate there is increasing concern for the safety of the 'nation state' and its citizens. While the so-called 'war on terror' has changed the world in critical ways, the impacts of these changes are, arguably, felt most strongly at the local level. Drawing from research rooted in local lives, this chapter demonstrates that although global insecurities have exposed and heightened some young peoples' sense of fear, the most salient of these fears are embedded in threats other than terrorism, and encountered by young people within their everyday lives. Where the global and the local dimensions are linked, however, is through the ways in which fear mediates young people's experience of (and inclusion in) the entitlements and practices of citizenship. This chapter focuses specifically upon the local dynamics of these other fears, and their implications for the kinds of social participation upon which active citizenship depends.

While the politics of citizenship can take many different shapes, an early and key formulation stresses the basic right of citizens to participate fully in the life of the society in which they reside. This chapter utilises this social and democratic notion of citizenship, taken from the influential work of Marshall (1950), who insisted that 'citizen rights' refer not only to the political and civil rights embedded in national constitutions, but also to a spectrum of *social* rights. Marshall therefore made an analytical distinction between different kinds of rights, and drew attention to the possibility that the practices associated with them might shape social, economic and political organisation in different ways. This setting of *individuals* into a *structured* relationship with the state (in terms of the *de jure* entitlements of the public), which can be interrogated empirically (to monitor whether, and to whom, such rights are effectively available), is the platform on which the concept of citizenship in social democratic theory lays its credentials (Smith 1989).

Citizenship as critique regards civil, political and social rights as entitlements whose universality in a *de jure* as well as a *de facto* sense remains to be realised. It offers a comprehensive vehicle through which to explore systematic discrepancies between the obligations required of, and the rights extended to, members of a nation state. Enduring variations in the availability of these rights, or in the opportunities to exercise them effectively can thus be conceptualised as forces shaping or structuring society (this stands in contrast to the more usual view that citizenship rights play an integrative role). At the heart of this idea is that all those who are part of the 'community' of a given jurisdiction should be able to participate fully in the social, political and economic life of that community. People should be able to enjoy life, influence the future, and earn a living (Smith 1989).

One challenge that this body of writing has issued is that nation states do not equally extend these rights in a *de jure* sense to all residents (or to all bona fide citizens) of the jurisdiction. This was Pateman's (1976) point when she referred to the patriarchal nature of the social contracts of even the more welfare orientated societies. However, another challenge is that there are a range of more and less informal mechanisms, policies, processes and practices in societies that curb even those citizenship rights that people formally possess. These practices are happening on a daily basis and at the micro-scale, and this chapter argues that fear is one of the most powerful of these processes. Amongst the most affected, I argue, are young people living within economically deprived and stigmatised urban areas.

Pantazis (2000) has employed the notion of vulnerability to demonstrate that the poorest people in society suffer most, both from insecurities relating to crime and from situations including job loss, financial debt and illness. Young people living in economically deprived areas are amongst those hit hardest, often growing up without many home comforts, and lacking the physical, social and legal protection available to other groups marginalised from mainstream activities in urban areas. Widely reported to be more fearful than the rest of the population, and most affected by the impacts of fear (Borooah and Carcach 1997; Pain 2001; Gordon and Pantazis 1997), young people may be additionally burdened with having to put on a brave face and 'just get on with it'. In this way, fear exerts a particularly powerful influence over young people's lives. This chapter demonstrates some of the tangible ways in which fear compounds the exclusion already experienced by young people living within disadvantaged areas, undermining their basic entitlements to citizenship and preventing their full participation as active citizens.

Fenham – the 'Ghetto' of Newcastle upon Tyne?

Empirical findings are drawn from the pilot study of my larger doctoral research project, undertaken with young people from a disadvantaged part of Newcastle upon Tyne in northeast England. Fenham is a ward within the west end of the city, which has suffered long term social and economic deprivation. Traditionally one of the city's main immigrant reception areas, Fenham contains Newcastle's highest population of black and minority ethnic households, most predominantly of South Asian descent. The ward also supports a large youth population; but there is considerable tension between the local youth with fairly low levels of educational achievement and the high number of university students who live there. Having lived in the area for three years, I have observed that Fenham has a strong reputation in the city and is associated with anxiety and social decline. As a consequence of these stereotypes, Fenham residents may suffer considerably from the effects of this stigmatisation and prejudice (Alexander, forthcoming).

The data are drawn from research conducted with three youth groups within the area. Participatory diagramming techniques were used to generate group discussions, and to encourage the young people to suggest issues of relevance to the research (for details see Alexander et al., forthcoming). I carried out focus groups and individual interviews, together with more relaxed, informal conversations, to gain a deeper insight into how the young people felt about their neighbourhood. The research has now developed into a longer term, collaborative research project. The three groups involved were:

- a young men's group (aged 16 to 25). They played for the football team of a youth club in a particularly stigmatised part of the ward. They described how they spent most of their time hanging out either at the club, or on the streets, but generally they spent their time together 'there's always three or four of us aboot';
- a young women's group (aged 15 to 17). They were all (or had recently been) involved in the youth justice system. Their youth workers shared a particularly close relationship with the young women, and were actively encouraging them to get involved in a 'Giving Back' project designed to 'Make Fenham Better'. Like the young men, they spent most of their time together, hanging out at the club, or at home;
- a mixed group (aged 16 to 20). The club met weekly at a programme designed specifically for young people with learning difficulties. Their only contact with each other was at this supervised youth group.

Using the young people's own words and frameworks of understanding, this chapter presents an insight into the practices and politics of fear affecting how these young people negotiate growing up and living in Fenham.

Fear (and Loathing) in the West End

Fear works in various ways within the neighbourhood, and is employed by a range of different groups to affect how young people act on a daily basis. One common theme was that the actions of the local police made them feel uncomfortable:

CA: I noticed a police car as I came into the estate ... do you often see the police around?

Joe[1]: Yeah, they're always round ...

---

1   All names in this chapter are pseudonyms for the young people who participated in my research.

CA:	Seeing them about a lot ... does that make you feel safe?
Mitch:	Nah man! They come round cos they're after us ... it's us they wanna catch!
Joe:	They're always following us around like, y'canna go nowhere w'out 'em following ...
Dave:	Ye'd think they'd have summat better t'do! (Men's football team, aged 16–25)

Their youth worker confirmed that the young men were routinely followed and questioned as they moved around the estate late at night. Yet this regular police patrolling does not appear to have installed any more of a sense of safety with the girls' group, who were even more suspicious of their presence:

CA:	Do you ever just hang out, and meet up on the neighbourhood?
Stace:	Nah. There's nee point. The lads just get mortal [drunk] ... or smoke tak [cannabis] ... that's when there's trouble...an' the police are always about, wantin' t'move you on. We always jus' hang out at Michelle's, watchin' tele' or havin' a drink. There's nee point gannin' [going] out anywhere, y'just get hassle ...
CA:	The police hassle you?
Stace:	Yeah. Especially Carly. She's always getting hassled
Jo:	The police won't leave her alone ... they're always drivin' round looking for her. The other day, she was at *a bus stop* she was, y'know, *waiting for the bus* and they arrested her. It's ridiculous man, she was waitin' for a bus! (Women's youth group, aged 15–17)

It would seem that in Fenham, as elsewhere, young people are subjected to pervasive levels of surveillance by the police, to enhance the feelings of safety and reduce the fear of crime of other local residents (Noaks 2004). This sense of security for the majority is 'premised on a targeting of the behaviour of minorities, thereby potentially reinforcing marginalisation effects and serving to exacerbate social and spatial exclusion' (Loader 1999, 384). Indeed, the level of targeting, harassment and victimisation by the police seemed to be even more pronounced within the girls' group. One particularly upsetting incident involved two police officers using heavy-handed measures to arrest a 15-year-old girl:

| Youth worker: | It's not on, like. She's only a four-foot-odd lass! How old were you, Carly, 15? To be fair you weren't holdin' your hands up and coming easily, but still! Two grown men jumpin' her, pushin' her to the floor an' then kickin' her and punching her in the face – that's not on. Y'can restrain a young girl wi'out usin' that kind of force ... |
| Carly: | I, had t'push meself forwards, like, cos my face was ganna smash onto the road, like, but instead I landed here (*lifts up top to show bruising*) I broke two ribs – it's still not right now, an' that were two month ago. (Women's youth group, aged 15–17) |

The young women's group voiced considerable anxieties about being arrested by the police for 'nee reason'. In group discussions, they talked about the ways in which the atmosphere of the area had changed, and that the increased police presence meant they no longer wanted to 'hang aboot' the local school or playground – instead they stayed at home to avoid confrontation. These young girls' narratives describe how they are actively discouraged from (and had modified their behaviour to avoid) socialising. Such moderations to their everyday lives have significant consequences for their basic civil rights, through affecting their self-esteem, confidence and general motivation to move about and make use of the neighbourhood in the ways that they would normally prefer to do.

Fear of being watched, bullied, moved on or hassled also worked to limit the social participation of the young people with learning difficulties, perhaps in even more pronounced ways:

CA:	So how d'ya feel on the walk home from school?
Mary:	Ya canna walk past the park, cos the high school kids pick on us.
Jim:	Y'gotta be careful not to look'em in the eye
Lisa:	Me Mam won't let me walk yem [home], I have to get a taxi to school and back every day.
Linda:	I can't go nowhere cos of my bullies.
CA:	Your bullies ...?
Linda:	My bullies follow me around everywhere. They call me names and try to beat me up. I canna dee nowt. Only place they canna get me is in here. (Mixed youth group with learning difficulties, aged 16–20)

The individuals' narratives told how verbal bullying had left these young people feeling very unsure of themselves. In particular, the torrent of abuse that Linda (16) had faced from a group of young people at school had provoked her to tear her hair out. This made matters much worse, as 'her bullies' targeted her all the more on account of her baldness. Linda told how she was unable to go to college, as one of 'ma bullies gans [goes] there' and since her learning difficulties prevented her from getting a job, her parents felt that the only option available to her was to stay at home all day. Like Linda, all the individuals in this group described various ways in which they had suffered relentlessly over time; and they overwhelmingly agreed that their general sense of wellbeing was controlled by the actions of other young people in her area. I had to reconcile myself to the fact that some young people in my other two research groups may have been party to the abuse that their particularly vulnerable peers have endured for some time.

Evidence is mounting of the proliferation of risks similar to those described by these young people. Violence and harassment that are specific to certain groups (for example based on physical and mental abilities, gender, sexual preference, age and ethnic groups) are a significant dimension of oppression, and have been labelled 'systemic violence' (Young 1990). Those who feel at risk may experience particular spaces as threatening, and the resulting restrictions, segregations and isolation play an important role in maintaining the social and spatial order of the city (Pain 2000). Avoidance strategies were even more pronounced in the group of young people with learning difficulties. They were by far the most fearful of the three groups, and described incidents which suggest their fears are well founded:

CA:	So what do you get up to on a night time?
Mary:	I just stay in.
CA:	Why is that?
Jim:	Y'canna gan out [go out] at night, y'get hassled off the Charvers and Ragies[2] ... they're really scary like ... and the scooters always whizzing past, they'd knock y'down, like
Lisa:	Me Mam used to let me walk home ... until the kids from the high school started on me ... they tore my school bag and punched me in the head. I thought I was gonna die ... it was awful. (Mixed youth group with learning difficulties, aged 16–20)

What might be regarded as a reasonably safe place during the daylight hours becomes a 'no go' zone after dark. The group told of being particularly afraid of 'local gangs' late at night. Overall, for these young people with learning difficulties, fear acts to limit where they feel safe to go. Taken together with the heavy supervision they received from their parents and guardians, these young people in particular endured a myriad of frustrations at having no say in, nor any control over, what they do on a day to day basis.

While there are certainly many problems in these socially and materially deprived neighbourhoods, the media rarely comments on the positive aspects of life. Instead, reports seem to reflect a pervasive sense of fear, which is heightened by a contemporary political agenda that stresses the need for 'tough on crime responses'. Far from accurately capturing the complex, multiple realities of peoples' experiences in the west end of Newcastle, the local media contribute to a broader discourse which positions certain suburbs and their residents as 'yobs', 'criminal' or 'antisocial'.

Jackie:	It were in the Chronicle 'n'all ... when Carly were arrested ... they're all jus' waitin' for her to put a foot wrong ...
Mandy:	'Local yob' was that what they called her? They had this photo of her, made her out to be a right chav [see fn 2]. She's givin' the finger ...
CA:	In the photo?
Mandy:	Yeah, but that was taken when she was *14*, it was in the paper from when she was sentenced ... it was a long time ago...she was just a kid y'know. She's grown up a lot since then, you'd neva see her do that now.
Jackie:	I didn't even recognise her in that photo, did I?!
Mandy:	Naw, I'know. But nee one's ever interested in our side of the story. It's pathetic man! (Women's youth group, aged 15–17)

The media reporting of the west end of Newcastle is part of the contextual backdrop against which to consider local people's heightened anxiety for their personal safety, as 'media representations of stigmatised suburbs can contribute

---

2   'Charver' (or 'Chav') and 'Ragie' are all derogatory slang terms in popular usage within northeast England. They refer to a subculture stereotype of a person who is uneducated, uncultured and prone to antisocial or immoral behaviour. The labels are typically applied by teenagers and young people towards white working-class or lower-middle-class residents living in and around their local areas.

to residents' fear of crime and its impact upon opportunities for social interaction' (Palmer et al. 2005). When they were younger, two of the girls involved in the youth justice system (Carly and Jackie) had committed several offences, and while their recent behaviour indicated a willingness to turn their lives around, they remained targeted by the media:

> Youth worker: Jackie was devastated by that piece. I've never seen her like that. Cried herself to sleep for nights – they just don't *think* about the effect these articles have on the kids – you were just a bairn when that was written! They forget you've got feelings too.
>
> Jackie: I never believe what I read in the *Chronicle* since then. I thought they'd print what I said, but there was only, like, two lines. The rest was made up! (Women's youth group, aged 15 – 17)

Clearly, there is a need for a more responsible approach to journalism, and an understanding of the damaging effect that a single newspaper article can have to the long-term well being and self esteem of these vulnerable young people.

Hope and Resistance to Fear

'Fear' can mean very different things to different people, and the term is 'often unreflective of the broad range of reactions of many people ... it may be interpreted as implying weakness and vulnerability rather than the commonplace resistance with which many people respond' (Pain 2000, 367). So far, this chapter has been concerned with the ways in which fear can be damaging to disadvantaged young people. However, young people in the research practised numerous alternative tactics and responses as they negotiated their everyday lives. These everyday practices and understandings of 'the way things are' can be viewed as resistance towards the exclusionary practices of others.

All the young people spoke passionately about the neighbourhood, and they were actively concerned with how people from outside the area viewed it:

> CA: What do people in Newcastle think of Fenham?
>
> Jo: They're afraid to come here. When I say I live in Fenham, people ... they like, they look at you funny ...
>
> Stace: What d'they know man? Bet they divn't even know where it is!
>
> CA: So if they've not been here, how do they know what it's like do you reckon?
>
> Mitch: All they know is from the *Chronicle*.
>
> Jo: They should be made to come here, and see what it's like for themselves! (Women's youth group, aged 15–17)

Lisa (17) was particularly insistent that the neighbourhood did not deserve its bad reputation, and argued that it was a nice place to live. Lisa had a 3-year-old son (Robbie), was expecting her second child, and had been given emergency housing in Fenham following a spilt from her violent ex-boyfriend. She had only lived in the neighbourhood for three months, and had not wanted to be placed there, because her family live at the opposite end of the city, and she knew it to be one of the 'roughest parts of Newcastle'. However, she soon made close friendships in the area, especially with the other girls in the group:

> Lisa: They're like a family to me ... I divn't know what I'd do without them. I was really dreading coming here, but the people are great, it's nothing like what I thought. Robbie's so happy here, all the lasses fuss over him, he canna wait to get to Carly's after school. She's great with him.
>
> CA: So do you feel it's a safe place ... are you happy for Robbie to grow up here?
>
> Lisa: Yeah, it's great, everyone looks out for one another, y'know. And everyone says 'hiya' when you walk past – even when I first arrived and I thought they don't know me, but they're still saying 'hiya'?! It's lush man. (Women's youth group, aged 15–17)

During one of the focus group sessions, Lisa's ex tried to get into the youth centre, and shouted abuse through the windows when he was not allowed access. All the young women and the youth workers retaliated, until he gave up and left. When I asked if Lisa was concerned that he would come back, she retorted 'let him try ... he'll get a shock'. Although the situation is far more complex than this momentary glimpse allows, the youth group is clearly a great support to Lisa, and has helped her to build on the encouragement, safety and strength that she needs to stay away from her ex. As Koskela (1997) has emphasised, women may respond to the threat of crime with boldness and defiance rather than fear, and, in the same way, women may lose the 'space of fearfulness' through certain life experiences. What meant most to Lisa about her reception in Fenham was the protection she felt, such that she said she was no longer afraid of her ex. Lisa's experience is not only an important example of resistance, but shows how an 'outsider' has been nurtured by the local community.

Often, communities with strong ties such as these can utilise the grassroots of social cohesion to exert informal social control, which is established and maintained via the implementation of norms to deter crime and promote feelings of safety (Palmer et al. 2005). A growing body of research suggests that the ways in which people perceive their neighbourhood can affect the degree to which they participate and interact in their community (Macintyre and Ellaway 2000; Austin et al. 2002; Ziersch et al. 2005). Much of this research indicates that there is a strong link between social interaction, 'local opportunity structures' and perceptions of crime and safety within neighbourhoods (Palmer et al. 2005). During my research, I noticed that how and why young people talk about crime is very influential upon how safe they feel within Fenham. Crime talk – and, more specifically, flows and tides of *rumour* – work in powerful and unique ways.

> CA: So what is it like to live here?
>
> Jo: It's canny [great] like. Everyone knows everyone, an' if summat's gannin doon [something's happening], we're the first t'hear aboot it.
>
> CA: How's that?

Neil: Everyone's textin' us what's gannin doon – we're always one step ahead!! (Men's football team, aged 16–25)

In Fenham, the very process of *talking* about crime enabled the young people to develop their own sense of place. It is well documented that whom and what we fear, and how we express and act upon these fearings, are constitutive of who we are (Firth 1956; Smith 1982; Sparks et al. 2001). A young person's ability to talk through their fears influences the formation of their sense of themselves, which connects to their wider, social and civic identity. In this way, rumour can be instrumental in the quest for resistance (when it is employed as a strategy for coping with fear, and working through it).

What counts as 'resistance' can be both complex and contradictory, and it can take on a number of different forms. As I described earlier, what is resistance for one person or group may also act to restrict the citizenship of another (Gilling 1997). However, it is encouraging to see instances where young people do act together to try to create more confident, resistant communities, boosting a sense of inclusion, and beginning to enable participation for all. In this way resistance can also mean – and can in practice be – a form of participation. I found numerous instances of young people actively involved with, and committed to, 'giving back' to their community, proud of Fenham and also opposed to the media portrayals and popular assumptions that continue to stigmatise it. In Fenham, the young people I spoke to prioritise their sense of safety, inclusion and belonging in their discussions of everyday life within the neighbourhood. Similarly, from research in an Australian suburb, 'while fear of crime may provide a backdrop to many of the experiences of residents ... to portray the entire area as being a 'suburb of fear' is to miss many of the complex, multiple realities of people's experiences of neighbourhood life' (Palmer et al. 2005, 403).

Conclusion

This chapter has considered some of the local dynamics of fear. The young people I spoke to talked about bullying, teasing, taunting, victimisation and harassment from peers at school, local gangs, police, community support workers, the media and, in some cases members of their own families. I have pointed to just a few of the many and varied ways that fear can work to mediate and shape young people's everyday lives, to compound exclusions and to limit the opportunity for the kinds of social participation on which active citizenship depends. I have also indicated some of the myriad of ways in which young people's practices and understandings demonstrate that they are also expert in resisting fear and stigmatising fear discourses, as they actively try to support one another and the wider community.

New times bring with them changes to the entitlements of residents in different nations, but what has been neglected in the literature is exactly what these changes mean on a local and everyday level. Recent shifts both in how citizenship is conceived and practiced, and in particular, in the reconstruction of the citizen as autonomous and responsible, mean different things to different people – especially at a local level. Critically, now more so than ever before, young people *need* to be accommodated in the city. Disadvantaged young people, especially, *need* to be 'embraced as moral subjects, and provided with opportunities to participate in responsible community life' (Stratford 2002, 202). Yet the inherent tensions operating between those who live in Fenham may also be rooted in more general conflicts about the various ways in which civic life and behaviour are constituted.

Given this complexity, it is surprising how little systematic work there is on the ways in which fear polices the boundaries of citizenship; on the character and meaning of victimisation and the long term effects it can have on the well-being of young people from disadvantaged areas; and on unpicking our understandings of 'the local yob', which are dense with metaphorical association and pregnant with political imagery, but rarely informed by patient empirical enquiry. If we wish to understand the filtration of generic social representations of crime into everyday sensibilities, and the very real and tangible affects these can have upon the individual experience of citizenship, we also need to comprehend the situated character of their reception and appropriation by people in the practical and mundane contexts of their daily life. This chapter is a starting point, and a call for further contributions to this project.

Bibliography

Alexander, C.L. (forthcoming), 'Rumour, Fear and Belonging: The everyday realities of the formation of a civic identity in Fenham, Newcastle upon Tyne', *ACME*.

Alexander, C.L., Beale, N., Kesby, M., Kindon, S., McMillan, J., Pain, R. and Ziegler, F. (forthcoming), 'Participatory Diagramming', in S. Kindon, R. Pain and M. Kesby (eds), *Participatory Action Research Approaches and Methods: Connecting people, participation and place* (London: Routledge).

Austin, D., Furr, L. and Spine, M. (2002), 'The Effects of Neighbourhood Conditions on Perceptions of Safety', *Journal of Criminal Justice* 30, 417–27.

Borooah, V.K. and Carcach, C.A. (1997), 'Crime and Fear: Evidence From Australia', *British Journal Of Criminology* 37, 635–57.

Firth, R. (1956), 'Rumour in a Primitive Society', *Journal of Abnormal and Social Psychology* 22, 122–32.

Gilling, D. (1997), *Crime Prevention* (London: UCL Press).

Gordon, D. and Pantazis, C. (1997), *Breadline Britain in the 1990s* (Aldershot: Ashgate).

Koskela, H. (1997), '"Bold Walk and Breakings": Women's spatial confidence versus fear of violence', *Gender, Place and Culture* 4, 301–19.

Loader, I. (1999), 'Consumer Culture and the Commodification of Policing and Security', *Sociology* 33:2, 373–92.

Macintyre, S. and Elllaway, A. (2000), 'Ecological Approaches: Rediscovering the role of the physical and social environment', in L. Berkman and I. Kawachi (eds), *Social Epidemiology* (Oxford: Oxford University Press).

Marshall, T.H. (1950), *Citizenship and Social Class: and other essays* (Cambridge: University Press).

Noaks, L. (2004), 'Diversification of British Policing: The citizen experience', *Policing: An International Journal of Police Strategies and Management* 27:2, 215–78.

Pain, R. (2000), 'Place, Social Relations and the Fear of Crime: A review', *Progress in Human Geography* 24:3, 365–87.

Pain, R. (2001), 'Gender, Race, Age and Fear in the City', *Urban Studies*, 38:5–6, 899–13.

Palmer, C., Ziersch, A., Arthurson, K. and Baum, F. (2005), '"Danger Lurks around Every Corner": Fear of crime and its impact on opportunities for social interaction in stigmatised Australian suburbs', *Urban Policy and Research* 23:4, 393–411.

Pantazis, C. (2000), '"Fear of Crime", Vulnerability and Poverty', *British Journal of Criminology* 40:3, 414–36.

Pateman, C. (1976), *Participation and Democratic Theory* (London: Cambridge University Press).

Smith, S.J. (1982), 'Victimisation in the Inner City', *British Journal of Criminology* 22, 386–402.

Smith, S.J. (1989), 'Society, Space and Citizenship: A human geography for the "New Times"?', *Transactions of the Institute of British Geographers* 14:2, 144–56.

Sparks, R., Girling, E. and Loader, I. (2001), 'Everyday Urban Lives', *Urban Studies* 38:5–6, 885–98.

Stratford, E. (2002), 'On the Edge: A tale of skaters and urban governance', *Social and Cultural Geography* 3:2, 193–206.

Young, I.M. (1990), *Justice and the Politics of Difference* (Princeton, NJ: Princeton University Press).

Ziersch, A.M., Baum, F.E., MacDougall, C. and Putland, C. (2005), 'Neighbourhood Life and Social Capital: The implications for health', *Social Science and Medicine* 60:1, 71–86.

Chapter 4

Fear and the Familial in the US War on Terror

Deborah Cowen and Emily Gilbert

At the start of this young century, America is once again engaged in a real war that is testing our nation's resolve. While there are important distinctions, today's war on terror is like the Cold War. It is an ideological struggle with an enemy that despises freedom and pursues totalitarian aims. Like the Cold War, our adversary is dismissive of free peoples, claiming that men and women who live in liberty are weak and decadent — and they lack the resolve to defend our way of life. Like the Cold War, America is once again answering history's call with confidence — and like the Cold War, freedom will prevail. (George Bush 2006)

George Bush made the above remarks in a speech at Johns Hopkins University, a day after the third anniversary of the 'liberation' of Iraq. With these few words he aimed to establish the nature of the war on terror – it is an 'ideological struggle' that opposes freedom and totalitarianism – and posits the need to defend the US way of life. As in so many other pronouncements, Bush suggests that the most important role for government in this world is to protect its people from an attack, and that to do so requires 'hunting' down the enemy, taking threats seriously and spreading freedom. The bluster is on the strong arm of the state which has long been associated with security and defence. But clearly there is an ideological battle being waged here that involves securing 'domestic values', on protecting American freedom and liberty, and the US way of life. The war on terror is thus double-pronged: it is not simply a war to stop terrorist 'acts' (terror as verb), but a war on the state of being terrified (terror as noun).

This chapter addresses the ways that the war on terror is not simply one that targets so-called terrorist *acts*, but the *feelings of terror* generated by a range of contemporary social and political insecurities, including, but certainly not limited to, terrorist attacks such as those of September 2001. As this and other chapters in this volume suggest, fear and insecurity are powerful emotions through which the state has sought to govern domestically and internationally, thus linking political geographies of fear at the national and global scale. At the same time, these very same fears have helped to cordon off the US state by justifying the entrenchment of immigration and border policies, and the exclusionary practices surrounding them, as anxieties over population have been heightened. But moreover, feelings of terror have not only been mobilised by the US state to entrench more severe border practices, but it is *through terror* that the US state has sought to govern.

This chapter thus takes emotion seriously, not simply as the feeling or experience of individuals or groups, but as an instrument of governance. As Sara Ahmed suggests, we need to address the politics of emotions for it is largely 'through emotions, or how we respond to objects and others, that surfaces or boundaries are made' (Ahmed 2004, 10). As Ahmed forcefully insists, this kind of analysis reveals that emotions are not simply personal or private, but are political and cultural practices that are constituted by and constitutive of social relations. As Divya Tolia-Kelly suggests, the emotional realm is not one of universals, but rather inflected with 'visual and social registers' such as race, which denote histories and trajectories of difference and power (Tolia-Kelly 2006, 215).

Images and narratives of 'the domestic' as both home and homeland, have figured large in this ideological battle between freedom and totalitarianism. 'Homeland' provides a provocative counterpoint to the 'monstrous' construction of the nation-state more typical of neoliberal antagonism towards central government in the early 1990s (Rose and Miller 1992). But perhaps even more importantly, the familial home/land is celebrated as a space of security. The home/land is cast as both the place of refuge in a dangerous world, and a threatened private social space in need of much greater defense. The fixing of the familial in national space may make possible the management of pain for globally privileged forms of injury, and yet also fuels the infliction of tremendous violence and suffering at 'home' and abroad. Indeed, the boosterism of the 'national family' cultivates new in/securities. It reassures some at the expense of those groups made 'foreign'; simultaneously racialised and of 'perverse' peoples, or as Puar and Rai (2002) argue, those constituted as 'monsters, terrorists, fags'. In much the same way, 'domestic' security measures such as the rise of secret prisons, the colour-coded terror watch system, the militarisation of the US border, the expansion of border wall construction and watchtowers are all designed to thwart insecurities, but paradoxically each contributes to a more firmly delineated 'us vs. them' that only perpetuates insecurities given that this simple dichotomisation is impossible in practice. Anxieties and insecurities proliferate, particularly where the distinction between friends and enemies has been unmoored from the territorial boundaries of nations as, for example, with 'homegrown terror.' When all space is potentially vulnerable, the resort to securing 'domestic' territory is dangerous work indeed.

Homeland Security

> Americans are asking: What is expected of us? I ask you to live your lives, and hug your children. I know many citizens have fears tonight, and I ask you to be calm and resolute, even in the face of a continuing threat. (George Bush, 2001a)

With these words, spoken on 20 September 2001, just days after the terrorist attacks on the US, President Bush suggested that Americans hold their families tight to drive away their fears. The emotional trauma of the events has been endlessly reiterated. Ritual commemorations both evoke the deceased and reinscribe the fears of the day, while new psychoses have erupted – such as 'Post

9/11 Traumatic Stress Disorder' – as a population continues to grapple with the emotional residue that such commemorations evoke. If the family was projected as a site of safety in the face of fear, so too on a much grander scale was the announcement of the formation of the Office of Homeland Security (OHS) designed to alleviate national insecurity. The OHS brings together the separate government departments dealing with security, immigration, natural hazard, health, and transportation, to help reconceptualise threat and emergency response and to help prevent future terrorist attacks. Its rationale is very much framed in terms of fear and weakness: 'The need for homeland security is tied to our enduring vulnerability. Terrorists wish to attack us and exploit our vulnerabilities because of the freedoms we hold dear' (Bush 2002).

The evocation of a US 'homeland,' with all its nationalist connotations, has already received much attention, particularly since it counters traditional US national narratives. Usually, narratives of homeland have been used to root national communities in a particular historic territory (Kaplan 2003; Pease 2003). The concept of homeland connotes familial ties that evoke common 'native origins, of birthplace and birthright' (Kaplan 2003, 86). Homeland, however, is also enveloped in nostalgia for it regularly refers to a place and a past that has been lost and needs to be reclaimed; hence, the homeland is always elusive, its realisation always deferred into the future. For the US nation, it was the terrorist attacks of 9/11 that created a rupture in the national consciousness, or what Bush called a '*wound* to our country' [emphasis added], that opened up the concept of the homeland but which also placed it just out of reach (Bush 2001b). Just months before, in his speech to the nation in January 2001, Bush had dismissed the idea of a US organised around bloodlines and birthright. Rather, in usual fashion, narratives of nation were framed in terms of 'spatial mobility' – progress, pluralism, futurity etc. – quite the opposite of the 'spatial fixedness and rootedness' of homeland (Kaplan 2003, 86). The terrorist attacks, however, prompted a new national narrative in which home was repositioned at the centre. As we will argue, the US homeland may not be ethno-nationalist but its violence is nevertheless deeply racialised and racist.

These national narratives are contested in a whole host of ways and their absolute acceptance should thus never be presumed. But what we want to explore here are the ways that these narratives of homeland and security have also worked to *generate* insecurities. Writing about the politics of home in a regime of 'neurotic' citizenship, Engin Isin (2004) has suggested that home has figured as a bastion for retreat from prevalent insecurities. Yet, as he points out, homes are increasingly over-securitised with an influx of home alarms, nanny-cams and gated communities, which suggests that they are also potent sites of anxiety. It is this idea of an anxious home, he suggests, that lies at the heart of the discourse of 'homeland'. Kaplan asks questions around a similar paradox with homeland: 'Does the word homeland itself do some of the cultural work of securing national borders? Might it also produce a kind of radical insecurity?' (Kaplan 2003, 85). While home and homeland are presented as the antidotes to global anxieties, they too are increasingly riddled with anxiety.

The affirmation of the 'traditional' western family in the Bush government is one manifestation of this anxiety. Under his administration, an earlier programme entitled 'Safe and Stable Families' was elevated to the status of an Act, Marriage Protection Week was declared in 2003 and, in 2004, administration officials announced plans to introduce a $240 million initiative to promote healthy marriages through 'research', and dubious-sounding 'demonstration projects, and technical assistance' (Pear and Kirkpatrick 2004). Marriage promotion has also become a key poverty alleviation strategy. As an extension of the Temporary Assistance to Needy Families (TANF) programme, the Administration for Children and Families (ACF) 'Healthy Marriage Initiative' was created, with targeted initiatives like the 'African American Healthy Marriage Initiative.' Echoing Moynihan's 1965 report 'The Negro Family', which argued that the failure of the black family caused welfare rates to rise, the ACF has declared a crisis of the black family. Boosting the rate of marriage among African Americans, the ACF promises, will decrease poverty, crime, child and sexual abuse and unemployment, while also raising the education levels of children and thereby raising their prospects for success. In this way, they claim they will improve communities and indeed the nation as a whole (ACF 2006).

Bush has furthermore given aid to groups that support 'traditional' family values as a federal priority. As one of his first acts as president, Bush instituted a policy that prohibits US family planning assistance to foreign NGOs that 'use money from any other source to perform abortion counselling or lobby to make abortion illegal' (Fritz 2006). In the fight against AIDS, nearly one quarter of Bush's $15 billion investment has been funnelled into religious groups including one run by the son of evangelist Billy Graham, and another by a Christian hunger relief agency (Beamish 2006). Dr Abeja Apunyo, the Ugandan representative of Pathfinder International, a reproductive health NGO, has been quoted as saying that Bush's 'abstinence before marriage' strategy is 'putting a lot of pressure on girls to get married earlier' (Beamish 2006). In fact, Bush created legislation that mandates that a third of US funds for STD prevention be reserved for abstinence programmes (Fritz 2006). Family form is increasingly the explicit subject of domestic policy debate. Debates over same sex marriage have been explosive, polarising the electorate but also giving rise to creative forms of political activism. It would not be an exaggeration to suggest that same sex marriage has become one of the most divisive issues in US politics. The Bush administration's support for a motion introduced by Iran that would ban gay and lesbian rights groups from Observer status at the UN raises pressing questions about the changing status of 'enemies' at home and abroad.

But more particularly with respect to 9/11, the 'traditional' western family has become the norm through which we are meant to understand the insecurities facing the American nation. When Bush proclaimed the first National Day of Prayer and Remembrance on 13 September 2001 he rallied his 'one nation under God' with the following words: 'I call on every American family and the family of America to observe a National Day of Prayer and Remembrance, honouring the memory of the thousands of victims of these brutal attacks and comforting those who lost loved ones' (Bush 2006). A day later, at the remembrance ceremony, when family members were asked to read out the names of the dead, this very concept of kinship was used to help differentiate between those 'with' and 'against' the US.[1] Surrounded by families of all colours and religions but only one nuclear shape and size, Bush (2001a) remarked that 'Our unity is a kinship of grief, and a steadfast resolve to prevail against our enemies and this unity against terror is now extending across the world.'

The form of the commemorations helped to affirm a white heteronormative family. As David Eng remarks:

> The rhetoric of the loss of 'fathers and mothers,' 'sons and daughters,' and 'brothers and sisters,' attempts to trace a smooth alignment between the nation-state and the nuclear family, the symbolics of blood relations and nationalist domesticity. This narrative of white heteronormativity leaves no public space, no public speech, for those liminal groups – gays and lesbians and undocumented migrant workers, for instance – who perished in the tragedies but whose degraded social status, hard to affirm in life, become impossible to acknowledge in death. (Eng 2002, 90)

These exclusions have very real material consequences, such as the difficulties that gay and lesbian partners of victims of the attacks have had accessing government benefits, and the work of Mexicano/labour organisations to procure documentation for the over 500 hundred workers who perished in the attacks (Eng 2002). At the same time, anxieties around non-normative families were perhaps most explicit in the days just after the attacks of 11 September, when Jerry Falwell proclaimed a link between the terrorist attacks and the anger of God. On The 700 Club, a Christian television programme, Falwell said that: 'I really believe that the pagans, and the abortionists, and the feminists, and the gays and the lesbians who are actively trying to make that an alternative lifestyle, the ACLU, People for the American Way, all of them who have tried to secularise America. I point the finger in their face and say "you helped this happen."' These were accusations with which host Pat Robertson concurred (see CNN 2001).[2]

The trope of the family has also been used to manage relations between the state and its Muslim citizens. At a 2004 Iftaar dinner, Bush defined the family as the glue of American society, and identified the parallels between Muslims and Americans of other faiths as rooted in family values. 'In recent years,'

---

1   Judith Butler also makes the important point that this remembrance of the loss of individual lives helps to frame the acts of terror as individual actions, thereby reducing terrorism to a personal pathology, rather than structure, that makes the events more understandable (Butler 2004, 5).

2   Falwell was forced to retract his statements a day later because of the uproar. But even those who condemned him persisted with understanding the acts of terror in an emotional register; hatred of another kind was determined to be the cause of the attacks, rather than any structural inequities. Lorri L. Jean, Director of the National Gay and Lesbian Task Force, for example, said that 'The tragedies that have occurred this week did not occur because someone made God mad, as Mr Falwell asserts. They occurred because of hate, pure and simple. It is time to move beyond a place of hate and to a place of healing. We hope that Mr Falwell will apologize to the US and world communities'.

Bush asserted, 'Americans of many faiths have come to learn more about our Muslim brothers and sisters. And the more we learn, the more we find that our commitments are broadly shared. As Americans, we all share a commitment to family – to protect and to love our children' (Bush 2004). This celebratory vision of the American family is contrasted with depictions of the failed and violent families of 'the enemy'. In the lead up to the invasion of Iraq, Bush made repeated references to Saddam Hussein's cruelty to families. Violence, towards his own family and other people's, served as indication and explanation for his general monstrosity. 'The dictator of Iraq is a student of Stalin, using murder as a tool of terror and control, within his own cabinet, within his own army, and even within his own family' Bush (2002) explained. He continued, 'On Saddam Hussein's orders, opponents have been decapitated, wives and mothers of political opponents have been systematically raped as a method of intimidation, and political prisoners have been forced to watch their own children being tortured'. First Lady Laura Bush, who typifies the conservative feminine ideal of stay-at-home mother, has also deployed a similar familial discourse that resists simple racisms and cultural stereotypes as it reconstitutes them. She said: 'We respect our mothers, our sisters and daughters. Fighting brutality against women and children is not the expression of a specific culture; it is the acceptance of our common humanity – a commitment shared by people of good will on every continent' (Ferguson 2005, 22). As Ferguson remarks, this phrasing enabled a positing of us vs. them that was not reducible to Muslims versus the west, but respect for families (the west and some 'good' Muslims) and the Taliban: 'This rhetoric obviously was politically useful at the time; it aimed to demonstrate that the Bush Administration was not anti-Muslim, only antiterror; it also helped to construct an image of a natural solidarity among 'civilized peoples' who ought to support a US-led war on terror' (Ferguson 2005, 23).

As Jasbir Puar (2006) has recently noted, this kind of logic is prevalent and dispersed. It is not just the administration, she argues, but even some leading feminist critics who are unintentionally developing problematic, even orientalist analyses of the gendered sexualities of terrorism. In their efforts to introduce a gendered analysis of terror, these critics, in different ways, have explained the acts and agents of terrorism by outlining their homosocial political networks, their patriarchal power relations, and even the unconventional family structures to which they ascribe. Puar (2006, 73–4) specifically mentions work by leading feminist scholars including Robin Morgan, Zillah Eisenstein, and Ros Petchesky; however, the problem is a broader one of how western feminism is sometimes complicit with, and even actively contributes to, imperialist doxa in analyses of gender and sexuality. This is a theme that Gayatri Spivak has explored in a different but equally salient register for our time, when war is rationalised on a supposedly feminist pretext to 'liberate' the women of Afghanistan. Spivak (1999, 303) assails the all-too-frequently rehearsed performance of 'white men seeking to save brown women from brown men' (see also Nast 2000). Judith Butler also picks up on the imperial uses of feminist claims in her recent work, *Precarious Life*. She asserts, with a hint of sarcasm, 'it would surely be a mistake to gauge the progress of feminism by its success as a colonial project' (2004, 41).

The normative family has helped to naturalise inequalities and allay fears and insecurities that are mapped onto the struggles within and against the US in the War on Terror. But this 'natural' social ordering has a history. During the WWII Vichy regime in France, the famous national motto that was coined during the French revolution – Liberté, Egalité, Fraternité – was replaced with the much more mundane and conservative 'Travail, Famille, Patrie.' The elision of work, family and nation in the new motto was meant to reorient France to the hard work of productive and reproductive life that would mitigate against resistance to the occupying state, as well as inculcate hatreds towards foreigners, such as the Jews, who were constituted as being outside the French family. Anne McClintock describes yet another example of this kind of social ordering. She explores the cult of domesticity of the British imperial project, and describes how then prevalent narratives of 'Family of Man' ordered national differences. 'The family as a *metaphor* offered a single genesis narrative for global history', McClintock explains, 'while the family as an *institution* became void of history. As the nineteenth century drew on, the family as an institution was figured as existing, naturally, beyond the commodity market, beyond politics and beyond history proper. The family thus became both the antithesis of history and history's organizing figure' (McClintock 1995, 44; emphasis in the original; see also Larner and Walters 2002, 398). The family hence naturalises differences within the national body, while projecting a particular de-contextualised and timeless model of the normative western family that helps to legitimise particular forms of exclusion and hierarchy. To put it more strongly, 'Projecting the family image onto national and imperial progress enabled what was often murderously violent change to be legitimized as the progressive unfolding of natural decree' (McClintock 1995, 45).

But in contrast to some popular arguments, we suggest that this political family is not *only* historical. The burgeoning scholarship on governmentality, while extremely helpful to this analysis given its concern for the role of models and metaphors in the constitution of political practice, nevertheless assumes that government has become less organised around a familial model over time. One of Michel Foucault's (1991) most noted arguments in his writing on governmentality suggests that the family was a definitive *historical* model of government that became *less important* with the rise of the modern nation state system in the eighteenth century. Our brief investigation of the elevation of the family as a model of government in the current period thus questions the finality of these historical shifts. We would like to suggest that this governmentality argument may be too final, and that we may indeed be witnessing the recasting of the familial as model for political relations at the national and other spatial scales, as we argue elsewhere (Cowen and Gilbert 2007). It is precisely through accounting for the affective dimensions of the political and specifically, the 'place' of fear in territoriality today, that we may yet add nuance to governmentality scholarship on the politics of family and 'home'.

Conclusions

With 9/11, the '*wounded*' culture that has been attributed to late-twentieth century citizen-formation (Brown 1995; Berlant 2000) has been expanded to include a wounded US nation. As Sara Ahmed writes with respect to the individual, 'Wound culture takes the injury of the individual as the grounds not only for an appeal (for compensation or redress), but as an identity claim, such that 'reaction' against the injury forms the very basis of politics, understood as the conflation of truth and injustice' (Ahmed 2004, 58). Although the US is not the only nation that frames itself in this way, the 'wound to our country' has been a powerful concept deployed by President Bush through which new forms of US identity have been configured. The overt political salve to the wound of 9/11 has been the Office of Homeland Security, but there is also at work, as we have demonstrated here, a more insidious appeal to a normative white heterosexual family. What we have tried to suggest, however, is that these tropes of home and family have only helped to encourage and perpetuate social anxieties. Engin Isin's model of the 'neurotic citizen' speaks to the affective subject who cannot be managed only in terms of a rational and calculating self, but is governed also through her emotions (Isin 2004). It is through anxieties and insecurities that the self and the nation are managed.

The political dangers of this wound culture are manifold, but particularly when the wound is fetishised, and the histories of being wounded and of wounding are forgotten (Ahmed 2004, 58–9). Donald Pease remarks that the nostalgia associated with homeland is rooted in an act of forgetting that eradicates other narratives of displacement and disruption, such as that of indigenous peoples (Pease 2003, 3). Or more broadly, as David Eng remarks, when the melancholia of the nation turns into mania: 'This mania transforms ungrievable loss into absolute disavowal – the refusal of the US to confront the silence of its past, its disavowed histories and policies that have helped to create specters of and for global terror. In the campaign for 'infinite justice/enduring freedom' history is shorn off from the past such that the horizon of the future disappears and prophecy remains a proposition yet to come' (Eng 2002, 92). Even though the question 'why do they hate us?' was raised by Bush himself in his speech of 20 September 2001, it was met with silence and with hostility. Those who sought to consider reasons for the attacks were criticised as 'exonerating' those attacks (Butler 2004, xiii), so that thinking about what brought about terrorism 'raised fears that to find a set of causes was to find a set of excuses' (Butler 2004, 2).

The politicisation and nationalisation of the family in times of war is not new. However, a focus on contemporary familial politics is crucial in any attempt to understand the specificity of our moment. This is especially the case with regards to the complex form of US nationalism that is simultaneously multicultural and racialised. This nationalism is defined, first and foremost, by its explicit casting of citizenship in anti-racist terms, even as it is centrally organised around a racialised imaginary and perpetuates racialised and racist economic, police and military violence. A highly normative model of the family that is historically white, western, middle class and heteronormative has been elevated to universal status as the core institution and values of American life. The nuclear family, not 'race' or religion, becomes the unifying principle of citizenship. It is through promotion of the family that government reproduces and responds to the racialised 'challenges' of black families at home, of fundamentalist terrorists abroad, and of the global AIDS epidemic. The 'traditional' family form works to normalise these 'problem' citizens. While war has made the security of the national family a popular obsession and a salient and powerful project, the politics of defence, organised in terms of a homeland constituted by nuclear families, threatens to augment violence in its most brutal forms.

Bibliography

Administration for Children and Families (ACF) (2006), <http://www.acf.hhs.gov/ healthymarriage/index.html>, accessed 22 February 2006 (updated 14 December 2006).

Ahmed, S. (2004), *The Cultural Politics of Emotion* (Edinburgh: Edinburgh University Press).

Beamish, R. (2006), 'Religious Groups Get Nearly One-Quarter of Bush Administration's AIDS Money', Associated Press, Online Edition, <http://www.microbicide.org/ publications/show_story.html?NewsID=183&print_story=1>, accessed 29 January.

Berlant, L. (2000), 'The Subject of True Feeling: Pain, privacy and politics', in S. Ahmed, J. Kilby, C. Lury, M. McNeil and B. Skeggs (eds),*Transformations: Thinking through feminism* (London: Routledge).

Brown, W. (1995), *States of Injury: Power and freedom in late modernity* (Princeton, NJ: Princeton University Press).

Bush, G.W. (2001a), 'National Day of Prayer and Remembrance for the Victims of the Terrorist Attacks on September 11, 2001', <http://www.whitehouse.gov/news/ releases/2001/09/20010913-7.html>, accessed 23 February 2006.

Bush, G.W. (2001b), 'Address to a Joint Session of Congress and the American People', September 20, <http://www.whitehouse.gov/news/releases/2001/09/20010920-8.html>, accessed 3 March 2006.

Bush, G.W. (2002), 'Preface', National Strategy for Homeland Security, Office of Homeland Security, <http://www.dhs.gov/interweb/assetlibrary/nat_strat_hls.pdf>, accessed 3 March 2006.

Bush, G.W. (2004), 'President hosts Iftaar Dinner', 10 November, <http://www.whitehouse. gov/news/releases/2004/11/20041110-9.html>, accessed 3 March 2006.

Bush, G.W. (2006), 'Remarks by President Bush on the Global War on Terror' at the Paul H. Nitze School of Advanced International Studies, The Johns Hopkins University, April 10, <http://www.state.gov/r/pa/ei/wh/rem/64287.htm>, accessed 5 August 2006.

Butler, J. (2004), *Precarious Life: The powers of mourning and violence* (London and New York: Verso).

CNN (2001), 'Falwell Apologizes to Gays, Feminists, Lesbians', <http://archives.cnn. com/2001/US/09/14/Falwell.apology>, accessed 3 March 2006.

Cowen, D. and Gilbert, E. (2007), 'Citizenship in the "Homeland": Families at war', in D. Cowen and E. Gilbert (eds). *War, Citizenship, Territory* (New York: Routledge).

Eng, D. (2002), 'The Value of Silence', *Theatre Journal* 54:1, 85–94.

Ferguson, M.L. (2005), '"W" Stands for Women: Feminism and security rhetoric in the post-9/11 Bush administration', *Politics and Gender* 1, 9–38.

Foucault, M. (1991), 'Governmentality', in C. Gordon, G. Burchell and P. Miller (eds), *The Foucault Effect: Studies in governmentality* (Chicago, IL: University of Chicago Press).

Fritz, N. (2006), 'Cash for Abstinence with Bush's No-sex Diplomacy', Business Day, <http://www.businessday.co.za/articles/topstories.aspx?ID=BD4A136774>, accessed 8 February 2006.

Isin, E. (2004), 'The Neurotic Citizen', *Citizenship Studies* 8:3, 217–35.

Kaplan, A. (2003), 'Homeland Insecurities: Reflections on language and space', *Radical History Review* 85 (Winter), 82–93.

Larner, W. and Walters, W. (2002), 'The Political Rationality of the "New Regionalism": Towards a genealogy of the "Region"', *Theory and Society* 31:3, 391–432.

McClintock, A. (1995), *Imperial Leather: Race, gender and sexuality in the colonial context* (New York: Routledge).

Nast, H. (2000), 'Mapping the "Unconscious": Racism and the Oedipal family', *Annals of the Association of American Geographers* 90:2, 215–55.

Pease, D.E. (2003), 'The Global Homeland State: Bush's biopolitical settlement', *Boundary 2* 30:3, 1–18.

Pear, R. and Kirkpatrick, D. (2004), 'Bush Plans $1.5 Billion Drive for Promotion of Marriage', *New York Times*, 14 January, A1.

Puar, J.K. (2006), 'Mapping US Homonormativities', *Gender, Place and Culture* 13:1, 67–88.

Puar J.K. and Rai A. S. (2002), 'Monster, Terrorist, Fag: The war on terrorism and the production of docile patriots', *Social Text* 20, 117–48.

Rose, N. and Miller, P. (1992), 'Political Power beyond the State: Problematics of government', *British Journal of Sociology* 43:2, 173–205.

Spivak, G. (1999), *A Critique of Postcolonial Reason: Toward a history of the vanishing present* (Cambridge, MA: Harvard University Press).

Tolia-Kelly, D. (2006), 'Comment – Affect: an Ethnocentric Encounter? Exploring the 'Universalist' Imperative of Emotional/Affectual Geographies', *Area* 38:2, 213–17.

Chapter 5

Me and My Monkey: What's Hiding in the Security State[1]

Cindi Katz

In the impulse purchase section next to the cash registers of my neighbourhood drugstore is a spindle of disposable camera packages that look a bit whimsical. Screaming 'child-friendly', the cartons, upon closer inspection, make a travesty of the term. Not at all the cameras for kids I imagined them to be, these were 'Child Safety Camera ID Kits' that contained a camera for taking mug and full body shots of up to three children, including their particular birth marks or unique characteristics; three 'DNA bags', otherwise known as 'ziplocs', for storing a lock of hair (missing from my kit); three 'personal profile sheets' for recording vital statistics such as the child's seemingly unchanging height and weight as well as their dental chart and medical conditions; and three 'non-toxic ink strips' for fingerprinting. Dragnet comes home.

By what logic has surreal fear been made so banal that such a hokey kit (Plate 5.1) might be picked up with some juicy fruit for your kid to take to camp? In what universe has such a commodity been produced, let alone positioned as an impulse purchase? In the world of post-11 September New York, is this the new normal? Yes and no. Yes, in the sense that the performance of security through objects, technologies and displays is meant to stage and foreground a pervasive sense of fear; and no, in the sense that most parents aren't yet buying this form of protection, though the fear-mongering strikes responsive chords associated with other domestic realms of hypervigilance, and seems to be authorising its broad attractiveness. In this chapter I fuse my concerns with social reproduction, precious parenting and what I call banal terrorism, to argue that the contemporary security state and the reign of trumped up paranoia it engenders have not simply altered the spaces and material social practices of contemporary childhood but have fed into a burgeoning regime of surveillance in which the household mirrors the practices of the state while softening its future subjects for what the Bush spin-meisters might call 'Operation Enduring Watchfulness'.

The amplified fear along with the moral panics with which it is associated provide ready means of distraction from the political economic, social,

1   This is an abridged version of a chapter with the same name published in Sorkin, M. (2007), *Indefensible Space: The Architecture of the National Insecurity State* by kind permission of Routledge.

Plate 5.1   Child safety camera ID kit

Source: author.

environmental and personal problems that face families of children coming of age in the US at present. These problems, as I have argued elsewhere, produce a pervasive sense of ontological insecurity that crosses class, race and gender lines with differentiated effects among various groups (Katz 2005). At the heart of this insecurity are the shifts associated with the globalisation of capitalist production, including an increasingly mobile and insecure employment landscape, wear and ruptures in the longstanding relationship between production and social reproduction, the precipitous rolling back of a century's worth of advances in the social wage, and new forms and arenas of militarisation and policing. These changes have led to increasing economic inequality among both classes and nations, the privatisation of formerly public or corporate responsibility for various elements of the social wage, and reworked geographies and temporalities of investment and disinvestment at a number of scales. The insecurities produced by these changes are palpable, and register in a variety of material social practices from the demise of welfare such as it was in the US to unsure and unstable job markets worldwide. But in rerouting as anxiety the political economic and social problems that produce it, the experience of ontological insecurity can derail potentially political responses as it rehearses the neoliberal tendency to privatise social concerns. In the thrall of insecurity, individuals as much as social formations are all the more vulnerable to fear-mongering, the machinations of banal terrorism and 'terror talk' (cf., Katz 2006a; 2006b). They tend to turn inward in response.

Rescripted as insecurity, the political, economic and social effects of capitalist globalism are individualised. At the same time the collective experience of insecurity around employment prospects and pensions; access to social services, healthcare, and housing; educational achievement; or social justice and self-determination – all included in the United Nations' initiatives to redefine 'security' as an issue of human health and well-being (for example, Commission on Human Security 2003) as much as with what I am calling ontological insecurity – is redirected, if not callously preyed upon, by the paranoia purveyed by the security state. Security in its hardened, bunkered form is built on and made more acceptable by the widespread and differentiated effects of insecurity of a completely different order. In another register, pervasive social insecurity and the individualised anxiety it engenders seem to call forth various mechanisms of securing the home and domestic environment that is played out with a particular vengeance around children. As people feel less and less secure in the nation, its future and the promises of capitalist modernity, they seem to struggle even harder to control what they can – their bodies, their domestic environment, the circumstances of their children's everyday lives – fraught as such efforts might be. The latter reflects, as much as it propels, the current spectacularisation of children and childhood in the US. It is the collision of a moment in which children have become spectacle (capital accumulation to the point where childhood becomes image (cf. Debord 1983) and an historical geography that channels social and ontological insecurity into discourses of fear and domestic vulnerability that creates ideal conditions for parental hypervigilance, among other things.

The regime of parental hypervigilance has much in common with that of the homeland security state. They both tend toward inappropriate strategies and targets, offering at best a false sense of security through overkill in one area and blithe disregard or ineptitude in others, and along these lines ignore or divert attention from grave problems of a wholly different order. The parallels in tactics, strategies and effects between the two scales of 'domestic' security are revealing, and examining them can help expose some of the alibis that underpin both realms as well as the limits of technologies of fear. It can also show the ways that material social practices of security at these two scales feed off of and help justify one another, reconfiguring daily life and legitimating practices unthinkable even a decade ago.

The technologies of fear are witnessed as the nation enacts broad and aggressive 'security' measures ranging from domestic wiretapping and other surveillance strategies through the 'war on terror', to the fantasy of a completely walled southern border. In the name of fear the public environment is monitored, bunkered and conspicuously patrolled while the home is increasingly fortressed. But the technologies of fear are also increasingly apparent in children's everyday lives as parents, teachers and others aspire to complete child safety if not total lockdown of children. In the contemporary US and elsewhere the market for child protection is growing as parents of all backgrounds are drawn to a host of means intended to shield children from perceived (but still quite rare) physical, social and (increasingly) metaphysical risks. Some of these strategies are familiar and fairly benign, but others are as disturbing as they are bizarre.

Among the familiar are privatised play areas, often associated with fast food restaurants, that come with fairly intense security protocols. For instance, 'Chuck E. Cheese', which bought out the free standing 'Discovery Zone', offers play equipment, entertainment, game arcades and prizes with its pizza which it proudly touts as its 'security measures to prevent child abduction'. Greeted by the always staffed 'Kid Check' booth, customers with children are stamped with a family identification number in invisible ink. Upon leaving, the black light in the booth ensures that 'everyone who comes together, leaves together' (http://www.chuckecheese.com/the-experience/kid-check-program.php). I always like a little creepiness with my pizza, to say nothing of the comparable threats to American children posed by obesity and abduction. Other familiar devices include the now ubiquitous room monitors that allow parents and others to hear, and increasingly to see, their child from other parts of the house or its surrounds. While the burgeoning number of means to ensure children's physical safety are not my focus here, it's worth noting that despite the importance and effectiveness of many of these measures, such as child safety seats or bicycle helmets, there is also much excess here that is resonate with protections in the realm of social danger. Even around physical harm, the manufacture of risk and the attraction to technological means of reducing it can get out of hand when studies have shown that parental monitoring and greater parent-child communication offer a more effective and long lasting means of ensuring children's well being (Hart and Iltus 1988).

The child protection industry, a thriving component of the home protection industry, offers a range of wares to parents bent on security. Visual systems figure prominently in the arsenal. Nanny cams, for instance, are an increasingly popular item as reflected both in sales and in growing attention in parent magazines and blogs. Nanny cams are concealed video cameras to view the activities of children, childcare workers and others – including parents – either through a live feed or recording. The best ones provide high-resolution color or black and white images and work in very low light (although infrared light emitters can be added). Most nanny cams do not record sound in part because it is illegal to do so without permission in several states. Images are transmitted through wireless devices from cameras hidden in all manner of mundane objects from clocks and pencil sharpeners to bad paintings and fake plants but, in the spirit of child protection, they are also in teddy bears and other innocuous toys. My favorite is a stuffed monkey wearing a black leather vest (Plate 5.2). Not exactly innocuous, but somehow appropriately perverse – a little biker monkey to spy on the person in whom trust should be paramount. Such ethical qualms apparently are rippling fewer and fewer parental ponds. 'Ethics, schmethics', sneers Rhyder McClure, a New York peddler of the cameras (Burson 2004). And indeed those selling surveillance seem to have little. They are not averse to staging scenes supposedly picked up on nanny cams that show child minders in various acts of negligence or keeping notorious incidents in people's minds. Nanny cam sales took off in

1997 after the British au pair Louise Woodward was accused of murdering one of the children in her care. As prices drop and the regime of paranoia grips more and more parents, sales have gotten stronger. According to technologies market analysts at Parks Associates in Dallas, the number of households with at least one child indicating interest in using a nanny cam more than doubled between 2002 and 2004 from 19 to 39 per cent (Haller 2006). While this does not translate directly as sales, of course, a number of internet businesses have reported substantial annual sales increases for nanny cams over the last five years. This trend is sure to accelerate as the technology gets cheaper. As the writer David Brin observed several years ago, $100 nanny cams will be 'utterly hopeless to resist' (Strauss 1998).

Plate 5.2   Stuffed monkey with hidden camera

Fear only begins at home. Its tentacles extend from there pretty much in inverse proportion to children's exposure to risk. One aspect of this phenomenon is web-camera systems in daycare centres and schools, which allow parents password protected access to either web-cam images or streaming live videos of their children's days. Parents can log on and view the images on any computer or various hand-held devices. Purveyors of these technologies promote them as means to both ameliorate the quotidian separations of contemporary family life and ensure that the services delivered meet expectations, but underneath they tap into the anxieties traced above (cf., Katz 2001). A small but growing number of childcare centres offer these systems, and those marketing them appeal to daycare operators' competitive advantage in demonstrating to consumers that they have nothing to hide. The contemporary penchant for security notwithstanding, these systems may not achieve the sort of market saturation that seems likely for nanny cams. Staff members often object to being under the watchful eyes of so many doting parents. But more to the point, it can be costly to install and maintain the security of these systems, and childcare businesses – to say nothing of public facilities – operate with relatively tight budgets. While it's a bit different for older children, where their own behaviour rather than exposure to risk seems to have led a growing number of public schools in the US and elsewhere to install surveillance cameras, security around young children remains more privatised, focused more on the home and the child's (mobile) body than anywhere else.

In the private realm things have intensified and become more strange at the same time as they echo the performative overreach of measures taken in the public sphere. A small but growing number of people are saddling their children with monitoring devices that allow parents and others to keep tabs on them using two-way radio type technology or more elaborately to locate them using GPS (geographic positioning systems). The former, which are widely available and inexpensive, consists of a transmitter encased in a child-friendly pendant or small stuffed toy worn by the child and a small receiver worn or held by the care-giver. The receiver beeps loudly when the child wanders beyond a certain distance. Thanks to 'smart' technology, the range varies according to density; in crowded situations the receiver will sound if the child goes further than about three meters, whereas in less busy conditions the child may reach ten meters before the alarm is sounded. The transmitters are also outfitted with 'panic buttons' so that children can alert their care givers with a 95 decibel alarm if something is awry (or they want ice cream). Promising peace of mind and the possibility of allaying panic for all involved, those promoting these devices routinely remind parents that they cannot replace actual supervision. Of course, one needs to be already pretty panic-prone to want to be alerted every time a child strays more than three meters in a commercial venue, to say nothing of the ways these devices – beeping as they will – are panic emollients.

First used in large water parks and the like, the digital angel has been marketed for private use since late 2001 for about $400 and a monthly subscription fee of about $30. Some models require a special tool to remove and thus are fixed on children until their caretakers take them off. Their pastel shades and floral or goofy motifs distinguish these devices from those used on people under house arrest. Surveillance technologies like the digital angel are obviously not (yet) for everybody, and have been acquired only by a minute segment of the population. But where privacy objections of all denominations – from civil liberties advocates, 'big brother' alarmists, and apocalypse-anticipating Christians who saw the implantable chip and its surrogates as the 'mark of the beast' – were raised around the development of the technology during the late 1990s and into the new century, these objections were muted in the security landscape that followed 11 September

2001. Not only did the manufacturer return to talking about implantation – a possibility they had previously seen wise to bury – but the corporation and its backers invigorated their discussion of the technology as a security tool, mentioning such things as chipping immigrants or tracking workers seen as posing a security risk in certain industries. 11 September also helped domesticate these technologies and enhanced their appeal to an already anxious public. Indeed, by chance the Digital Angel came on the market just in the wake of 11 September and the manufacturer immediately noted an upsurge in demand. 'Peace of mind' was now imagined as the possibility of a 'happy ending' to a catastrophe ('A "Digital Angel" for Troubling Times' 2001). Getting a leg up on the surveillance systems and invasions of corporeal privacy that became the new normal after 11 September, Digital Angel quickly stepped up its production process to meet the new demand. With its potential to transmit biological and location data through building materials with extraordinary accuracy, the Digital Angel seemed to some at least the perfect technology for horrific times.

If most people remain resistant to chipping their loved ones and themselves, despite the appealing fantasy of complete protection, it is clear that mobile telephones are increasingly used to provide similar kinds of information both within the family and more broadly. Telephones tether and locate loved ones as well as co-workers and others, calling forth co-presence at any time of the day or night while identifying the source – if not necessarily the geographic location – of the call. As the potential for constant contact has become commonplace and the mobile phone market saturated, a growing number of wireless phones have been outfitted with GPS technology so that users can be located with pinpoint accuracy. This feature has been used to track workers as well as for law enforcement and in emergency situations, but it is now being marketed as an easy way to keep tabs on family members. Indeed, child protection has been packaged as an add-on to various family calling plans. For $10 a month, services such as Verizon's 'Chaperone' or Sprint's 'Family Locator' enable parents to locate their child's 'kid-friendly wireless phone' on a small map visible on their own phone or through the web. For an additional ten dollars, the Verizon plan allows the parent to define a geographic area from which the child cannot stray without their being alerted. When the 'Child Zone' is breached the parent will receive a text message. What happens next is unclear, because as the fine print cautions, these systems are not suitable for 'child management' and are no substitute for supervision and actual communication.

These services are supposed to offer 'peace of mind' – the phrase is ubiquitous in the child protection industry – but if their use catches on, Big Mother will have done a lot to soften Big Brother's future subjects. Sprint, for one, takes pains to reassure that theirs is not an Orwellian operation – children must agree at the outset to have their parents check on their whereabouts. They are sent a text message each time the parent does a 'safety check' and locates their cell phone. Of course if the phone is off it cannot be located, and I've already read accounts of children passing their phones to one another at least in part to foil their parents. Like so many security technologies, these devices for all their sophistication are easily thwarted. All of this begs the question of 'child management', and the serious issues of open communication and trust it raises. As in the larger society, the distorted focus on an ever present – but most unlikely – threat authorises and provides an alibi for a range of invasive, inadequate and often inappropriate measures (cf., Kelly 2003).

It is by now a commonplace that families are yoked by 'electronic leashes' through mobile phones and other devices. Much of this tethering enables children and young people to have a bit more spatial autonomy than they might as it gives parents (and children) the 'peace of mind' that comes with ready contact, although the virtual base touching of some parents can render this freedom moot. If young people use mobile phones to stay on top of constantly evolving social situations, parents view them as a way to make sure their children negotiate their travels and schedules smoothly and safely. But just as the borders between work and home are blurred by cell phones, so too are the newly charted boundaries between young people and their parents, which are shaky at best. The phones may be a means of granting kids some autonomy, but the constant contact they enable can just as easily hem it in. As Rachel Pain and her colleagues suggest, mobile phones may simply 'reshape' rather than reduce parental fears (Pain et al. 2005, 826). Some parents cannot rest unless they are called at every transition – on the bus, off the bus, leaving school, arriving home, whatever – and are informed of every change in plans however small. As cell phones become latter-day umbilical cords, young people's facility to make sound judgments about their social activity space and everyday engagements may be hobbled by such micromanagement as the burgeoning concern from colleges and universities about 'helicopter' parents suggests.

Just as the spectre of abduction and other extremely rare crimes against children are trotted out to legitimate parental hypervigilance, so too the looming threat of terrorism has been added to the repertoire of rationales for a cell phone on every body. These issues were all out in force in April 2006 as the New York City public schools began to enforce their longstanding ban on cell phones. As Tim Johnson, chair of the Chancellor's Parent Advisory Council, made clear, 'In the times we are living in, this is completely a safety issue for the overwhelming number of families' (Hartocollis 2006). The Council filed a suit against the Department of Education within a few months to get the ban lifted. I agree that the ban is problematic (and unrealistic), but the hysteria it produced is inseparable from the paranoid regime of domestic terror that only became more apparent following 11 September 2001. Typical was the parent of a sixth grader who fumed, 'The Chancellor will have civil disobedience on his hands. No one in New York is going to let their child go to school without a cellphone' (Gootman 2006). Far from her mind in the throes of this crisis was that plenty of kids in New York City public schools go to school without breakfast, let alone a cell phone. A little civil disobedience on those grounds would be a fine thing. Of course, in the private schools things are ratchetted up a notch – there it's a question of 'rights'. But somewhat hilariously the rights in question were those of worry. In the words of Alexandra Peters, former President of the Parents League, they 'feel pretty strongly that parents have a right to be concerned about their kids' safety, and that cellphones are a good way for them to make sure' (Hartocollis 2006).

Speaking of worry, the manufacturers and marketers of most of these technologies warn of their creating a 'false sense of security' just as frequently as they offer them as means toward 'peace of mind'. But it seems that a false sense of security is what people have been reduced to – or have learned to find solace in – in the absence of anything resembling true security. Here the parallels between the state and home are direct and obvious. In several venues, I have pointed out the absurdity of desert camouflaged soldiers guarding the public environments of New York City and elsewhere. Their attire – the antithesis of camouflage – makes them readily apparent to everyone, and that seems to be the point. While undercover police work the same environments unnoticed, the military *performs* homeland security. This display of security is no doubt meant to reassure the public, but it is a reassurance that rehearses and reinstates a sense of constant threat. And it's that everyday production of fear that gets camouflaged. The performance secures docility while the fear exacerbates and excuses all manner of hypervigilance, including parental.

Yet even as these novel strategies of child protection become the norm, the broad promises of the social wage achieved by the late twentieth century (their unevenness notwithstanding) continue to be worn away by a neoliberal state consumed by its own security and a corporate sector bent on reducing labor costs. Nothing in any of these security measures at whatever scale can redress the sorts of insecurities these shifts provoke. But these insecurities – and the deeper ontological insecurity with which they are associated – seem to be sublimated in the false sense of security on offer. The technologies of homeland (as well as home-based) security essentially respond to the symptoms and not the causes of most of the serious problems facing young people in the US. But worse, these measures in themselves propel a state of insecurity, first by making a paranoid regime pervasive at every scale from the body to the nation, second by absorbing funds that might be spent on more constructive arenas of social reproduction, and third by drawing young people, especially those with few job prospects, into the maw of 'the war on terrorism' itself.

Beyond all of these issues, it is neither possible nor desirable to protect children from everything as much as we might like to. The practices of hypervigilance and other variants of 'hyperparenting' miss this point entirely. In the flurry of overprotection, children and adolescents may not be learning to make their own sound judgments, to adjudicate various disputes, or to develop a sense of trust in themselves and others. Moreover, focusing on the insecurities bred of fear – whether of nannies, criminals, terrorists or others – diverts attention and resources away from less dramatic but much more common problems faced by children and families. These problems – which encompass everything from the failures of public education, the inadequacies of public play environments, the lack of work or community-based childcare centres, the dearth of affordable housing, or the number of children and families without health insurance, to things like the regimentation of everyday life, the epidemic of eating disorders in the midst of hunger and the persistence of domestic violence – actually might have a chance of being ameliorated if the energy and resources expended on troubles that almost by definition transcend resolution were redirected toward them.

Parallels with the urban, national and global scales are clear. As in the home, so with the state. It is a fantasy that any mode of security can safeguard the public from everything. Moreover, the metastasising security charade under which we currently live puts even greater resources at the disposal of the military, the police, the prison system and the surveillance complex. All the while in the home, as in the US state, many of the most pernicious threats to security and well-being come from within. If what was spent on 'security' were redirected toward the goods, services and spaces that comprise the social wage, it might temper some of the free range insecurity – ontological and material – that pervades contemporary life in the United States. The erosive toll of revanchist globalisation should be counted among the terrors of everyday life; it takes the lives of far more people – in slow seeping ways – than the horrifying but exceedingly rare terrors that command so much attention. As suggested above, there is a great and growing divide between rich and poor households in the face of these erosions and how their toll is extracted. These shifts seem to provoke wealthier families to further fetishise their children, while poorer families often have to scramble just to secure the means of their children's existence. As inequality is exacerbated, so too is the nature of childhood troubled in different ways by these circumstances. Childhood itself is compromised on the one hand by material insecurity and on the other by the fetishised enactments of fear and security as young people are denied the promise of a secure future. And as the war in Iraq continues, even the possibility of a future is tragically foreclosed for all too many.

These problems will not be solved by piecemeal private strategies that at best try to compensate for an eviscerated social realm, and at worst take the pervasive individualism of neoliberalism to heart. Even in the problematic realm of the conjured and too easily stoked fears around childhood, there is a difference between a campaign that hails some notion of community by asking, 'have you seen this child?' and a drive that would clamp an RFID tag on one's own child. It is time to attend to the circumstances that underlie contemporary insecurities around children, rather than fritter around the insecurities themselves. These circumstances demand a reinvigorated politics around the social wage in all its permutations. Elaborations of hypervigilance are a diversion. And not only that. It is also time to recognise the creeping neoliberalisation of the security state. Not only are we witnessing the downscaling of the security state into the home, and thus the parallels I've been tracing here, but also and increasingly the technologies of the state security apparatus are being privatised (cf., Katz 2001 and 2005). As more and more households avail themselves of cellular telephones that offer GPS tracking services, for instance, the more people can be tracked by law enforcement agencies or in the vague interests of homeland security. Likewise the growing number of home-based DNA and fingerprint archives, such as those produced with the 'Child Safety ID Kits' found in my local drugstore, which most people would readily share with their local police department if asked in the interests of child safety. These are not benign bits of mom and pop data, as the overreach of the office of homeland security around cell phone records should make clear, but how convenient that they are provided at your expense. Meanwhile in the interests of preventing 'passport fraud' and meeting US visa requirements, the European

Union has reportedly been debating mandatory fingerprinting of all children six and older, with plans to store the information on a centralised database (Doward 2006). Whether through an American style 'do it yourself' impulse or a more state centreed approach as in Europe, the trend is clearly to produce massive amounts of personal data and make it available to the state. The (con)fusion of personal security and national security is breathtaking, as is the way the interests of the former can so easily be made to serve the latter. These troubling practices are only the beginning of what may come of the conjuncture between heightened individual anxiety and a strong security state. What is already clear is that home and childhood are remade in this twisted space.

There are several parallels in security practices at the national, urban and home scales that bear reflection. In each arena, security is framed in relation to externalised threats rather than home grown troubles, and in ways that produce flattened and demonised others – whether as 'terrorists', 'foreigners', 'gang members', 'Arabs' or 'illegal aliens.' But also at each scale these practices come at the expense of dealing with 'security' problems of another order entirely. This distinction might be understood as attending to the (exaggerated) concerns of 'security *from*' at the expense of attending to the more widespread problems of social reproduction that can be framed as the 'security *of*'. Focusing on selected dramatic – but exceedingly rare – risks diverts attention and resources from other less dramatic but more common and erosive problems such as those produced by the retreats in the social wage associated with the globalisation of capitalist production and the ascendance of neoliberal public policy. Perhaps worse, as these sorts of disinvestments in social reproduction take place they are masked and rationalised by the stepped up discourse of fear and the apparatus of security that is attendant upon it. Children and young people pay dearly either way. As Inderpal Grewal (2006, 37) points out, the heightened state of security displaces the violence of the family onto various racialised, classed, gendered and otherwise flattened others, and then calls upon and reinstates patriarchal authority to protect against these dangers. This dynamic works across scales, wedding the differentiated but often mutually reinforcing interests of US imperialism, biopolitics and capital accumulation. Just as patriarchal authority is called forth to 'protect' the home – smuggling in a host of material social practices that attempt to control the bodies and minds of women and children – so too does the security state assert its authority around the biopolitics of heteronormativity, racism and sexism as it promulgates its 'surveillant assemblage' and militarises the spaces of everyday life (cf., Grewal 2006).

It is time to refuse the bait of fear and its erosive consequences at all scales. The strategies associated with hypervigilance as much as the performance of security cannot redress the serious problems provoked by the imperatives of capitalist globalism, violent imperialism and neoliberal retreats from the social wage. These imperatives produce a broad range of material insecurities and for many a deep sense of ontological insecurity about the future. These insecurities help make people receptive to the promises of security in whatever precious or bunkered form it's offered, but they can only be countered by returning to notions of security rooted in social justice and focused on the broadest concerns of social reproduction and restoration of the social wage. Everything else is indefensible.

Bibliography

'A "Digital Angel" for Troubling Times' (2001), M2 Communications Ltd, 9 November, <http://web.lexis-nexis.com.ezproxy.gc.cuny.edu:2048/universe/document?_m= bbe111d408e0954344930ea0704bdf15&_docnum=2&wchp=dGLbVlz-zSkVA&_ md5=18f523dc9a0fb14cfc92c9a780d099cb>, accessed 3 July 2007.

Burson, P. (2004), 'Parents Have No Qualms in Using Nanny Spy Cams', *Tulsa World*, 27 December.

Chuck, E. Cheese [website], <http://www.chuckecheese.com/the-experience/kid-check-program.php>, accessed 3 July 2007.

Commission on Human Security (2003), *Human Security Now* (New York: Commission on Human Security), <http://www.humansecurity-chs.org/finalreport/English/ FinalReport.pdf>, accessed 3 July 2007.

Debord, G. (1983), *Society of the Spectacle* (Detroit: Red and Black).

Doward, J. (2006), 'Millions of Children to be Fingerprinted', Observer, 30 June, <http:// observer.guardian.co.uk/uk_news/story/0,,1833407,00.html>, accessed 3 July 2007.

Gootman, E. (2006), 'City Schools Cut Parents' Lifeline (The Cellphone)', *New York Times* A1, B5, 27 April.

Grewal, I. (2006), '"Security Moms" in the Early Twenty-First-Century United States: The gender of security in neoliberalism', *WSQ: Women's Studies Quarterly* 34:1 and 34:2, 25–39.

Haller, S. (2006), 'Parents Monitor Kids, Nanny from Afar with Tiny, Increasingly Popular Cameras', *Associated Press State and Local Wire*, 17 April.

Hart, R. and Iltus, S. (1988), 'Developing a Model of Families as Safety Management Systems for Children at Home', in J.D. Sime (ed.), *Safety in the Built Environment* (London: E. & F.N. Spon.).

Hartocollis, A. (2006), 'Parents to Sue Over Schools' Cellphone Ban', *New York Times* 13 July, <www.nytimes.com/2006/07/13/nyregion/13phones.html>, accessed 3 July 2007.

Katz, C. (2001), 'The State Comes Home: Social reproduction and the global retreat from social reproduction', *Social Justice* 28: 3, 47–56.

Katz, C. (2005), 'The Terrors of Hypervigilance: Security and the Compromised Spaces of Contemporary Childhood', in J. Qvortrup (ed.), *Studies in Modern Childhood: Society, agency, culture* (New York: Palgrave Macmillan).

Katz, C. (2006a), 'Power, Space, and Terror: Social Reproduction and the public environment', in S. Low and N. Smith (eds), *The Politics of Public Space* (New York: Routledge).

Katz, C. (2006b), 'Banal Terrorism: Spatial Fetishism and Everyday Insecurity', in D. Gregory and A. Pred (eds). *Violent Geographies* (New York: Routledge).

Kelly, P. (2003), 'Growing Up as Risky Business? Risks, Surveillance and the Institutionalized Mistrust of Youth', *Journal of Youth Studies* 6:2, 165–80.

Pain, R., Grundy, S. and Gill, S. with Towner, E., Sparks, G. and Hughes, K. (2005), '"So Long as I Take my Mobile": Mobile phones, urban life and geographies of young people's safety', *International Journal of Urban and Regional Research* 29:4, 814–30.

Strauss, G. (1998), 'Nanny Cams Ease Parental Angst', *USA Today 1–2A*, 27 February.

SECTION 2

Fear of Nature and the Nature of Fear

The two chapters in this section address an important, if often neglected, aspect of fear: how it relates to what is considered as 'natural' in different ways. The core idea is that fears which are commonly perceived to be 'natural' in fact reflect and retain certain social and political orders. Fears of 'natural' phenomena – such as darkness, flooding, landslides – also encapsulate much wider issues of personal and societal security. The impacts of even the most 'natural' disaster are mediated, and amplified, by vulnerability, just as they are dampened in the context of resilience; both resilience and vulnerability are profoundly shaped by economic, social and political contexts. As recent scholarship has elaborated, geopolitical events, processes and discourses are an important part of the constitution of nature, as well as fear.

Alan Ingram offers a powerful example of this. Globalisation in its various forms has brought us all closer to danger, he suggests, with the threat of those deadly transmissible diseases that western societies had hoped were things of the past re-emerging alongside new killer viruses; some real and some still incubating in the scientific imaginary (but no less, and perhaps even more, fear-provoking for that). The global reach of some of these diseases – both practically and by association with places where human behaviour and existence are precarious and different – makes them seem more frightening and less controllable. One consequence, as Ingram shows, is that the re-emergence of infectious disease is being harnessed to a politics of international migration. Fear of infection has always been used to control where people live and to curtail their mobility: incarceration, the use of quarantine, the requirement of segregation, the barriers to immigration, have all been used throughout human history to curb human rights in the name of disease prevention. All this slipped off the political agenda during the mid twentieth century, thanks to the prospect and reality of eradicating the major infectious diseases and tightly controlling the rest. But a decade of spectacular failure has seen these fears taking centre stage again, provoking a tension between policies which really tackle their roots, and those which use disease management as a smokescreen for other political ends.

Likewise, a focus in recent research on the nature of fears in rural areas throws the largely urban-dominated focus of most enquiry into perspective. It underlines, again, that place is a crucial part of the shape of fear, and that potentially risky environments are read with their social connotations firmly in mind. As Jo Little draws out in a thought-provoking argument about nature, fear and rurality, political issues of identity, othering and exclusion are central in how people think and feel about the landscapes around them (see also Askins in Section 5). Using examples from her research in New Zealand, Little shows how fear of nature can be used as an exclusionary device, to identify, name and eject those 'out-of-place' Others in the countryside, to protect the exclusivity and character of rural residential enclaves, as well as to guard the fact and ideal of wilderness.

Both chapters – in common with others in this collection – add fuel to the question 'what is the nature of fear'? While concern about the physical and emotional well-being of ourselves and those who are close might seem the most natural thing on earth, the shape of these fears is never far from the wider social and political fabric comprising everyday life. Part of the materiality and efficacy of fear is the way it inhabits place: both those that seem different or strange and (as we heard in Section 1, and as the chapters in Section 3 also make clear) those much closer to home. This creeping materiality of fear is actively transforming the social landscape. Simply observing it is an act of explicit compliance. Making the landscape otherwise is where the challenge lies.

Chapter 6

Pandemic Anxiety and Global Health Security

Alan Ingram

In an age of interdependence, when threats can cross borders in an instant, we are mutually vulnerable, and our defences are only as good as our weakest link. That holds true whether we are talking about terrorism or the spread of disease.

(Louise Fréchette, Deputy Secretary-General of the United Nations, addressing the European Parliament in 2005)

Introduction

Geographies of infectious disease are shifting in ways that menace global society. The apprehension, if not the fact, of this has become increasingly widespread over the last 30 years. Epidemic diseases, once thought to be eradicated as a significant threat to modern societies, or at least confined largely to the more unfortunate parts of the world, are now foregrounded by a sense that global transformations have remade the world as a single epidemiological community. Fear of pandemic has, as a result, been disseminated throughout scientific, policy, corporate and media networks, and much of the world is now primed to dread the emergence or re-emergence of infectious diseases into the 'global arena'.

The development of a specifically *global* consciousness about infectious disease is fraught with ambiguities. Infectious diseases are responsible for far more death and suffering than, say, terrorism; they account for more than ten million deaths annually, with the burden concentrated overwhelmingly in poor countries. A focus on infectious disease might, on the one hand, prompt greater engagement with questions of global equity and solidarity than even the threat of terror. On the other hand, as with other 'global dangers', there are risks that this engagement will be triangulated disproportionately around the 'fears and fantasies of the already affluent', reinforcing rather than ameliorating global divisions (Ó Tuathail 1996, 253).

In this chapter I draw on a growing critical literature on global health to explore the spatialisation of fears about infectious disease and of associated strategies of security in terms of three main issues. The first is the emergence of 'the global' as the definitive context for understanding infectious disease since the 1970s. The second deals with an enduring tendency to locate the causes, origins and responsibility for the threat of infectious disease outside, elsewhere and with others, regardless of epidemiology. The third deals with the concern that pandemic anxieties are serving as a vehicle for the consolidation of hegemonic interests in the guise of global health security. In conclusion, I outline in brief three considerations for critical geopolitics as it addresses geographies of pandemic anxiety and global health security.

Globalisation, Geography and Germs

> Plagues are as certain as death and taxes. (Richard Krause cited in Garrett 1995, 5)

The context for current epidemic and pandemic fears has been formed by concerns about the nature of relations between epidemiology and modernity. In particular, an epistemic shift has taken place from a linear view whereby humanity would in time prevail over pathogenic microbes, to a non-linear understanding whereby humans, animals, plants and microbes are seen as engaged in shifting interactions whose outcomes are not predetermined. However, the precise form in which this understanding has crystallised and gained significance is closely related to the geopolitical coordinates of contemporary globalisation.

By the middle of the twentieth century, it seemed to many medical and public health experts that the control of infectious diseases in all countries was within reach or at least conceivable. This confidence has since been shattered by a number of developments since the 1970s. First, a growing number of hitherto unknown infectious diseases (such as Ebola and HIV) began to be identified by western science. Second, it became increasingly apparent that some well known diseases (like tuberculosis and cholera) were 're-emerging' in unanticipated ways in a variety of places. Third, resistance to existing pharmaceutical therapies also became increasingly apparent (for example, in the case of multi-drug resistant tuberculosis – MDR-TB, and now an extensively drug resistant form – XDR-TB).

These troubling developments are bound up with the triumph of neoliberal globalisation. Indeed, the national public health and welfare programmes that were central to the health gains achieved during the twentieth century came under sustained neoliberal assault. In this context the response of scientific and medical communities in the US was particularly significant, as they turned increasingly towards national security discourse as a way of dramatising and rationalising the need for political commitment to public health, giving rise to a particular discursive regime around emerging diseases within scientific, entertainment, journalistic and policy circles in the US during the 1990s. Schell (1997) for example draws attention to the 'foreign viral geography' common to accounts of emerging infections in virology, science journalism and popular culture. King (2002; 2004) notes both the distinctive scale politics of the US Institute of Medicine's (IoM) campaign on emerging infectious disease threats and the way it appealed to connections between public health, national security and economic interests, as signaled in the title of a key report: *America's Vital Interest in Global Health: Protecting Our People, Enhancing Our Economy, and Advancing Our International Interests* (IoM 1997).

By 2000, the US National Intelligence Council (NIC) was recognising publicly a global infectious disease threat to the United States (NIC 2000).

This worldview was mobilised particularly forcefully around a number of events held to be indicative of the new epidemiological reality, including an outbreak of Ebola among monkeys imported from the Philippines at a Reston, Virginia research facility in 1989; the outbreak of pneumonic plague in Surat in India in 1994 and the major Ebola outbreak among humans in the Democratic Republic of Congo in 1995. A recurring motif was the fact that with increased global connectivity, disease was 'only a plane ride away'. Its twin was the idea, prominent in a range of post-Cold War conservative dystopias, that first world cities were undergoing a process of 'third-worldisation', accounting, it would seem, for events such as the tuberculosis crisis in New York in the early 1990s (Gandy and Zumla 2003). Indeed, for Garrett (1995), emerging infectious diseases were a symptom of a 'world out of balance', where the collapse of public health systems, chaotic urbanisation, environmental degradation, travel, migration and trade were conspiring to produce 'microbial traffic' of a new order. Such analyses, which offered many alarming examples but little in the way of serious social, economic or political analysis, chimed with the conservative dystopianism peddled by authors such as Robert Kaplan (the title of Garrett's book, *The Coming Plague*, is a telling echo of that of Kaplan's notorious 1994 essay, *The Coming Anarchy*).

The turn towards security in public health was reinforced by anxieties about the proliferation of bioweapons among rogue states and terrorist groups. Although the US had apparently halted its bioweapons programmes in the 1970s, having concluded that they held little military utility, concerns were raised during the 1990s that the Soviet Union had continued research and development in this field and that its bioweapons complex had not been secured during the collapse of communism. When anthrax spores were mailed to members of the US Congress in October 2001, public health moved definitively onto the frontline of homeland security. As the Bush administration sought to mobilise international opinion for the invasion of Iraq in 2003, speculation about the possibility of terrorist strikes employing smallpox served to reinforce a sense of homeland insecurity.

This easy discursive slippage between the pathogen of terrorism and the terror of pathogens referenced truly existential dreads that even the 9/11 attacks could not evoke. After all, Joshua Lederberg, the Nobel prize-winning geneticist and a key proponent of the emerging infectious disease worldview, had stated:

> Some people think I am being hysterical, but there are catastrophes ahead. We live in evolutionary competition with microbes ... There is no guarantee that we will be the survivors. (Cited in Schell 1997, 94)

From western vantage points, contemporary globalisation, far from bringing about the end of history, meant global health crisis, national insecurity, and, perhaps, the end of humanity itself.

Cartographies of Contagion

Naming a risk amounts to an accusation. (Douglas 2002, xix)

As the restaurants of the city's China-towns remained empty and as cases of exclusion against Torontonians from Asia abounded, our proud mixed social fabric was ripped. (Keil and Harris Ali 2006, 109)

The experience of SARS in Toronto was one of profound geographical dislocation, as a western city encountered the kind of exoticisation typically reserved for places outside the first world (Strange 2006). This experience was not limited to Toronto, with, for example, the epidemic being recruited by certain Taiwanese commentators into their arguments for maintaining isolation from the Chinese mainland (Ching-chih 2005). SARS demonstrated once again the social power of contagion, of transmission (in this case transnational) by contact with others.

What accounts for this power? Bashford and Hooker argue that the idea of contagion is particularly threatening because it 'implies absorption, invasion, vulnerability, the breaking of a boundary imagined as secure, in which the other becomes part of the self' (Bashford and Hooker 2001, 2). Modern societal responses to contagion have consequently involved 'all kinds of anxious practices in which selves and societies sought (vainly) to secure clear boundaries' (Bashford and Hooker 2001, 5). Indeed, the association between infectious disease and various ideas of the other is pervasive and resistant.

It has become a commonplace of critical histories of medicine to observe that medical knowledge was a key component in the assertion of western superiority over colonised peoples. The connection with racialised otherness has been manifested particularly clearly in the biopolitics of colonial nationhood; the struggle for a healthy and secure Australia has been intimately and problematically bound up with the struggle for a white Australia (Bashford 2001). Markel and Stern (2002) have shown how ideas of the least valued social identities, disease and foreign-ness have tended to attract each other during particular periods of immigration in US history, regardless of the actual associations between immigration and disease. This tendency is no less visible in the recent history of HIV/AIDS in the colonial present.

For example, it was a specifically racialised understanding of HIV/AIDS that made possible the detention by the US government at the military base at Guantanamo Bay in Cuba of hundreds of HIV-positive Haitians fleeing dictatorship in the early 1990s (Farmer 2005). But the consequences of racialised discourses and control strategies have ranged wider than the often ineffective (though politically attractive) practices such as quarantine and *cordon sanitaire*. The US Centers for Disease Control had already in 1983 inferred that 'Haitians' were a 'risk group' (a medically dubious term) for HIV/AIDS, with devastating consequences for Haitian migrant workers in the United States and for the tourist trade in Haiti where it is a major source of national income (Farmer 2001). In a different context, the reactionary panic among British right-wing newspapers between 2003 and 2005 to evidence of associations between rising rates of immigration, tuberculosis and HIV/AIDS cannot be understood outside the preceding territorialisation of public and 'national' health, and the extensive symbolic and material work done to stigmatise and police migrants who do not conform to specific templates (Hampshire 2005; Coker and Ingram 2006). Responses to HIV/AIDS also turn in a particularly direct way upon the sexualisation and gendering of infectious disease (Schell 1997). There is something about infectious disease that seems to call forth particularly masculine narratives of war and conquest, protection and security. These in turn, in metropolitan post-imperial societies at least, call white colonial subjectivities into play.

This tendency towards other-blaming has been analysed in the context of social psychology by Joffe (1999), who argues that people often respond to threats by recourse to existing representations and in ways that protect themselves and the groups they identify with from fragmentation and negative associations. In particular, in times of crisis regard for the other is liable to shift from suspicion towards a sense that they pose a material threat or are 'purveyors of chaos' (1999, 23). However, this only accounts for initial reactions. Whether more alarmist responses take hold depends on whether individual fears are ratified by others and by society at large. Here Ungar's (1998) study of US media responses to emerging infectious diseases and the 1995 Ebola epidemic in Kikwit, Zaire (now the Democratic Republic of Congo) is particularly instructive.

Ungar distinguishes between 'crises' (which may be identified by certain actors but which do not receive wide attention) and 'panics', the latter being episodes of acute collective or 'grassroots' fear (1998, 37). He suggests that the Ebola epidemic in particular met the conditions for a 'crisis'. But when the possibility of grassroots panic began to appear, media outlets and elite actors shifted from a 'mutation-contagion' narrative that placed the US itself within a potentially expanding circle of threat, to a more reassuring 'containment' narrative that emphasised the social and geographical distance of Kikwit from the United States.

More generally, Ungar suggests six factors affecting the development of panics out of initial crises: the number of dramatic precipitating events; the potency and vividness of the underlying dread; recent cultural preoccupations and resonances; the timing and location of critical events; the level of consensus in the definition of the threat; and the renewal or disappearance of the fear-inducing events. Among these factors lies recognition of the interplay between the materiality and the social construction of epidemics. As the quotation from Keil and Harris-Ali at the top of this section suggests, the power of certain diseases seemingly to undo the social as well as the body to some extent calls into question the validity of this distinction and reinforces the need to see epidemics and responses to them in terms of 'more-than-human geographies' (Whatmore 2006). However, for the moment I want to return to a particular way of thinking about the sociospatial politics of epidemics.

I have suggested that while the tendency to other-blaming appears in a wide variety of historical and geographical contexts, and while the framing of disease as a security issue in the United States in particular is perhaps reflective of the orientation of elites within a particular kind of capitalist and imperial society that accords little space to social rights, the extent to which fear and other-blaming dominates in any particular instance is not beyond the reach of politics. Consistent with her psychoanalytic approach, Joffe suggests that the risks of other-blaming can be countered by a less idealised view of the self and a less denigrated view of the other. Epidemics can be the occasion for tolerance, social criticism and reform. The extent to which those considered to be other can express agency and voice is also significant. Similarly, just as media and elite actors can switch between more threatening and more reassuring narratives as circumstances shift, a variety of actors can pursue alternative representations and performances of space, holding out the possibility, at least, of different kinds of health politics.

The Geopolitics of Global Health Security

> Public health has experienced a governance revolution of such significance that infectious disease control now represents an important criterion of 'good governance' in world affairs. (Fidler 2004a, 799)

> In contrast to the panoptic institutional surveillance of a single prison or the clinic, which is easily identified as coercive or violent, this surveillance is imagined to be everywhere, at all times, producing data available to everyone: a global clinic. (King 2002, 776)

The SARS epidemic of 2002–2003 made a significant contribution to the validation of the idea of global health security as an international policy imperative. SARS, or Severe Acute Respiratory Syndrome was first recognised in Guangdong province in China in late 2002. It was carried to Hong Kong by a Chinese doctor who infected a number of other travellers in the hotel where he stayed, triggering an epidemic that resulted in 8096 probable cases and 774 deaths in 27 countries (the majority in China itself) by its conclusion in summer of 2003 (WHO 2004).

In global and historical terms this was a tiny toll of morbidity and mortality, but the epidemic displayed a number of the features identified by Ungar as conducive to panic. First, it was dramatic in a number of ways: the disease had a high case fatality rate; it appeared to be new; it spread in ways that were for a time unknown; it spread across international borders; and it proved fatal for many medical personnel treating it (including Carlo Urbani, the doctor who first identified it). Second, it raised dread of a long-expected influenza pandemic, reactivating cultural anxieties around emerging infections. Third, SARS arrived in the climate of generalised western post-9/11 anxiety, intensified in the US by the subsequent anthrax attacks. Fourth, daily reports of spread to new locations and countries validated the cliché that 'germs respect no borders', but also carried the message that Oriental microbes threatened western societies (Washer 2004). The appearance of SARS in Toronto, the subsequent WHO advisory against travel to that city and the consequent diplomatic storm was particularly telling in this regard (Hooker 2006). Furthermore, SARS appeared to move through air travel and strike at global cities, key pathways and nodes of global interconnection

(Keil and Harris Ali 2006). Fifth, there was near-universal consensus about the seriousness of the threat signified by SARS. Its impact on travel and tourism, the way it played into domestic crisis in China, and the fact that it impinged on international diplomacy, validated SARS as an economic and geopolitical event as much as a public health emergency. Finally, in early 2003 fear was sustained beyond the initial events by a continual rise in new cases over a period of weeks and months.

The epidemic was therefore held to be indicative of the 'new reality' of global epidemiological connectivity. But it was also an occasion when the ability of public health to 'act global' was demonstrated. Indeed, the international response to SARS, led by WHO, has been interpreted as a seminal event in global public health governance, a 'post-Westphalian' moment of transnational collective action (Fidler 2004b).

SARS provided a compelling demonstration that states could no longer conceal information about unusual outbreaks from the international community and expect to maintain legitimacy. It showed that WHO was able and willing to use non-governmental information sources and censure individual states (here China) for their failures. The epidemic also lent impetus to discussions about new International Health Regulations (IHRs) that had dragged on for a decade, with agreement reached by all WHO member states in 2005. The new IHRs require all states to achieve basic standards in public health surveillance and response and mandate international notification of 'public health emergencies of international concern' (WHO 2005; Fidler 2006; Chan 2007). The idea of WHO as guardian against transnational disease threats has been reflected in the reform of its own institutions and self-presentation around what is now termed 'epidemic and pandemic alert and response'. This includes the creation of a 'Strategic Health Operations Centre', a crisis management facility for the coordination of a wide variety of activities. Finally, SARS and pandemic influenza have reinforced concern about the emergence of new pathogens from animal species into human populations, necessitating closer cooperation between the WHO, Food and Agricultural Organisation (FAO), and the World Organisation for Animal Health (OIE) (Karesh and Cook 2005).

Global health security has therefore emerged as a complex set of practices through which global life is to be protected from epidemic and pandemic threats and the anxieties they generate. But although it has been described as a new kind of policy space where states set aside conventional rules of international politics to engage in new kinds of collaboration (Fidler 2005), global health security is hardly immune from power relations.

First, global health security raises questions about global health equity. Despite international pressure to upgrade surveillance and response capabilities in all countries, vast disparities and gaps are evident in both spheres and the world appears decidedly unprepared for all-too-plausible global health scenarios. Fidler (2006) suggests that the 'surveillance gap' between developed and developing countries has if anything widened since 2001, not least because the former have ploughed hundreds of millions of dollars into their own national systems. In the case of the USA, much of this has been focused around low-probability bioweapons threats of little general relevance to national or international public health. The widespread concern about pandemic influenza has also highlighted stark inequalities in likely access to anti-viral drugs, vaccines and healthcare facilities within and between countries (Davis 2005; Garrett 2005; Osterholm 2005; 2007).

Second, there are grounds for tension between those countries that are seen as the most likely sources of new epidemics, particularly pandemic influenza, which are less affluent, and the demands advanced by richer countries and the WHO that they invest substantial resources in biosecurity and incur significant economic costs by culling animal populations believed to pose a wider threat. Global health security requires the transformation of poorer societies in the name of the global good (Braun 2007). In a further threat to the idea of global health security as a public good, in early 2007 it was reported that Indonesia had stopped sharing samples of influenza virus (a vital component of global public health surveillance) with WHO and had signed a commercial agreement with Baxter Health Care, a private US corporation. Recognising the hard edge of what Fidler (2001) has called *microbialpolitik*, Margaret Chan, Director General of WHO stated that 'we will have the best chance of winning support when we appeal to national self-interest' (2007). It is far from clear that states and private corporations would abide by the putative ethics of global health security in the event of something like pandemic influenza (Osterholm 2007).

Third, there are questions about connections between global health security and other northern global security agencies and interests. Currently the US Department of Defense provides a significant component in influenza surveillance with a network of surveillance sites in 56 countries through its Global Emerging Infections Surveillance and Response System (DoD-GEIS) (2006). What is at issue are the ways that these, and other, web-based, surveillance capabilities relate to hegemonic security interests more generally. It seems obvious that possession of privileged epidemiological intelligence would constitute a material advantage during health crises impacting on international relations. The combination of this kind of knowledge with growing corporate interests in influenza preparedness points ominously towards a kind of biosecurity industrial complex (Fidler 2006).

It has thus been argued that global health security involves a new geopolitics of surveillance that is not just post-Westphalian but actively imperial. Weir and Mykhalovsky (2006) draw attention to the interest shown since 2001 by intelligence agencies towards the Global Public Health Intelligence Network (GPHIN), a Canada-based initiative that has since 1997 used webcrawler technology to identify media reports of unusual public health events. They suggest that GPHIN has also been used to identify 'terrorist' activities. Recalling Hardt and Negri, they argue that global public health surveillance 'is "empire" without an outside rapidly being integrated into the intelligence needs of the Global North' (2006, 259). Troubling though this is, it is perhaps analytically misleading, not to say disempowering, to exaggerate the novelty of the present. The association between public health and national security is longstanding, and while their present connections have yet to be traced in full, the increasing interest in doing so perhaps lends some impetus to hopes for a more equitable global health politics.

Conclusion

It is over a decade since calls were issued for critical sociologies of emerging infectious diseases (Farmer 1996). This task has become still more pressing with the recent salience of fear in governing rationalities. Epidemic and pandemic anxieties have been added to the continuum of things to be feared that is available to opportunist political strategies, and questions must continue to be asked about the extent to which global health security is contributing to global health equity. In this sense the governmentality of disease intersects with the governmentality of unease (Bigo 2002). There are many different ways that geographers can contribute to the critical interrogation of this field, but in conclusion I would like to offer three observations that might be made in relation to critical geopolitics in particular.

The first is to recognise the enduring relevance of the task outlined by Ó Tuathail (1996), to problematise the ways that global space is written by centres of power and authority. But research must go beyond this, to consider how global health is also constituted and contested by diverse material practices (not to mention strategies of accumulation). Second, consideration of emerging infectious disease raises again the whole variety of ways in which critical geopolitics needs to take greater account of embodied experience in everyday life (Hyndman 2004). Third, it is necessary to acknowledge the extent to which contemporary understandings of emerging infectious disease locate geopolitics in relation to nature. This poses in a particular way the challenge of moving beyond anthropocene geopolitics (Dalby 2007) to a more-than-human geopolitics of infectious disease and global health security.

The turn to security in public health, occasioned by epidemiological and societal insecurities and fears, carries multiple valences, not all of them necessarily ominous. There are more than enough reasons to be seriously concerned about today's global health situation. In that sense the emergence of global health security cannot be regarded as a simple projection of an ethnocentric anxiety or imperial drive to control. But neither is it adequate to assume that such impulses play no role at all, or that pandemic anxieties and global health security are anything other than deeply political.

Bibliography

Bashford, A. (2001), 'Foreign Bodies: Vaccination, contagion and colonialism in the nineteenth century', in A, Bashford and C, Hooker (eds), *Contagion: Historical and Cultural Studies* (London: Routledge).

Bashford, A. and Hooker, C. (2001), 'Contagion, Modernity and Postmodernity', in A. Bashford and C. Hooker (eds), *Contagion: Historical and Cultural Studies* (London: Routledge).

Bigo, D. (2002), 'Security and Immigration: Toward a critique of the governmentality of unease', *Alternatives* 27:1, 63–92.

Braun, B. (2007), 'Biopolitics and the Molecularization of Life', *Cultural Geographies* 14:1, 6–28.

Chan, M. (2007), 'Health Diplomacy in the 21st Century', 13 February, <http://www.who.int/dg/speeches/2007/130207_norway/en/index.html>, accessed 26 March 2007.

Ching-chih, C. (2005), 'Why Quarantine is the Best Policy', *Taipei Times*, 26 January, <http://www.taipeitimes.com/News/editorials/archives/2005/01/26/2003221041>, accessed 6 July 2005.

Coker, R. and Ingram, A. (2006), 'Passports and Pestilence: Migration, Security And Contemporary Border Control Of Infectious Diseases', in A, Bashford (ed.), *Medicine at the Border: Disease, globalization and security, 1850 to the present* (London: Palgrave).

Dalby, S. (2007), 'Anthropocene Geopolitics: Globalisation, empire, environment and critique', *Geography Compass* 1:1, 103–18.

Davis, M. (2005), *The Monster at Our Door: The global threat of avian flu* (London: New Press).

Department of Defense (2006), *DoD Global Emerging Infections Surveillance and Response System: Annual Report fiscal year 2006* (Silver Spring, MD: DoD-GEIS).

Douglas, M. (2002), *Purity and Danger: An analysis of the concepts of pollution and taboo* (London: Routledge).

Farmer, P. (1996), 'Social Inequalities and Emerging Infectious Diseases', *Emerging Infectious Diseases* 2:4, 259–69.

Farmer, P. (2001), *Infections and Inequalities: The Modern Plagues* (London: University of California Press).

Farmer, P. (2005), *Pathologies of Power: Health, human rights and the new war on the poor* (London: University of California Press).

Fidler, D. (2001), 'The Return of "Microbialpolitik"', *Foreign Policy* 122, 80–81.

Fidler, D. (2004a), 'Germs, Governance and Global Public Health in the Wake of SARS', *Journal of Clinical Investigation* 113:6, 799–804.

Fidler, D. (2004b), 'SARS: Political pathology of the first post-Westphalian pathogen', *Journal of Law, Medicine and Ethics* 31, 485–505.

Fidler, D. (2005), 'From International Sanitary Conventions to Global Health Security: The new international health regulations', *Chinese Journal of International Law* 4:2, 325–92.

Fidler, D. (2006), 'Biosecurity: Friend or foe of public health governance', in A. Bashford (ed.), *Medicine at the Border: Disease, globalization and security, 1850 to the present* (London: Palgrave).

Fréchette, L. (2005), Remarks to Foreign Affairs Committee of European Parliament, Strasbourg, 23 February 2005, <http://i-newswirpe.com/pr8038.html>, accessed 29 July 2005.

Gandy, M. and Zumla, A. (eds) (2003), *The Return of the White Plague: Global poverty and the 'new' tuberculosis* (London: Verso).

Garrett, L. (1995), *The Coming Plague: Newly emerging diseases in a world out of balance* (New York: Penguin Books).

Garrett, L. (2005), 'The Next Pandemic?', *Foreign Affairs* 84:4, 3–23.

Hampshire, J. (2005), 'The Politics of Immigration and Public Health', *The Political Quarterly* 76:2, 190–98.

Hooker, C. (2006), 'Drawing the Lines: Danger and risk in the age of SARS', in A. Bashford (ed.), *Medicine at the Border: Disease, globalization and security, 1850 to the present* (London: Palgrave).

Hyndman, J. (2004), 'Mind the Gap: Bridging feminist and political geography through geopolitics', *Political Geography* 23:3, 307–22.

Institute of Medicine (1997), *America's Vital Interest in Global Health: Protecting our people, enhancing our economy, and advancing our international interests* (Washington, DC: National Academy Press).

Joffe, H. (1999), *Risk and 'the Other'* (Cambridge: Cambridge University Press).

Karesh, W. and Cook, R. (2005), 'The Human-Animal Link', *Foreign Affairs* 84:4, 38–50.

Keil, R. and Harris Ali, S. (2006), 'The Avian Flu: Lessons learned from the 2003 SARS outbreak in Toronto', *Area* 38:1, 107–9.

King, N. (2002), 'Security, Disease, Commerce: Ideologies of post-colonial global health', *Social Studies of Science* 32:5/6, 763–89.

King, N. (2004), 'The Scale Politics of Emerging Diseases', *Osiris* 19, 62–76.

Markel, H. and Stern, A. (2002), 'The Foreignness of Germs: The persistent association of immigrants and disease in American society', *The Millbank Quarterly* 80:4, 757–88.

National Intelligence Council (2000), *The Global Infectious Disease Threat and its Implications for the United States* (Washington, DC: NIC).

Osterholm (2005), 'Preparing for the Next Pandemic', *Foreign Affairs* 84:4, 24–37.

Osterholm (2007), 'Unprepared for a Pandemic', *Foreign Affairs* 86:2, 47-57.

Ó Tuathail, G. (1996), *Critical Geopolitics: The politics of writing global space* (London: Routledge).

Schell, H. (1997), 'Outburst! A Chilling True Story about Emerging-Virus Narratives and Pandemic Social Change', *Configurations* 5:1, 93–133.

Strange, C. (2006), 'Postcard from Plaguetown: SARS and the exoticization of Toronto', in A. Bashford (ed.), *Medicine at the Border: Disease, globalization and security, 1850 to the present* (London: Palgrave).

Ungar, S. (1998), 'Hot Crises and Media Reassurance: A comparison of emerging diseases and Ebola Zaire', *The British Journal of Sociology* 49:1, 36–56.

Washer, P. (2004), 'Representations of SARS in the British Newspapers', *Social Science and Medicine* 59:12, 2561–71.

Weir, L. and Mykhalovsky, B. (2006), 'The Geopolitics of Global Public Health Surveillance in the Twenty-First Century', in A. Bashford (ed.), *Medicine at the Border: Disease, globalization and security, 1850 to the present* (London: Palgrave).

Whatmore, S. (2006), 'Materialist Returns: Practising cultural geography in and for a more-than-human world', *Cultural Geographies* 10:13, 600–609.

World Health Organization (2004), *Summary of Probable SARS Cases With Onset of Illness from 1 November 2002 to 31 July 2003*, WHO: Geneva, <http://www.who.int/csr/sars/country/table2004_04_21/en/print.html>, accessed 26 March 2007.

World Health Organization (2005), *Revision of the International Health Regulations* (WHA58.3) (Geneva: WHO).

Chapter 7

Nature, Fear and Rurality

Jo Little

Introduction

The purpose of this chapter is to examine the relationship between the geographies of fear and nature. The chapter argues that studies of fear have incorporated the idea and the practical realities of nature in complicated, confused and often contradictory ways. Nature has been seen variously as both the source of fear and as a protector against fear; inflicting huge damage and destruction when it acts beyond the 'control' of human society but also providing security against an unpredictable human threat. As poststructuralist geographies have opened up new ways of conceptualising the relationship between nature and society, challenging the dominance of binary thinking and the assumption of discrete categories (see for example, Doel 1999; Murdoch 2006), so space has been created for rethinking the social construction of nature and the ways in which ecology and the environment are incorporated within human experience of space.

The chapter differs from many of the others in this volume in that it is not about a specific fear affecting a defined group of people. Indeed, nature itself may, at first sight, be rather remote from geopolitical concerns about struggles over land and security felt by individuals and groups. It is telling that any discussions of nature tend to be couched in terms of global environmental questions and sustainability within the geopolitics literature. While such issues are clearly hugely important (and very firmly related, as Castree (2003) points out, to power knowledge and global inequality at the local level) they do not often engage with the local experience of nature and with the emotions that shape our responses to it. In this chapter I show how the global and the local are woven together in people's understanding of nature and how their day to day concerns help to shape ideas of nature in a whole variety of ways that serve to influence global environmental politics. The examples used show the importance of emotional responses to nature. They also highlight the interrelatedness of nature and emotion reminding us that nature does not simply create an emotional response but is, in turn, a construction that emerges from our emotions.

Much of the discussion here is set within a rural context, emerging as it does from previous work that looked directly at fear in rural communities in the UK and New Zealand (see Little et al. 2005a; Panelli et al. 2004). That work noted the many differing ways in which nature was incorporated into rural residents' feelings of and responses to fear. It recognised at the time, however, that a separate focus drawing more fully on debates around the co-construction of nature and society and making use of emerging emotional geographies in understanding the relationship between fear, nature and space was required. The work also noted the particular importance of these debates within a rural context where heightened connections to and understandings of the 'natural world' made more meaningful beliefs about the interconnectivity of emotion and nature. This chapter suggests some of the ways in which nature and fear are intertwined in rural settings. The examples used are fairly wide ranging but they all stem from the contention that we need to take seriously the co-construction of nature and fear and, in so doing, recognise and begin to unpack the complexity of nature as part of our understanding of and emotional response to place.

Geographies of Nature, Rurality and Emotion

Nature-society relations have become one of the key areas of academic attention within recent human geography. In particular theoretical debate aimed at breaking down the separation of the natural from the social has opened up exciting avenues of enquiry about the meaning of nature and its social construction (see for example, Anderson 1995; Castree 2005; Haraway 1991; Watts 2005; Whatmore 2002). The starting point for these debates has been a recognition of the exclusion of nature from the study of social, cultural, political and subjective relations. If included at all nature was conceptualised as passive and inert, a timeless, unchanging raw material governed by the universal and predictive laws. It was thus 'the background against which culture elaborates itself, the contrast that distinguished variation, difference, becoming from the given, the unchanging and the inevitable' (Grosz 2005, 45). As some writers have articulated, however, recognising the need to break down binaries of the natural and the social is one thing, but actually finding ways of doing this is another.

It is clear that *how* we put this into *practice* depends on how we understand the idea of nature. For Grosz (2005) nature must be viewed as the 'force outside that incites culture', 'unpredictable and open ended', as a form of perpetual becoming rather than the static and contained backdrop for a more animated, ever-changing culture. Nature-culture relations are thus defined by emergence and not containment with culture as the 'open product of nature', not taking nature as its origin and basis but constantly in dialogue with a continually evolving nature. Grosz suggests that the idea of nature as reiterative and generative sets up a series of problems that culture must address, centering on the notions of temporality, of difference and complexity, the ever increasing diversity of populations and the relations between the self and other.

Geographers, working with new understandings of nature-culture relations have drawn on a range of concepts and theories to inform the new directions in their research and these have been reviewed at some length elsewhere (see for example Braun and Castree 1998; Castree 2005; Cloke and Perkins 2005; Instone 2004). Within these new approaches geographers have started to think about different ways of understanding nature in the construction of place, recognising the role of human/non-human interactions and of the need to employ different ways of conceptualising the world. Recently they have started to draw on non-representational theory to develop understandings based on practice and performance.

Linked to this work, geographers have also begun to pay much more attention to the role of emotion – indeed Bondi (2005) has recently gone so far as to identify an 'emotional turn' in geographical approaches seeing this development very much in keeping with broader social, cultural and political trends in which emotions have become more central to public life. The move to attend to emotions in understandings of social and physical environments derives from the same kind of questioning of traditional forms of knowledge that lies behind the revalorisation of nature. In particular the deconstruction of accepted binaries such as mind/body, nature/culture, rational/emotional, has been important in developing a holistic approach to subjectivity and troubling the boundaries between the environment and the individual (Bondi 2005).

While some past work in both humanistic and feminist geography has sought to encourage a greater emphasis on people's feelings about place in understandings of experience and identity, it is through more recent non-representational approaches that geographers have been encouraged to focus specifically on emotions. In seeking to move away from approaches that rely on representation, geographers have paid much greater attention to those 'myriad of transient and unarticulable practices that constitute everyday lives' (Bondi 2005, 437). Thus they have become more engaged with the performative and with embodied practices that provide a different kind of intelligence about the world (Thrift 2004). Although there has been debate concerning how such non-representative approaches can actually convey emotion, it is clear that these kinds of new approaches as developed by cultural geographers have helped to raise awareness of alternative ways of understanding people's relationship with place. Emphasis has also been placed, in such work, on the relational nature of emotions and on the fluidity and diversity of human subjectivity.

This chapter argues the importance of emotions in our understanding of nature and of the relationship between identity and place. It suggests that how we respond to nature is part of (and informs) our emotional relationship with rurality that lies at the heart of the ways in which we perform the rural. In focusing here on fear, the relational aspects of nature, rurality and emotion are evident – as the examples show, our fears are not simply a response to the kinds of nature we encounter in rural areas, but are also part of a construction of rurality that demands and valorises a particular way of seeing nature. Thus, as I shall show, while we may fear certain forces and acts attributed to 'nature', we also manage and respond to nature in a way that privileges a certain view of the rural. In particular, as Buller (2006) notes, the notion of nature as wild is both highly selective and carefully selected – only allowed in designated physical places or defined species categories. In other words, our understanding of rurality (in the western world) rests on certain fears around nature being permissible, or even encouraged, while others are not. Rural nature as wild and untamed demands a very different emotional response to rural nature out of control.

Perspectives on the Relationship between Nature and Fear

With this idea of nature and fear as relational, the following discussion is divided into two main sections. The first examines the concept of nature as a buffer against fear, a protector of rural spaces and communities and as a counter to the evil influences of progress, modernity and the urban. The second perspective explores the concept of nature as the instigator or cause of fear, and the ways in which such fears have also been built into how which we think about and understand the rural as well as into the more material aspects of performance and identity within rural spaces. The chapter refers to a variety of research findings, as appropriate – some where fear is a direct focus of the research but others where emotion is encountered while investigating broader issues around rural nature.

Nature as Protector

One key way in which nature can been seen as acting to counteract feelings of fear and increase safety in rural areas is by providing a barrier between the rural and the urban. At a very simplistic level distance can insulate rural communities, the sheer remoteness seeming to isolate them from harm. Such an idea clearly relies on the idea that danger comes from outside the rural community – so rural areas are not simply remote but rather remote *from* a particular danger. This notion of the dangerous 'other' has permeated accounts of cultural constructions of rurality in which social exclusion or marginalisation (and the fear of and resulting from it) has been seen as rooted in a fear or dislike of difference and a wish to protect rural people and communities from those who do not belong (see also Yarwood and Gardner 2000). Valentine's (1997) research on rural childhood, for example, showed how fears about child safety from parents were largely couched in terms of stranger-danger and related to fears of the unfamiliar 'other'. While not unique to rural areas, such fears in the case of Valentine's research seemed to hinge on a much more specific and spatialised sense of the other as 'not rural'. Moreover, protection from such dangerous 'others' was provided by the remoteness and self-contained nature of the rural space and its lack of connection to the urban.

The rural may be seen, too, as a source of relief from fears around terror/security which are viewed as predominantly urban (Graham 2004). Although as yet unsubstantiated by detailed research, there is an indication that remoter rural areas, particularly those distant from the USA, are seen as safer and more attractive places to live, with places such as rural New Zealand seeing an increase in migration by those wishing to escape the threat of terrorism.

A similar view of danger and the insulating effect of remoteness was found amongst residents of communities in rural Otago, New Zealand in research into women's feelings of fear and safety (see Panelli et al. 2004; Little et al. 2005a). The research[1] found that those living in the remoter rural areas appeared to consider themselves protected from the more common everyday dangers associated in more populated areas. They considered that the remoteness (together with the size of the community) meant that they rarely encountered strangers and thus were less at risk. This was enhanced by a feeling of knowing and being known by other residents and consequently being able to identify those who did not belong and of whom they should be fearful. The positive comments about remoteness were tempered amongst some residents by the fact that this could also lead to a lack of surveillance and also a problem of securing assistance if needed. One resident living in a remote valley in Otago summed up the contradictions in the relationship between fear and rurality as follows:

> In some ways its [the countryside] is safer. Less crime because of the isolation but more dangerous if it does happen [as it] takes too long for the emergency services to get here.[2]

Again, the notion that it was outsiders that should be feared came over strongly in the New Zealand research – the presence in the case study villages of a seasonal migrant labour force provided an easily identifiable group of 'others' and tended to be the target for fear amongst 'permanent' villagers. As one respondent claimed:

> Most of the crime committed in our area seems to be by outsiders. Fruit pickers, pruners, packers etc. More and more people are employed as orchards are growing to maturity.

While another continued:

> In Central [Otago] the crime rates go up in the summer due to the influx of seasonal workers ... I could feel unsafe on my own at night in summer.

It is worth noting that such fear of the outsider, particularly the migrant worker, was not, so the local Central Otago police claimed, supported by levels of arrests amongst the itinerant groups. Indeed, it served in some cases to mask incidents of violence from within the community and, more frequently, the family. Authors such as Kristeva (1991) and Sibley (1998) have argued that it is the stranger's unnatural presence that renders them abject and consequently threatening to the rural community. They are feared as individuals but it is their

---

1   The research was undertaken in 2002 with Ruth Panelli and funded by the University of Otago. It explored rural women's feelings of fear and safety and drew on questionnaires and interviews with rural women and key actors in Central Otago and Devon. I am indebted to Ruth for her input on this joint project.

2   All the quotes used in this section are drawn from the questionnaire survey undertaken as part of the New Zealand research in Central Otago (see Panelli et al. 2004 and 2005).

collective presence that threatens community and the protection this provides from danger and fear.

As well as reflecting a view that the stranger to be feared was from 'outside', the comments recorded in the research also demonstrated a strong belief that it was the urban that represented the greatest threat. Fear seemed to correspond not only to the physical isolation of the rural but also reflected a belief in the social and cultural division between country and town. The urban was identified partly for its lack of connection to nature and to what the rural respondents understood as 'country values'. The culture of the urban was depicted as unnatural and alien and thus to be feared. In today's global world it was also recognised that, however physically remote, nowhere was really 'safe' from urban values and culture. Such views clearly play on a familiar urban rural dichotomy and on the association of the urban with the modern and with the unnatural. To the rural dwellers of remote Otago, fears of isolation, harsh winters and the force of nature were relatively insignificant compared to those associated with the encroachment of the town and the invasion of the unpredictable urban stranger.

Interestingly, in the research, nature was also recruited by the rural women as working with them and against the strangers. Not only were strangers out of place in the countryside (and thus to be feared), but their presence was an active threat to the harmony of nature (see also Yarwood and Gardener 2000). This was emphasised in their belief that outsiders lacked certain competences to deal with nature. *Understanding* nature was the characteristic that marked out 'genuine country people' and a lack of understanding indicated a potential lack of other shared values. In our research we encountered many women whose fear appeared mediated by the belief that the stranger did not have the skills and competences to live comfortably in a rural community. Such outsiders would end up disliking the environment and/or community and moving away. The lack of competence in nature was not only undesirable in terms of the lifestyle and happiness of the outsider but also likely to endanger the existing country folk whose own understanding may be compromised in having to deal with problems caused by outsiders.

These findings resonate with ideas discussed elsewhere, for example by Edensor (2001) and McNaughten and Urry (2001), concerning the way familiarity with, and competence within, nature in relation to hill walking and other outdoor recreation have traditionally been connected with ideas of health and the body. Again, such work argues that nature is constructed as uninviting and potentially dangerous to those who are unfamiliar with its moods and power, yet therapeutic and health giving to those with understanding. Nature, it is argued, needs to be understood and respected and those who learn skills such as map reading and survival techniques are safe and comfortable in nature. The fit, healthy body can benefit from nature's calm and tranquil qualities because it is a body that has the ability to withstand fear and dominate the cause of fear. It is a safe body. Nature is also complicit in the production of that body through providing the environment for exercise and the development of strength as well as peace and solitude.

The relationship between nature and competence, the body, and fear are also touched on in work on gender and recreation. Burgess (1995), for example, discusses the fear felt by women exercising in woodland in the urban fringe, commenting on the sense in which their responses to the environment were shaped by a combination of fears concerning an unfamiliarity with nature but also the ways in which nature might conceal threat from strangers. In research undertaken on women running/jogging in rural areas, Wesley and Gaarder (2004) show how women may be fearful of exercising in remote locations but also gain strength and courage from being competent in such locations – knowing the area and the terrain, and having confidence in their bodies. This claim is supported by Bialeschki and Hicks (1998) in their work on women, the outdoors and fear. They write:

> Also included as a part of planning (hiking trips) was acquiring skills and experiences that made the woman feel more competent and able to take care of herself in threatening situations. One older woman said 'other people who don't feel safe in the wilderness type of environment, it is maybe because it's unfamiliar to them... it's a lot unknown so the more you have that experience the younger you get that experience, the more comfortable you feel.

The chapter now turns to look at opposing constructions and representations of nature in which, rather than protecting against fear, nature can be the cause of fear. It should be stressed, however, that although the idea of nature as causing fear is set up here as oppositional to nature as protector, these two constructions are not mutually exclusive; nature is rarely one or the other but evokes a complex, multiple and shifting reaction in terms of fear, as is shown below.

Nature as Fear

While in Central Otago nature or wilderness was seen as providing a barrier to dangerous strangers whose inability to comprehend or cope with remoteness would act to increase the safety of those living there, remoteness also might serve to conceal the dangerous stranger from surveillance by neighbours. Thus some respondents spoke of feeling more vulnerable to home invasion because there were fewer people around to watch out for strangers and nobody to call for help. In addition, the sheer distances that emergency services needed to travel to get to the remoter properties was seen by some as a potential cause of fear. While it is not nature here that is the source of fear, the rural environment itself is an obvious factor in its creation.

This sense of fear being associated with wilderness conditions was more directly obvious in the research in comments about the state of farming and the vulnerable livelihoods of individuals. Here nature was much more likely to be seen as responsible (and thus feared), mainly in its control over the weather, for the fortunes of the farming industry in general and also the plight of particular enterprises and individuals. While 'good farmers' were able to predict and cope with the 'whims of nature' to some extent, there was always a sense that, for farming in fairly marginal and extreme environments, nature was easily capable of some dramatic gesture that could destroy a crop or threaten an entire enterprise. Against such gestures, people were ultimately helpless and all attempts to battle nature would prove fruitless. There was a clear message amongst those living in remoter Otago that nature has the power to kill, devastate and to ruin livelihoods through destroying agriculture and, less frequently, the buildings and infrastructure of contemporary economic and social life.

Nature as beyond the control of humans clearly has the greatest power in terms of the ability to induce fear. There are seemingly numerous instances where 'natural disasters' remind us of the vulnerability of humans and the enormity of some physical processes, whether in relation to sudden events such as earthquakes or tsunami or more gradual long-term conditions such as the loss of an eco-system or climate change. Although fear here is about the helplessness of humans against nature, fears seem heightened where there is some suggestion of human cause or intervention. Where humans have tampered with nature, the suggestion of loss of control appears more frightening. Such concerns serve to link the more nebulous fears about global level damage inflicted by humans on the environment with the immediate, day to day fears surrounding the obvious impact of damage on natural systems.

A clear example of this kind of fear of nature out of control can be seen in responses to developments in agriculture and food production. Recent outbreaks of BSE and foot and mouth disease in UK agriculture have reinforced growing concerns about the potential risks of changing or interfering with nature. Such diseases are seen as an indication that agricultural practices have sought to inflict too drastic a change on natural systems in the name of profit. Writing in the Guardian newspaper, the journalist Paul Evans (2001) makes the link between fear, nature and agricultural disease, stressing the way in which current fear relates to a long-term sense of human interference in nature and a loss of control.

> Fear is what the virus brings. Fear shuts down the footpaths. Fear slaughters the animals. Specifically this is a fear that wild nature will respond violently to our presence on Earth and our intervention in natural processes. This is not just what we feel about nature – this is our experience of how nature is.

He goes on:

> This year [2001] … we have already had storms, floods and blizzards. Agriculture is linked to BSE, e-coli, salmonella, bovine tuberculosis and swine fever. Now there's a visitation from a virus (FMD), reappearing from a painful long-ago memory, and burning through the ecology of commerce like wildfire. All these things are perfectly natural. A fear of them is a fear of nature's answering violence.

Globalisation speeds up and exacerbates these threats in the way that Ingram describes in this volume. The nature of the cultural and political relations between the west and other countries predisposes our emotional reaction to one of fear.

Although such dramatic cases raise very specific fears, they also relate to broader worries about the risks associated with food production processes generally and a belief that current practices are unsustainable in terms of their effects on nature. Debates about genetically modified (GM) crops and animals have famously referred to 'Frankenstein foods', conjuring up a monster out of control, a disturbed or distorted nature that humans have helped to create. In recent research on the consumption of local and organic foods, ideas of risk and safety are seen as growing influences on consumer choice of food (see Little et al. 2005b). The idea that 'local food' with short supply chains is more likely to be 'natural', produced in a way that is different from the dominant practices of conventional agriculture (for example not treated with chemicals to last or to appear homogenous like supermarket food), means to some consumers that it is less risky.

This work on the relationship between risk, local food and nature brings us back to the earlier discussion about the role of knowledge and competences about nature in the reduction of fear. The local food research has shown how concern amongst some consumers about our lack of understanding about food production, and our disconnectedness from agricultural practices, is seen to lie at the heart of broader worries about food quality, health and risk. In one study, consumers claimed that children in particular were losing touch with knowledge about food production and its connection with nature. Such fears were themselves related to broader concerns about the lack of connectivity between young people and nature, and moral panics about health, fitness, exercise and childhood obesity.

Throughout history 'natural disasters' have been linked in both a religious and secular context with the idea that society is being punished by the wrath of nature. This notion of nature as beyond human power is also something that humans take comfort from. Thus Buller (2006), for example, in recent work on the sighting of supposed 'big cats' in the British countryside, talks about the enduring importance of the mythical to notions of nature. He draws on Michel Serres' concept of angels to describe the way alien big cats establish, mix, order and disorder the connections between society and nature, human and non-human, wild and domesticated nature. Buller argues that, in the UK at least, we still need the wild. Deprived of the wild in our countryside we are increasingly forced to invent and imagine it – hence the sightings of big cats and a fear of wilderness invading residential areas. We also seek out fear of nature in other ways – through, for example, adventure tourism where 'overcoming' fear of nature is part of the challenge that activities such as bungee jumping, white water rafting and sky diving represent (Cater and Smith 2003).

Conclusion

The aim of this chapter has been to explore (somewhat speculatively) ways in which geographical debates about nature and fear inform one another. Specifically the chapter has looked at the different roles that nature can play as either a cause of fear or a protector against fear. The feared objects involved may be environmental, social, human-made or not; and the degree of threat or protection perceived is increasingly affected by connections and flows between rural, urban, local and global. Focusing on the rural, the chapter has highlighted the complex and often contradictory relationship between fear and nature and argued that understanding more about this relationship is important not only for our understanding of rurality as a cultural and social construct but, perhaps more importantly, for our attempts to break down the binary distinction between nature and culture and recognise the interconnectivity of these concepts. 'Rural' is not just a local indigenous construction, but its affective experience is constituted by relations with and imaginaries of the 'urban' and 'global' scales too.

Nature has long been seen as intimately tied in to emotions surrounding rurality – for example evoking feelings of peace and tranquillity. Fear is a complex and many-faceted dimension of this emotional response and is evident at times in easily recognisable and direct ways. It is also, however, present in the construction of a whole range of values surrounding the ways in which we think about and understand rurality, particularly in terms of access to and behaviour within the countryside. Fear of nature is used as an exclusionary device to identify those 'out-of-place others' in rural space – the urban stranger or the walker lacking in 'rural' skills, for example. In this sense it is clear that fear is not always a negative emotion but can be used by certain groups to secure their own interests and protect the rural as a space of privilege and exclusivity. Fear of nature is also important in terms of retaining the notion of wilderness and of a greater power than human-kind. Such power, as others have noted, is appealing in both a religious and secular context within societies providing a sense of a force beyond the human.

Focusing on the co-construction of nature and fear in the ways discussed in the chapter has highlighted the growing recognition of emotions in geographical research and writing. It has also demonstrated that emotions need to be seen not just as psychological states but as social and cultural relations (see Ahmed 2004). Moreover, emotions are not simply rooted in the individual but move and are negotiated between bodies. Hopefully the issues raised in this chapter will encourage the development of research on our emotional responses to nature, and a greater acknowledgement of how this may be incorporated into geographical analyses.

Bibliography

Ahmed, S. (2004), *The Cultural Politics of Emotion* (Edinburgh: Edinburgh University Press).

Anderson, K. (1995), 'Culture and Nature at the Adelaide Zoo: At the frontiers of "human geography"', *Transactions of the Institute of British Geographers* 20, 275–94.

Bialeschki, M. and Hicks, H. (1998), '"I Refuse to Live in Fear": The influence of fear of violence on women's outdoor recreation activities', paper presented at the annual conference of Leisure Studies Association, Leeds Metropolitan University.

Bondi, L. (2005), 'Making Connections and Thinking through Emotions', *Transactions of the Institute of British Geographers* 30, 433–8.

Braun, B. and Castree, N. (eds) (1998), *Remaking Reality: Nature at the millenium* (London: Sage).

Buller, H. (2006), 'The Woozle's Return: Angels, monsters and imaginary spaces', seminar paper, University of Exeter. Copy from the author.

Burgess, J (1995), *Growing in Confidence: Understanding people's perceptions of urban fringe woodlands*, Report to the Countryside Commission (Cheltenham: Countryside Commission).

Cater, C. and Smith, L. (2003), 'New Country Visions: Adventurous bodies in rural tourism', in P. Cloke (ed.) *Country Visions* (London: Pearson).

Castree, N. (2003), 'The Geopolitics of Nature', in J. Agnew, K. Mitchell and G. Toal (eds), *A Companion to Political Geography* (London: Blackwell).

Castree, N. (2005), *Nature* (Routledge: London).

Cloke, P. and Perkins, H. (2005), 'Cetacean Performance and Tourism in Kaikoura, New Zealand', *Environment and Planning D: Society and Space* 23, 903–24.

Doel, M. (1999), *Poststructural Geographies: The diabolical art of spatial science* (Edinburgh: Edinburgh University Press).

Edensor, T. (2001), 'Walking in the British Countryside: Reflexivity, embodied practices and ways to escape', in P. McNaughten and J. Urry (eds), *Bodies of Nature* (London: Sage).

Evans, P. (2001), 'The silent Spring: Why do we fear nature's retribution', *The Guardian*, 7 March 2001.

Graham, S. (2004), *Cities, War and Terrorism* (Oxford: Blackwell).

Grosz, E. (2005), *Time Travels: Feminism, nature, power* (Durham, NC: Duke University Press).

Haraway, D. (1991), *Simians, Cyborgs and Women: The reinvention of nature* (New York: Routledge).

Instone, L. (2004), 'Situating Nature: On doing cultural geographies of Australian nature', *Australian Geographer* 35, 131–40.

Kristeva, J. (1991), *Strangers to Ourselves* (London: Harvester Wheatsheaf).

Little, J., Panelli, R. and Kraack, A. (2005a), 'Women's Fear of Crime: A rural perspective', *Journal of Rural Studies* 21, 151–63.

Little, J., Gilg, A., Simpson, S., Ilbery, B and Watts, D. (2005b), 'Consumption, Consumer Behaviour and Alternative Food Networks', Working Paper 4, *Relocalisation and Alternative Food Networks Research*, Universities of Coventry and Exeter.

McNaughten, P. and Urry, J. (eds) (2001), *Bodies of Nature* (London: Sage).

Murdoch, J. (2006), *Post-structuralist Geography* (London: Sage).

Panelli, R., Kraack, A. and Little, J. (2005), 'Claiming Space and Community Rural Women's Strategies for Living with, and Beyond, Fear', *Geoforum* 36, 495–508.

Panelli, R., Little, J. and Kraack, A. (2004), 'A Community Issue? Rural Women's Feelings of Safety and Fear in New Zealand', *Gender, Place and Culture* 11, 445–66.

Sibley, D. (1998), 'The Problematic Nature of Exclusion', *Geoforum* 29, 119–21.

Thrift, N. (2004), 'Intensities of Feeling: Towards a spatial politics of affect', *Geografiska Annaler* 86B, 57–78.

Valentine, G. (1997), 'A Safe Place to Grow Up? Parenting, Perceptions of Children's Safety and the Rural Idyll', *Journal of Rural Studies* 13, 137–48.

Watts, M. (2005), 'Nature Culture', in P. Cloke and R. Johnston (eds), *Spaces of Geographical Thought* (London: Sage).

Wesley, J. and Gaarder, E. (2004), 'The Gendered Nature of the Urban Outdoors. Women Negotiating Fear of Violence', *Gender and Society* 18, 645–63.

Whatmore, S. (2002), *Hybrid Geographies* (London: Sage).

Yarwood, R. and Gardner, G. (2000), 'Fear of Crime, Culture and the Countryside', *Area* 32:4, 403–11.

SECTION 3

Encountering Fear and Otherness

The four chapters in this section are bound by a common aim, which is to examine how so-called 'global' fears play out and are experienced in everyday life. The concern of the contributors is how people encounter, practice and live fear and other emotions everyday, and the assorted ways in which these are intertwined with geopolitical conflicts. In so doing, these accounts expose how fear of 'Others' leads to prejudice or is used as an excuse for prejudice, and how people who are feared may themselves become fearful of attack and discrimination. While similar arguments have been made in relation to issues such as homophobia, homelessness, and those with mental health problems, it is the social politics of race, ethnicity and religion which are the main concerns of these chapters. Some investigate the treatment of newcomers to the countries under examination, while others focus on the ways in which longstanding minority groups deal with longstanding, but subtly shifting, abuse. All of the chapters draw out the effects of recent global fears, for example the ways in which terrorism, the 'war on terror' and international migration can exacerbate historical conflicts or mark changes in direction, disrupting any sense of linear progression towards multicultural societies. The contributors provide rich empirical material in support from migrants, asylum seekers, Muslims and young people in western contexts.

Peter Hopkins and Susan Smith track the ways in which 'fear is entangled with the racist practices involved in defining and controlling global positioning, national space and local lives', both in a particular context – Scotland, with a particular history and an image of having fewer tensions than England – and over time. They argue that there is both continuity and revision, as the politics and practices of fear hinge on racial essentialisms in old and new ways. In particular, religion has become more prominent as a point of racial distinction between young Muslim men and other young people in Scotland, and segregation is being reinscribed rather than gradually dissolving.

Likewise, Michael Haldrup, Lasse Koefoed and Kirsten Simonson examine how fear provides one way of enacting 'practical orientalism'. Their focus is on encounters of Danish-born people with recent migrants, and they demonstrate how hegemonic geopolitical discourses are connected to racism and discrimination. The 'mooding' of these discourses, or the way that bodies take on and act on emotions, is one way in which other bodies (their appearance, dress and behaviour) are encountered in negative and harmful ways: 'scapegoating, for instance, enables a group to convert an anxiety into a fear, thus legitimizing hostile utterances and actions against bodies "out-of-place."' Their Otherness, on which geopolitical relations rely, is produced through these material encounters as well as pre-dating it (see also Askins in Section 5). Greg Noble and Scott Poynting take further the notion of national identity and security as underpinning hostility towards migrants, with a scathing critique of the portrayal of Australia as 'a relaxed and comfortable nation'. The abuse that migrants may experience on a daily basis serves to exclude them further from citizenship and equal participation (see also Alexander on young people in Section 1). Examining the risks of harm faced by migrants in everyday life, rather than hazy assertions about the circulation of cultural fear, helps to ground our understandings of the hard edge of neoliberal geopolitics in this (perhaps, for some observers, unexpected) location.

The picture that the chapters in this section paint is partly a bleak one, of hostility, fear, material risk and harm. Yet that is not the only conclusion they point to, for as we might expect, their respondents' accounts do not simply confirm taken-for-granted assumptions about the flow of fear from global events into everyday life. For the young Muslim men quoted in Hopkins and Smith's chapter, it is clear that fear is situated and contingent: some local neighbourhoods and cities predominantly reflect safety and comfort rather than danger, and family and community life are a rich source of happiness and security. These young men's balanced appraisal and engagement with the situation in which they find themselves provides a fresh foil to more popular geopolitical discourses. And in Kathrin Hörschelmann's work, a more hopeful narrative is also developed. The young people in her research recognise the complex and plural consequences of the 'war on terror'. Without romanticising the young people involved – most see their own agency to effect change as quite limited – Hörschelmann mounts a persuasive argument that challenges a number of stereotypes about young people, presenting them as thoughtful political beings enmeshed in systems of care for others, both near and far.

Chapter 8

Scaling Segregation; Racialising Fear

Peter E. Hopkins and Susan J. Smith

Introduction

There is a sense in some parts of the literature, as well as across the mass media, that life in the affluent west is characterised by a growing culture of fear; that anxiety, insecurity and uncertainty constitute a relatively new and increasingly pervasive way of being. And this may be true in some walks of life, perhaps because the power relations which differentiate (in complex ways) between feared and fearful are changing. However, the structures of anxiety that characterise what Noble (2005, 108) calls 'the affective regulation of belonging' are not new. They are implicated in the long game of racialisation, and in the segregationisms which – far from being the declining legacy of a colonial past – remain a powerful tool of cultural politics.

On the one hand, terror was part of the mechanics of slavery; it was the engine of apartheid; it is still the driving force of 'ethnic cleansing' and xenophobia in many parts of the world. On the other hand, closer to 'home', moral panic, the fears of the feared – enacted in case 'the Empire strikes back' – has been at the core of an accumulation of racist immigration legislation together with a range of strategies of containment and control by every political administration in the UK for nearly 50 years (Smith 1989; Baumber 2004).

This chapter is about a politics and practice of fear that makes religion a point of racial distinction between young Muslim men and other young people in Scotland.[1] We are concerned with the elision of race and religion which is taking place as the politics of recognition (the dignification and celebration of difference in all its fine-grained subtlety) are displaced by the power-brokerage of terror whose tendency is to revise, recast and, in the end, reassert, a divide between the West and the Rest. Our argument is that, in one sense, what is happening today

---

1 This chapter is based on data collected during eleven focus groups and twenty-two interviews conducted between March 2002 and July 2003 (Hopkins 2004). All of the young men were aged 16–25 and identified as Muslims. They were contacted through a process of snowballing where initial contacts at schools, colleges and universities, mosques, community and voluntary organisations, and youth groups were asked to identify other young Muslim men who might agree to participate in the research. All of the focus groups and interviews involved discussions that focused on Scotland, the local community, being a young man as well as being Muslim, concentrating in particular upon the young men's senses of belonging, identity and in/exclusion.

is not new at all: the constant threat and material reality of harm has always had, and continues to evoke, regulatory and segregative consequences. But in another way, everything has changed, at least in respect of the way constructions of scale are deployed to frame, legitimise, and manage the mechanisms of offense and defense that mark out and unequalise difference. A rescaling of fear is taking place, dividing communities of interest that might once have been allies; and engendering profound discomfort as it fragments homespace and the lives it contains among continents, between institutions and across a splintered political landscape.

Continuities

There are two kinds of continuity that we wish to emphasise here, both bringing the real threat and enduring fear of attack to bear on processes of essentialism around conceptions of biological and cultural difference.

On the one hand we note that the demonisation of racialised Others drives all scales of politics, and has historically been used politically to assert power over territory: over neighbourhoods (especially through struggles over housing), over national boundaries (through exclusive immigration legislation) and across entire world regions (for example in the coordination of diverse national strategies around labour and refugee migration to create the effect of 'fortress Europe'). The 'respectable' face of this kind of politics is inextricably bound up with a politics of terror that plays on the fears of the included by criminalising their 'Other'. Looking back over more than twenty years of racial politics in the UK, there are numerous ways to illustrate this. In a bid for racial exclusivity, for example, Enoch Powell evoked the spectre of an English urban landscape studded with 'Citadels of Urban Terrorism' in a speech to the Monday Club delivered in 1980; at the third reading of the British Nationality Act in 1981, Harvey Proctor spoke of the 'dreadful and inevitable racial strife' facing Britain's cities; in a debate on race relations in the same year, Ivor Stanbrook told how 'some areas of this country are inhabited by people who ... openly reject lawful authority'. This is the tip of an iceberg more fully excavated in Smith (1989; 1993a): whether explicitly, in the language of old racisms, or implicitly in the euphemisms of the new, there is a politics of fear which hinges around racial (and other) essentialisms in divisive and exclusionary ways.

On the other hand, there is a long list of ways in which lay perspectives and everyday behaviours – actions which are rude and insulting, ignorant and undignified, threatening or violent – conspire to racialise, exclude and mark out differences on the basis of bodily markings, adornments and behaviours. The fact that some of these racist activities are banal or 'low-level', routinised, not overtly hateful, and not even at the forefront of people's mind for much of the time, does not mean they cause no-one to suffer. It is the prospect of any encounter turning sour – the constant threat of violence simply because of some combination of location and appearance – that makes fear so powerful an impulse to separation, that implicates fear in the multi-stranded segregation of society and the complex scaling of space. This broad point is reasonably well demonstrated in the literature and has been for some years. A history of the 'common sense' racisms that sustain geographies of inequality set out in Smith (1989), for example, when viewed in the light of today's news headlines, suggests that as far as the motivation for defensive withdrawal and the basis for strategies of resistance are concerned, there are as many continuities as there are differences.

The Scottish example we are working with does bring out some of the nuances in this, not least because of the distinctiveness of Scottish history and the complex racialisation of politics that has been a part of it. Here, a political preoccupation with the religious divide between Catholic and Protestant Christians displaced the racisms at the centre of English political affairs from Scottish affairs, producing what is now recognised as unwarranted complacency among Scottish decision-takers. As Miles and Dunlop (1987, 199) point out, 'what distinguishes Scotland from England is the absense of a racialization of the political process since 1945, rather than an absense of racism *per se'*. So although the character of racism in Scotland is distinctive in some important ways (Smith 1993b), in Scotland as in England there is an all too familiar catalogue of insults, assaults, damage and harm, effected through both personal racism and political extremism, undermining health, welfare and wellbeing, and contributing to the separation and segregation of social life. Recent interviews with a relatively middle-class sample of young Muslim men in Glasgow and Edinburgh tell of the legacy this has left in their description of two styles of withdrawal from Scottish public life.

The first, perhaps more conventional, narrative is contained in the accounts of 47 Glaswegian interviewees. Glasgow accommodates 31 per cent of Scotland's minority ethnic population, 23 per cent of whom live in the relatively segregated space of Pollokshields. This is the most residentially segregated area in Scotland in terms of ethnic group membership, with around 50 per cent of the local population identifying with a South Asian heritage, and 40 per cent identifying as Muslim. Here the young men describe their experience of residential segregation as protective, specifically against the threat of racism.

For example, Shafqat and Michael talk about the safety effect of numbers on a local scale – numbers which are protective in a symbolic and, if necessary, practical sense.

Shafqat: Pollokshields is the Asian person's safe haven. Pollokshields is: the Asian person, black or ethnic minority, can walk through Pollokshields knowing that nothing racist is going to happen to them, it just won't happen in Pollokshields … I like Pollokshields. I've lived here, grew up here, I quite like it. For me, it is a really safe place to be … maybe because of who I am, because I am the kind of guy that everyone knows in Pollokshields. (Interview, Glasgow, 17 June 2003)

Michael: See in Pollokshields nobody is racist because they know they'll get knocked out because there are more Asians there … (Focus group, Glasgow, 3 April 2003)

Discourses about safety in numbers, and the haven effect of living in an 'Asian area' litter discussions with the young men from Pollokshields. Consider this focus group extract:

Saeed:	It's just that there are not very many Asians in other areas, so you just get an unwelcome feeling.
Nasser:	Yeah, people kind of look at you, as if you shouldn't be there ...
Peter:	So, do you think it is important to have a lot of Asians about?
Saeed:	Yeah, it's safer ... you feel more welcome ...
Peter:	So you definitely feel safer going into an Asian area, like even in another city, say in London?
Saeed:	I've never been to London before so I can't really say.
Nasser:	No, I think that with Asians around it is safer wherever you go, yeah ... (Focus group, Glasgow, 24 July 2002)

Here, the young men prioritise their sense of safety, inclusion and belonging – of being 'welcome' – in their discussion of life in Pollokshields. Their narratives give precedence to these themes, and stress the importance of residential segregation as a strategy for minimising anxieties, uncertainties and insecurities. It is, indeed, the combination of numbers and residential location that defines the local in these narratives of safekeeping.

This style of (safely segregated) living is, moreover, located as a point of distinction, marking Pollokshields as different from other, less segregated neighbourhoods which are depicted as inherently more risky. The young men therefore hold similar views to some of the participants in Phillips' (2006, 33) research, who suggested that they would not like to live in 'all white' or 'white working class' areas because of fears about 'racism, ethnic tensions and racist harassment'. These strategies of defensive withdrawal are typical of times and places where institutional responses to racism have been ineffective, prompting resistance itself to be segregationist. We restate them here to make two points. First, the scale of 'local' is, to an extent, interchangeable with spaces of residential segregation, as locational decisions are drawn into a suite of strategies for safekeeping. Second, the impetus towards strategic withdrawal is no less alarming now than at any time in the last half century; it is no less pervasive, and no more novel than it has been in the past. It is 'more of the same' surrounded by the same breathtaking political complacency.

The Scottish example, whose 'numbers' debate has always been different to England's, contains a further dimension of defensive withdrawal, best thought of as a strategy of 'invisibilisation'. While English racial (racist) politics hinges crucially around strategies tackling 'the problem' of (large) numbers and (segregated) locations of visible minority populations (Smith 1988), Scottish politics has always justified a 'hands-off' approach to race and racism with reference to low numbers and relatively low indices of residential integration. The epitome of this is the case of Edinburgh. Here, the highest levels of segregation of the distinctively small visible minority population of Edinburgh – the national capital – live in South Edinburgh, where in the 'most segregated' wards the minority ethnic population accounts for 3 per cent or less of the total. The 30 young men from South Edinburgh whose narratives inform our comments here occupy spaces that are thought of as 'white', and their strategy is to maintain this 'balance' – to invisibilise their own presence – in order to avoid being perceived as a threat, and being placed, as a consequence, at risk:

Anwar: It's probably, probably better if there's maybe fewer because then, you know, you feel less of a threat. That's sort of ... the argument, you know ... because, like, if there tends to be quite a lot in one area, you think they're trying to take over and things like that ... so probably better off in small numbers. (Interview, Edinburgh, 17 December 2002)

Nadeem: The Scottish people that live there, they might not like it like that. They won't like being dominated by Asians. (Focus group, Edinburgh, 19 June 2002)

Mohammed: ... in Edinburgh, there are like no places that are like full of Asians or whatever ... at the moment if there is only the odd ethnic minority person here and there, then people don't seem to bother, but when there becomes a lot then that could create problems because people feel threatened you know ... (Interview, Edinburgh, 16 May 2002)

Omar: The problems in Scotland are very minimal because there are very few Asians in Scotland. (Focus group, Edinburgh, 14 November 2002)

These four young men place high priority on minimising the perceived 'threat' to white Edinburgh that large, residentially segregated and visibly distinctive ethnic minority populations 'impose' on others. There is a logic then to becoming invisible – to avoid being noticed and picked out for bodily markings, personal appearance and cultural behaviour and to blend into areas with low levels of ethnic minority residential clustering. The interests of the young men appear to be focused on lessening the chance of experiences of exclusion and disconnection, while giving primacy to personal safety, minimising the fear and anxiety associated with potential experiences of racism. Again, the local is experienced through conceptions of neighbourhood life; the scale of the local is constructed around an ideal of integrated residential space as a springboard for an integrated, effectively undifferentiated, social life.

In this study, there are, then, two views and two sets of tactics around neighbourhood: both about minimising risk; both about responding to fear; both prioritising the drive to safety, security and belonging. One stresses the importance of safety in numbers, prizing residential segregation as a source of security. The other is a tactic of safety in scarcity, seeking invisibility through dispersal. It would be a mistake to over-emphasise these tactics, as if the whole of all the young men's lives were about fear and withdrawal. Our point rather is that there is an undercurrent of threat, and an undercurrent of anxiety which – although mingled with other affects and experiences – produce tendencies towards segregation and invisibilisation which play off against other ways of living and weave into other strands of personal biography in all kinds of ways.

Both the segregative tendencies we have documented are effected by people who are young Scots: young men who are Scottish; they belong to Scotland; Scotland belongs to them. Yet there is a sense running through their discussions that this belonging is conditional. A sense of belonging is conditional, for example, on subscribing to what Back (1996, 111) describes as a 'harmony discourse' – an ideological claim for a locality free of racism and its attendant threats. An inclination here is to identify right wing extremism as the main source of risk, and to locate that extremism in an 'Other' space (in this case in urban England):

> Kabir: Something could happen quite soon in Bradford ... Burnley and so on because the BNP came, but I personally don't see that it would happen in Glasgow and even less likely in Edinburgh ... in Scotland there are some things that haven't really been touched on in a big way, for example, especially like the BNP. They haven't been very successful in Scotland. (Interview, Glasgow, 12 December 2002)

The inclination, then, is to relocate the source of harm, the feeling of discomfort and the threat of racism by placing it beyond the pale: by positioning its source in the heart of English nationalism and in the activities of English right wing extremism.[2] This by definition removes some part of the racist threat from the immediacies of daily life, making space for the comings and goings which are required when people work, play, worship and exist beyond the spaces of housing and home. This 'harmony'-talk may be as much an expression of hope as an articulation of fear, but either way it indicates a sense of belonging that is qualified and provisional rather than taken-for-granted.

To *summa*rise: there are some important ways in which this recent study of the life and experiences of young Muslim men in Scotland continues and elaborates the narrative of 'old' British racisms and the segregationism with which that became associated during the twentieth century. Fears anchored on racist practices and intentions – and on all the physical and psychosocial harm that flows from these – underpin a tendency to separatism whether by segregationism or invisibilisation (which are, in effect, two sides of a single coin). These localised, material, spatial strategies are accompanied by symbolic claims made in the interests of psycho-social wellbeing. There is an inclination to regard 'belonging' as something conditional on displacing the main source of risk onto the racism of English urban extremists, onto the actions and intent of people who live beyond the bounds of Scottish nationhood.

---

2   This notion that the worst of racism is to be found in the ravages of urban England, rather than the niceties of Scottish life, is also found in the discourse of other areas of Scottish affairs as discussed in Smith (1993b).

Revisions

The tactics of withdrawal associated with the fears inspired by racism are encouraged in a setting where the bases of religious, cultural, and ethnic differentiation are denied positive recognition. On this, two things have changed in recent years.

First, as the language of race, which gained momentum across the 1980s, blurred into new discourses of ethnicity in the 1990s, and as a rethinking of religion cut across the race debate towards the close of the millennium, theory and practice around difference produced a concerted move in the direction of positive recognition. One of the ethical achievements of social research and public life in the closing years of the twentieth century was to begin to accommodate this: to look to ways to extend positive recognition as part of the project of social justice. In the late 1980s and early 1990s, for example, Tariq Modood (1988; 1994) criticised the use of singular 'black' identity label, asserting that such a categorisation did not do justice to the uniqueness of the 'Asian' experience. As Alexander (2002, 562) observes:

> Tariq Modood thus argued that 'black' erased cultural differences and economic successes; that it ignored the specificities of emergent forms of 'cultural racism', especially in relation to Islam and Islamophobia; and that it privileged an African-Caribbean agenda masquerading as an inclusive political movement (1992a). More than this, Asians have simply never been seen, or have ever seen themselves, as 'black'.

While Modood might equally be criticised for homogenising an idea of 'Asian' which refers to people whose personal or family background is rooted in South (not East) Asia, and which lumps Muslims, Sikhs and Hindus together, this sensitivity to (and politicisation of) difference is indicative of the move to recognition that feminism, anti-racism, and a range of political theorising (around, for example, the idea of group as well as individual rights) has favoured, elaborated and fought for – with a considerable degree of success – across the last decade.

On the other hand, with the events of 11 September 2001 – and a sweep of subsequent terrorist attacks – came recognition of a different and far less welcome kind.

Kabir: It was really after September 11 that ... they went from simply talking about Asian and racial issues, to turning specifically on the Muslims. (Interview, Edinburgh, 12 November 2002)

Abdul: ... there was a backlash against Muslims after September 11 and I felt quite isolated and I'd never felt like that before. (Interview, Edinburgh, 6 November 2002)

This most recent turn of world events has gone global and has recast old racialisations – those organised around the presumed geographical origins and affiliations of those whose bodies are marked out as coloniser/colonised – into a different kind of role. Old markers of race have been drawn instead, or additionally, into a new set of essentialisms around signifiers of religious affiliation, as the 'war on terror' has developed hand in hand with the demonisation of Muslim and all its markers, wherever they are found and whoever bears them. With recent world events, the idea of a unified 'Asian' identity has been prised apart at the same time as the recognition and dignification of all kinds of difference has been subdued. Instead Muslims – depicted as being epitomised in certain fractions of South Asian, Middle Eastern and African cultures – have 'become the ultimate 'Other', transfixed through the racialization of religious identity to stand at the margins, undesired, irredeemable, alien' (Alexander 2002, 564).

The world has changed, then; it has been made different, cynically as well as by default, since 11 September 2001. These changes have local, national and global consequences. Indeed, they are part of a redefinition of the politics and practice of scale, as the questionable idea of global threat is drawn into the material reality of local life. What has changed, though, is an ethical trajectory, as 'the West' once again lines up against 'the Rest', displacing the niceties of recognition with the indignity of biometric profiling, tagging, tracking and targeting. Diversity has been displaced by difference; and the divide is of world proportions.

There is an extent to which the translation of all this into the anxieties of everyday life is inspired by the same kind of 'moral panic' that underpinned the criminalisation of black people of African-Caribbean origin or heritage in Britain in the late 1970s (Hall et al. 1978). Cohen (1972, 9 in Valentine 2001, 181) defines a moral panic as occurring when:

> A condition, episode, person or group of persons emerges to become defined as a threat to societal values and interests; its nature presented in a stylized and stereotypical fashion by the mass media, the moral barricades are manned by editors, bishops, politicians and other right-thinking people; socially accredited experts pronounce their diagnoses and solutions; ways of coping are evolved or (more often) resorted to; the condition then disappears, submerges or deteriorates and becomes more visible.

The narratives of young Muslim men in Scotland, spoken fresh from the aftermath of 11 September 2001, point insistently to the power of the media to define and circumscribe their lives in this way. As Valentine (2001, 181) notes, 'the media play a pivotal role in moral panics by representing a deviant group or event and their effects in an exaggerated way'. That this kind of media signification has influenced the lives of young Muslims has been reported elsewhere (see for example, Dwyer 1998; Samad 1998), and participants in many studies are aware that they have been identified as society's 'Ultimate Others' (Phoenix 1997). Participants in the Scottish study are therefore aware that there has been, and continues to be a 'moral panic' about Muslims, and in particular about young Muslim men.

| Faruk: | People have got the wrong impression of Islam at the moment with this terrorism and all this crap going on, and all of this bad press that we are getting at the moment. Everyone can just blame anything that happens on Muslims. (Interview, Glasgow, 25 June 2003) |

Although the events of 11 September 2001 in New York, and more recently those of 7 July in London, may have been a catalyst for moral panic, it is hard to link media imagery and political culture directly into the everyday experience of local life. Nevertheless, Muslims in Scotland have reported increases across a range of subtle and less subtle exclusions, threats and attacks which they attribute (in this study) to 11 September and its aftermath, as well as (in more recent reports) to 7 July. The Annandale Street mosque in Edinburgh was firebombed on 5 October 2001 causing £20,000 worth of damage; lower level vandalism is also discussed in some of the transcripts. Babar (interview, Glasgow, 24 June 2003) identified 11 September 2001 as the root cause of a series of thefts of money from the mosque he attended at university. Michael recalled eggs being thrown at the central mosque in Glasgow (focus group, Glasgow, 3 April 2003), while the sister of Kabir's friend was spat at in the underground (interview, Edinburgh, 12 December 2002) and so on.

In short, young Muslim men's attempts to locate the source of racist threat in England (beyond Scotland), and their downplay of local racism, which we interpreted (above) as part of a strategy of 'invisibilisation' has been subverted by a global politics which demonises key markers of Muslim life. The symbols and markers of Muslim lives and bodies – dress, skin pigment, beards – now mark out those who bear them as both different and threatening. The detail of this is elaborated elsewhere (Hopkins 2004; 2006; 2007a), and similar findings reported in a range of other national contexts and urban settings. Noble's (2005) work focussing on Sydney, for example, points to the negative effects of this new recognition which: 'might include name-calling, sometimes said aggressively, sometimes not, jokes in bad taste, bad manners, provocative and offensive gestures or even just a sense of social distance or unfriendliness or an excessive focus on someone's ethnicity' (110). Lori Peek (2003, 271) similarly recounts how Muslim students in New York 'became the victims of discrimination, harassment, racial and religious profiling, and verbal and physical assault' following the events of 11 September 2001. There are many examples, but the point here is that young Muslim men speak of a new style of exclusion and new impetus towards segregation which takes separatist practices a step beyond the structures of residential space and into a world of bodily tactics around interpersonal distinction and separation.

What we are seeing is the triumph of the 'wrong' sort of recognition; a set of tactics concerned not with valorising difference but rather with creating an atmosphere of illegitimacy. We suggest further that these new processes and practices of recognition conspire to edge the markers of Muslim identity, and the bodies that bear them, away from public life and into the private, yet increasingly uncomfortable, spaces of home and mosque. The fear and practice of violence and harassment polices the boundary of public and private in all kinds of ways, nudging the lives of young Muslims towards these separate spheres through a complex racialising of fear. As Noble (2005, 114) contends 'our ability to be comfortable in public settings also rests on our ability to be acknowledged as rightfully existing there: to be recognised as belonging'. Where this right is challenged, interviewees experience a lack of 'fit' with public life and turn to other spaces for a sense of community, identity and comfort. This sums up Saeed's account of his day:

> Saeed: Yeah, wake up in the morning, normal kind of thing, and I do my morning prayer and then I might go back to sleep, that's at about four or five in the morning ... and then I wake up again about seven or eight o'clock, have breakfast and get ready to go to work ... and then go home, and then either go home for prayer or go to the mosque for prayer, sit with the family, have dinner, talk and do things and then it's time to go back to bed. I try to split my time between work and family and mosque ... and at night I do my night prayer and then go to sleep and start again in the morning ... so a normal day is like that. (Interview, Edinburgh, 14 June 2002)

Turning first to the idea of home. Noble (2005) has argued that where people are marked as being out of place in particular public spaces, 'objects of belonging and their domestic spaces' become 'important elements of making oneself at home' (Noble 2005, 112). Claire Dwyer (2000) has drawn attention to the ways in which homespace is gendered, and how young Muslim women are expected to promote the religious and cultural integrity of the family. A traditional refuge for times of distress is, of course, home, whose meanings are tied up with ideas of shelter, safety and belonging. Certainly the space of home is one place of retreat for young Muslim men in the Scottish study. Many see the street as a place where they are, especially after 11 September 2001, increasingly likely to experience racism, harassment and discrimination (Hopkins 2007b). Some go out only in a group with family members or friends; others felt uncomfortable even attending school shortly following the events of 11 September 2001.

> Aktahr: ... I had people calling me Osama Bin Laden and things like that ... After the bombing happened and you walked into registration class, you could feel the tension and atmosphere against you ... it was rough ... (Focus group, Edinburgh, 19 June 2002)

Home in contrast provides a safe place: young men report withdrawing from wider social networks and concentrating on the (domestic) space of family because of the fear of being attacked whilst negotiating local streets.

> Kaukab: I like always spend time with my family in the house, so I don't spend time out in the community. (Interview, Edinburgh, 16 December 2002)

> Sabir: I tend not to go out that much. I did go out a lot more last year. (Interview, Edinburgh, 10 December 2002)

Home is one sanctuary from this kind of recognition, which is by no means full of niceties. But, as Blunt and Varley (2004, 3) have argued, it is 'invested with meanings, emotions, experiences and relationships that lie at the heart of human life'. Home is then a space of potential which can, as Noble (2005) points out, inspire a sense of 'comfort'; it can increase the 'fit' we experience in relation to the spaces we inhabit and the practices we perform' (114). That is why, although home is 'a material and an affective space, shaped by everyday practices, lived experiences, social relations, memories and emotions' it is also 'intensely political, both in its internal intimacies and through its interfaces with the wider world' (Blunt 2005, 506, 510). For young Muslim men, one of these interfaces is the politics of fear:

> Kabir: You know, you worry about what may happen to your family ... I was walking down the street after and I just didn't feel very safe walking around and it was a terrible feeling ... I didn't feel very safe at all, you know ... these things shouldn't affect us on an individual level but they do. I mean, they shouldn't make us change our habits, but they do ... they change your pattern of behaviour. (Interview, Glasgow, 12 December 2002)

Mosque also has a special, and particular, place in the lives of young Muslim men. Whereas home is the locus of family life – a focus for all the elements of everyday family practices – Mosque is a link not just to local affairs but also to a global community. It is the focus of an emotional bond with Muslims across the world – affinity with *umma* provides a link to the hopes as well as the fears of a 'brotherhood'; it is a source of empowerment, a sense of belonging and it is a strong bond. Some see themselves as being 'a Muslim first', and others, like Ifty:

> Ifty: ... love mosque, there's a brilliant atmosphere and community there, so I try to go five times a day, but I normally go four times a day at least ... (Interview, Glasgow, 16 July 2002)

> Saeed: ... the mosque as well ... that is a very important part of being a Muslim. (Interview, Edinburgh, 14 June 2004)

Other studies of Muslim youth have highlighted the importance of *umma* as a global network of identification (Dwyer 1998; Archer 2003; Alexander 2000), the flip side of which is a safe space for local life:

> Asadullah: Yeah, you can walk past another Muslim in the street and you will know. You shake hands with him and say Islam to him.
> John: When someone walks into the mosque, just like anyone right, like any of us, you just shake hands. (Focus group, Glasgow, 3 April 2003)

> Abdul: ... if two Muslims meet each other ... there is already a level of intimacy there. (Interview, Edinburgh, 6 November 2002)

However, the geopolitical shift of 11 September 2001 and beyond has not only impacted on local living in a range of problematic ways, but it has disrupted young Muslims' own 'global scale' resource for countering this, by alienating them from the *umma* – or global community of Muslims – which might otherwise have offered an alternative to affiliating with national or local life in Scotland.

> Latif: Yeah, I mean would you be proud to say that you are the same religion as like Osama Bin Laden or Saddam Hussein? (Focus group, Edinburgh, 4 February 2003).

11 September 2001 has broken a bond: not with local Muslims but with the global network that might once have been experienced as a resource. Hence, although there is a set of ideas across the transcripts for this study that emphasise the positive identification of Islam (for example, Talib: Islam, it is a peaceful religion yeah, but Islam is about justice [focus group, Glasgow, 5 September 2002]), there is also a marked ambivalence towards a global *umma* in many of the narratives. Affiliating with *umma* exposes the young men to potential experiences of marginalisation, blame and hatred. Reflecting on this, one of us has noted: 'By standing outside of the *umma* and distancing themselves from notions of global brotherhood and the scale of the global, the young men can resist, oppose and reject the connections that might be made between their religious beliefs and practices and those of the people involved in certain global events' (Hopkins 2007a, 1126). In the transcripts, then, there is often more emphasis on what divides Muslims than on what unites them: on the cultural differences between Muslims living in different parts of the world and on religious differences between Sunni and Shia Muslims.

While the gist of this study and our argument is that young Muslim men feel an impulse, inspired by threat, fear and desire for safekeeping, to withdraw to the segregated space of the home and mosque, we reiterate that this is a tendency, an impulse. Other tactics and responses are evident in the study and other emotional geographies are part of the negotiation of daily life.

Conclusion

Fear is, and has historically been, racialised in all kinds of ways. What we have tried to tease out in this account of the racialisation of religion is the way that fear is entangled with the racist practices involved in defining and controlling global positioning, national space and local lives. As the niceties of positive recognition are increasingly displaced by a repositioning of 'the (morally outraged) West' against 'the (potentially terrorising) Rest' the politics of fear are overlaying old segregationisms with new separatisms. The demonisation of global connectedness as implied by affinity with *umma*, struggles over national belonging in UK and Scottish space, and the newfound visibility of key cultural and bodily markers, are not only underlining an old drive to residential segregationism but are providing impetus for a whole range of separatist tactics around withdrawal: from the open streets of the city to the enclosed spaces of home; from the public arena of civic participation to the more particular, partially privatised domains of mosque. In short, the complex imbrication of a politics of fear with a politics of scale is redefining the structure and experience of segregation. This confirms the centrality of segregation – widely recognised by historians – to the dynamic of racism in the modern world.

Bibliography

Alexander, C. (2000), *The Asian Gang: Ethnicity, identity, masculinity* (Oxford: Berg).

Alexander, C. (2002), 'Beyond Black: Re-thinking the colour/culture divide', *Ethnic and Racial Studies* 25:4, 552–71.

Archer, L. (2003), *Race, Masculinity and Schooling: Muslim Boys and Education* (Maidenhead: Open University Press).

Back, L. (1996), *New Ethnicities and Urban Culture* (London: UCL Press).

Baumber, S. (2004), 'The Problems of Refuge: Socio-spatial construction of 'the refugee problem' in Fortress Britain', unpublished MSc thesis, University of Edinburgh.

Blunt, A. (2005), 'Cultural Geography: Cultural geographies of home', *Progress in Human Geography* 29:4, 505–15.

Blunt, A. and Varley, A. (2004), 'Introduction: Geographies of home', *Cultural Geographies* 11:1, 3–6.

Dwyer, C. (1998), 'Contested Identities: Challenging dominant representations of young British Muslim women', in T. Skelton and G. Valentine (eds), *Cool Places: Geographies of youth cultures* (London: Routledge).

Dwyer, C. (2000), 'Negotiating Diasporic Identities: Young British South Asian Muslim women', *Women's International Studies Forum* 23:4, 475–86.

Hall, S., Critcher, C., Jefferson, T., Clarke, J. and Roberts, B. (1978), *Policing the Crisis: Mugging, the state and, law and order* (London: Macmillan Press Ltd).

Hopkins, P.E. (2004), 'Young Muslim Men in Scotland: Inclusions and exclusions', *Children's Geographies* 2:2, 257–72.

Hopkins, P.E. (2006), 'Youthful Muslim Masculinities: Gender and generational relations', *Transactions of the Institute of British Geographers* 31, 337–52.

Hopkins, P.E. (2007a), 'Global Events, National Politics, Local Lives: Young Muslim men in Scotland' *Environment and Planning A* 39:5, 1119–33.

Hopkins, P.E. (2007b), 'Young Muslim Men's Experiences of Local Landscapes after September 11 2001', in C. Aitchison, P.E. Hopkins and M.-P. Kwan (eds), *Geographies of Muslim Identities: Representations of gender, diaspora and belonging* (Aldershot: Ashgate).

Miles, R. and Dunlop, A. (1987), 'Racism in Britain: The Scottish dimension', in P. Jackson (ed.), *Race and Racism* (London: Unwin Hyman).

Modood, T. (1988), '"Black", Racial Equality and Asian Identity', *New Community* 14:3, 397–404.

Modood, T. (1994), 'Political Blackness and British Asians', *Sociology* 28:4, 859–76.

Noble, G. (2005), 'The Discomfort of Strangers: Racism, incivility and ontological security in a relaxed and comfortable nation', *Journal of Intercultural Studies* 26:1, 107–20.

Peek, L.A. (2003), 'Reactions and Response: Muslim students' experiences on New York City campuses post 9/11', *Journal of Muslim Minority Affairs* 23:3, 271–83.

Phillips, D. (2006), 'Parallel Lives? Challenging Discourses of Self-Segregation in the British Muslim Population', *Environment and Planning D: Society and Space* 24:1, 25–40.

Phoenix, A. (1997), 'The Place of "Race" and Ethnicity in the Lives of Children and Young People, *Educational and Child Psychology* 14:3, 5–24.

Samad, Y. (1998), 'Media and Muslim Identity: Intersections of generation and gender', *Innovation* 11:4, 425–38.

Smith, S.J. (1988), 'Political Interpretations of Racial Segregation', *Environment and Planning D: Society and Space* 6, 423–44.

Smith, S.J. (1989), *The Politics of 'Race' and Residence* (Cambridge: Polity Press).

Smith, S.J. (1993a), 'Residential Segregation and the Politics of Racialisation', in M. Cross and M. Keith (eds) *Racism, the City and the State* (London: Unwin Hyman).

Smith, S.J. (1993b) 'Bounding the Borders. Claiming Space and Making Place in Rural Scotland', *Transactions of the Institute of British Geographers NS* 18, 291–308.

Valentine, G. (2001), *Social Geographies* (Essex: Pearson Education Limited).

Chapter 9

Practising Fear:
Encountering O/other Bodies

Michael Haldrup, Lasse Koefoed and Kirsten Simonsen

Introduction: Fear and Orientalism

While fear of the Other has always been a prominent element in regulating the daily practices of people in modern Nation-States, the first decade of the twenty-first century has seen a profound re-working and re-scaling of such fears. Fears have been 'globalised' along new lines of conflict, for example, the global US-led 'war on terror'. While it may be argued that this re-scaling of fear is rooted in an American foreign policy driven by 'the desire to avenge 9/11 and reassert the fantasy of a world in which America is forever "the sole remaining superpower"' (Ó Tuathail 2003) it is also necessary to resist such reductions. The current production of a generalised geopolitical fear of 'the Muslim Other' is not entirely new but draws in important ways on a long historical colonial legacy.

The author who has contributed to this insight more than anybody else is Edward Said. He observed that the function of denominators such as 'Islam' and 'the Orient' in western public discourse is/was 'part fiction, part ideological label' (1997, x) merely serving as a kind of 'scapegoat for everything we do not happen to like' (1997, xv). Taking the late eighteenth century as a rough starting point, Said suggest that this discursive system of dominance and authority in the uneven relation between the Orient and the Occident can be understood as a regime of knowledge – a systematic, disciplined system of power – that not only describes, teaches, and rules but also *produces* the Orient (1995). The background to this, as Said emphasises, is 'that neither the Orient nor the concept of the west has any ontological stability; each is made up by human effort – partly through the identification of the Other and partly through affirmation'. It is a supreme fabricated fiction, 'lending itself to collective passion that has never been more evident than in our time with mobilisation of fear, hatred, disgust and a resurgent in self-pride and arrogance' (Said 2004, 870). Much analysis following Said (1995; 1997) has tended to focus on Orientalism mostly as a 'regime of knowledge', thereby placing the analytical scope on the workings of institutions, discourse and texts. It has repeatedly (and justly) been fleshed out that acts of representation are not innocent. The degree to which Orientalism is (re)produced and negotiated in banal, bodily and sensuous practices, on the contrary, has been less prominent in the discussion. However, Orientalism is not only established by 'institutions' and regimes of knowledge, it is also centrally performed, practised and (re)negotiated in daily life. The everyday (re)negotiation of Orientalism in complex ways (re)produce the discursive system of power and dominance that establish it as a natural, self evident, 'taken for granted' global moral order. Orientalism is not just passively reflected in everyday life – it is rather distributed, manipulated, reproduced and opposed. It is linking the little banal social poetic with the grand dramas where contrasting images between the Orient and the west is fought in real visible wars, exclusions and repressions.

Likewise, the current re-scaling of fear does not only take place through distant and disembodied discourse but is articulated through processes of Othering developed and enacted in everyday life (Nielsen and Simonsen 2003). In the light of post-9/11 changes across the world, Said's observations on the power of Orientalism have gained new relevance. As Gregory argues, the way we see, perceive, picture, imagine and speak of others is what in the last instance also legitimises the violent fight against the Other (Gregory 2004, 20). Hence, there are close interdependencies between the Orientalism of the eighteenth and nineteenth centuries, the current 'war on terror' and animosities towards Muslims in (some) western societies. Increasingly, control and surveillance measures taken by national governments, animosity towards Muslim migrants and public discourse in support of current American-led foreign policy in the Middle East, merge and produce a generalised geopolitical fear in the midst of everyday life experiences.

This generalised antagonism has attracted increasing academic attention. However, much of the literature pursues a hierarchical model in its treatment, seeing it as a one-way flooding down from geopolitics and media treatment into everyday life. Or, if the embodied and 'affective' side is taken up, it is as a 'spontaneous mass coordination of affect' (Massumi 2005). In this chapter, we want to highlight how the production of fear (and other emotions) enters into the banal and intimate spheres of everyday life. In this, we want to emphasise how hegemonic geopolitical discourse is not only hierarchically translated into everyday life, but also (re)produced through banal, embodied experiences and practices. We do that, firstly, by pursuing a theoretical understanding of everyday practices and bodily encounters, arguing that encounters with O/others are 'mooded' with emotions, passions and attitudes such as fear, love, hatred and so on. Secondly, we illustrate this by discussing how Danish citizens account for their everyday encounters with Muslim Others and the emotions produced by these encounters. In doing this we show how affective experiences of fear and indignation add to a diversity of emotional and sensual geographies; geographies that in turn afford particular utterances of difference and even racism. Hence, we argue that constructions of otherness used to legitimate discrimination, neonationalism and even pure racism are not only 'scaled down' from global media discourse, but enabled through such 'mooded' and embodied geographies of difference.

Banality, Practice and Emotions

We pursue our theoretical goal in two steps. First we stretch the notion of Orientalism beyond its institutional meaning by focusing on the *banal* and *intimate* means by which it is (re)produced in everyday life. The entrance to this move follows the idea of 'banal nationalism' forwarded by Billig (1995). This notion describes how, in established nations like the European ones, everyday practices reproduce national identity in ways so ordinary, so commonplace, that they escape attention altogether. It can be in speech through routinely and unconsciously using homeland-making phrases; small unnoticed words such as 'we', 'the' people, 'this' country, 'here', 'society' etc., or media announcements such as 'the' weather, 'home' news and 'foreign' news etc. Or it can be in material symbolic items such as coins, banknotes and flags, hanging unnoticed from public buildings or used at birthday parties and other informal celebrations.

Billig developed his ideas in relation to the (re)production of nation-states. However, we do think that the relatively unexamined concept of banality in Cultural Studies (see also Seigworth 2000) also proves a possible starting point for our extension of the ideas of Orientalism. Said is open to the idea that Orientalism can be 'a practice that designates in one's mind a familiar space which is "ours" and an unfamiliar space beyond "ours" which is "theirs"' (1995, 54). This offers the opportunity to talk about a 'banal' Orientalism; an everyday routine way of talking and acting, a language that forces people to think in 'us'/'them' dichotomies, or a 'habit' that enables an internal orientalisation to be (re)produced as a natural form of life. Banal Orientalism is evident in the everyday use of linguistic markers, small unnoticed words such as 'us' and 'them', 'theirs' and 'ours' naturally appearing in everyday talk that produces non-European immigrants as the Other – so regularly that it has escaped out of sight.

If we follow Billig's idea of banality, then the institutionalised system of Orientalism not only circulates in texts. It becomes part of ordinary life, of the search for social meaning and coherence: a narrative and poetic everyday practice that at the same time creates the background for powerful political discourse. Banal Orientalism equips people with an identity and an ideological consciousness, and internalises these into a complex series of themes about 'us' and 'them', about the 'homeland' and the world at large. It is a daily reproduction that is instrumental in positioning everybody in time and space, in a moral international world order. This means that Orientalism is a form of identity that is not always consciously 'flagged'; it is based in doxa (Bourdieu 1994) – the undisputed, pre-reflexive presuppositions of 'the game' of everyday life. The idea of banality suggests that we study Orientalism as a routine way of speaking about the world – a geopolitical consciousness circulating not only institutionally and in textual bodies, but also in narrative practices and the way in which 'we' think about the world in our everyday life.

Our next theoretical step is to supplement Said's (and Billig's) predominantly textualist perspective with a more practice-oriented view on Orientalism, where bodily practice and embodied experiences come into a central position. We have earlier suggested the notion of *practical orientalism* to illustrate this point

(Haldrup et al. 2006). It concerns the translation of hegemonic discourses into everyday practices or rather their active (re)production in the habitual spaces of ordinary experience. It is about the way in which cultural difference is performed in the encompassing field of everyday sociality and sensual habit – how it colours the visual, flavours the olfactory and tempers the emotional (Herzfeld 1997). The development of this notion, then, requires a stronger emphasis on bodily encounters and emotions.

This effort might start from Merleau-Ponty's phenomenology of practice, which identifies the body as part of a pre-discursive social realm based on perception, practice and bodily movement (Merleau-Ponty 1962). Lived experience, to him, is always and necessarily embodied, located in the 'mid-point' between mind and body, or subject and object. In it, perception is based on *practice*; that is, on looking, listening and touching etc, as acquired, cultural, habit-based forms of conduct. Perception, from this perspective, is not seen as an inner representation of the outer world, but rather as a practical bodily involvement. It is an active process relating to our ongoing projects and practices, and it concerns the whole sensing body. This means that the human body takes up a dual role as both the vehicle of perception and the object perceived, as a body-in-the-world – *a lived body* – which 'knows' itself by virtue of its involvement and active relation to this world. The bodies are not locked into their private world, but are in a world that is shared with 'others'. Consequently, to meet or to see the other is not to have an inner representation of him/her either, it is to be-with-him/her. This underlines the understanding of the world as a genuine human interworld and of subjectivity as publicly available; the subjects are sentient-sensuous bodies whose subjectivity assumes embodied and public forms. Merleau-Ponty uses the notion 'body-subject' to underline this idea of embodiment. However, the corporeality of social practices concerns not only this sensuous, generative and creative nature of lived experiences, but also the way in which these embodied experiences themselves form a basis for social action. Bourdieu (1977; 1990) expresses that when seeing 'habitus' as embodied history, which is internalised as a second nature. That is, social structures and cultural schemes are *incorporated* in the agents and function as generative dispositions behind their schemes of action. Two aspects of these ideas of embodiment are of particular interest in the present connection.

The first of these is the public character or the radical intersubjectivity of the 'body-subjects'. Their practices and perceptions enjoin them to an interworld or 'intermundane space' (Merleau-Ponty 1968, 269). This space is constituted by the 'reversibility' of the perceiving subject. Body-subjects are visible-seers, tangible-touchers, audible-listeners etc. They form a part of the perceptual world that they open onto. In this way, the concept of intersubjectivity can be amplified by one of *intercorporeality*. It is however not the sheer sensibility of the body-subjects that institutes intercorporeality. It is as well the meaning involved in the bodily practices of the other that counts. One does not just perceive another body as a physical object; rather one is affected by the meaning of its appearance. The other body-subject is animated and its animation communicates, and furthermore, as a communication, its manners call for a response. You do not contemplate the communications of the other, they affect you and you reply to them.

Following from this, the other important aspect of embodiment informing everyday meetings with other bodies is emotion. Robins (1995) stresses this aspect in relation to urban culture. Encounters with 'strangers' in public space, which many urbanists see as the crucial aspect of 'the urban', are for him loaded with passions, whether these are enjoyment and desire or rather anxiety, fear and aggression. In approaching this issue, Merleau-Ponty (1962) argues that our relations with others (and with objects) are always 'mooded' and that there is no escape from such moodedness. Moods and emotions, then, are basic human attributes, but they are not inner physical or sensuous states. We should rather see them as the contextual significance of sensations, that is, as associated with practices and social situation. Emotions are, with Merleau-Ponty, *situated corporeal attitudes*, ways of being and acting in relation to the world. They are inseparable from other aspects of subjectivity, such as perception, speech/talk, gestures, practices and interpretations of the surrounding world, and they primordially function at the pre-reflexive level. Emotion, then, is a way of relating. It is part of the 'system' that body-subjects form with others. That means that they must be intersubjectively constituted, they shape and are shaped by relations between body-subjects. This relational view might suggest some overlap (but definitely not identity) with contemporary discussions of affect (see for example Massumi 2002; Anderson 2006).

Thus, everyday encounters with other fleshy and sensuous bodies affect us, and this affection can take the form of different feelings such as love, desire, hate or fear. So the sense of mutuality involved in the phenomenological account should not be mistaken for harmony. Nevertheless, the approach remains limited insofar as it does not appreciate differences among bodies and power relations involved in intercorporeal meetings. This deficiency is more than anywhere else pointed out in feminist critiques (see for example Irigaray 1984; Young 1990; Grosz 1994). An interesting attempt to deal with the problem is the contribution from Young (1990) in which she explores the possibility of a specifically 'feminine' body comportment and relation in space. She displays a contradictory spatiality primarily based on the historical and cultural fact that women live their bodies as subjects and objects simultaneously. A woman in 'our' culture experiences her body on the one hand as background and means for her projects in life. On the other hand she lives with the ever-present possibility of being gazed upon as a potential object of others' intentions. This ambiguous bodily existence tends to 'keep her in her place', and it influences her manner of movement, her relationship to her surroundings and her appropriation of space. Young's argument then implies that feminine spatiality involves not only an experience of spatial constitution, but also one of being 'positioned' in space. That is why feminine existence tends to construct an enclosure around herself, at the same time restricting her movements and functioning as a defense against bodily invasion. This is about power relations, and in the last instance about fear of violence.

More generally, this development concerns the way in which gazes are involved in objectification of the Other and/or feelings of being objectified by the Other.

Such power relations do not of course refer to female bodies only, but also to other deviations from the 'neutral' body – such as skin colour (see Fanon 1986), age, disability and sexuality. It challenges Merleau-Ponty's idea of the social body as a body opening up into the fleshy world of other bodies. For this world is a differentiated world, and in such a world what is meant by the social body is more often than not 'precisely the effect of being with some others over Other others' (Ahmed 2000, 49). The social body is also an imaginary body that is created through the relations of touch between bodies recognisable as friendly and/or strange. Familiar bodies can be incorporated through a sense of community, being with each other as like bodies, while strange bodies more likely are expelled from bodily space and moved apart as different bodies. In this way 'like' bodies and 'different' bodies do not just precede the bodily encounters of incorporation or expulsion, likeness and difference are also produced through these encounters. What Sara Ahmed calls 'strange encounters' are hence not only *visual*, but also *tactile*: just as some bodies are seen and recognised as stranger than others, so too are some skins touched as stranger than other skins. This of course also involves 'situated corporeal attitudes' or emotions. Various familial relations involves particular forms of emotion and ways of touch, while the recognition of some-body as a stranger – a body that is 'out-of-place' because it has come too close – might involve a fear of touching.

This suggests that, in accordance with the general concept of Orientalism, fear emerges as an important element of the sensual encounters of practical orientalism. Living in an unstable world and encountering 'strange' Others can cause both *anxiety* and *fear*. Most commentators, inspired by Heidegger and/ or Freud, make a clear distinction between anxiety and fear, seeing anxiety as a generalised state and fear as more directed towards specific entities in the world. Bourke (2003) interestingly questions this clear distinction. Historically, she says, anxiety from time to time is converted to fear and vice versa. The uncertainty of anxiety might be removed by the process of naming an enemy – whether a plausible or implausible one. Scapegoating, for instance, enables a group to convert an anxiety into a fear, thus legitimising hostile utterances and actions against bodies 'out-of-place'. In the section to come, we will illustrate the way in which practical orientalism (and connected emotions) emerges in bodily encounters and the sociality of everyday life, through drawing on a few examples from Denmark.

Embodied Imaginations of Otherness

In the following we will illustrate our point by means of examples taken from two interview analyses of our own; one performed in a medium-sized Danish provincial town (Koefoed 2006), one in the city of Copenhagen (Simonsen 2005). Both analyses used narrative in-depth interviews. We will of course not generalise these findings, just identify their content and argue that they are important in understanding current conflicts over 'cultural' difference and the fears and emotions related to these. In doing this we emphasise how both visual and tactile encounters with the other produce both anxiety and fear.

Most strikingly we find practical orientalism enacted in relation to the visual perception of the other. The visual comes into the everyday meetings with/ affections by Other bodies in many ways. Appearances of bodies and visual objectification of Others are major inputs to the processes of othering. More than anything else, however, it appears in connection with gender, sexuality and the work of the 'male gaze'. The woman being objectified and positioned in space is the process put into play, and so is the traditional 'blame the victim' claim saying that it is her responsibility to consider her appearance and clothing so as not to act as a temptation to male sexuality. It is however used in a strange converted way:

> I don't want to be Turkish. I don't want to be a Muslim. I don't want to be marked by the Muslim community. I mean, the freedom we have achieved. And now the girls in Denmark are supposed to put on more clothing. Our morality, it might not be too good. I mean, maybe we could behave ourselves better, and dress more decent and not expose the skin of the stomach. But actually I can't see that it is anybody's business if I want to have my stomach uncovered, because why should I stop doing that just because some foreigners that think it is an invitation have come into the country? But then they have to stay out of here. I mean, it is such things. And this is about values, because this is absolute. It has something to do with women's liberation. (Interview extract, our translation)

The woman speaking here talks about women being in public space and exposed to the male gaze, but this is the gaze of the Other man, the Muslim man. The process of objectification that we mentioned above is here turned around and used to signify the Other man who, in her saying, cannot deal with the bodily appearance of Danish girls, he 'thinks it is an invitation', and whose culture therefore does not accord with Danish (western) values. In this, she is drawing on (and contributing to) a rather widespread discourse in the public opinion in Denmark saying that women's liberation is something 'we' have and 'they' do not have – 'they' being (Muslim) immigrants deeply embedded in their 'medieval' culture. Questions of gendered power relations and visual dominance are changed into an 'immigrant problem', and at the same time rendering invisible power in 'Danish' gender relations and reinforcing distinctions between 'Danes' and 'immigrants', and in that way using feminism in the process of orientalisation.

This process of orientalisation does however not restrict itself to the Muslim man. It takes yet another turn and involves the Muslim woman as well. This can be illustrated by a feature article with the title 'Whore and Madonna again' published in the Danish (leftist) newspaper *Information*, where a 'feminist' author blames Muslim women wearing a scarf for sexual assaults conducted by Muslim men (Thomsen 2000). She connects such assaults to a gendered practicing of Islam and not, for instance, to social marginalisation. Muslim men become the violating ones, and Muslim women, through their religious bodily markers as 'pure women', are claimed to legitimise the men's violating actions. Wearing a scarf embodies the traditional, the patriarchal and the suppressive. It desexualises its wearer by rendering her unapproachable and in the same move sexualises the (Danish) non-wearers. In Thomsen's optic, then, 'we' (Danish emancipated women) become 'the sexualised Others', and in some strange way Danish men become invisible in the analysis. Bodies wearing this piece of clothing, the scarf, are then articulated as unacceptable in the encounter with modern, secularised, emancipated 'Danishness', and made to symbolise 'the alien' and 'the backwards' which undermines gender equality and exposes Danish women to the threatening 'male gaze'. In this sense the visual and the tactile are connected in the (above-mentioned) fear of the threatening body of the Other.

Both these examples show how recognizable visible markers of difference, which are worked out as stereotyped objects of fantasy and fear, inhabit practical orientalism. This is 'the suppressed immigrant woman', who is not only suppressed but also positioning herself as 'pure' in relation to the Danish woman, and 'the threatening immigrant man', who is patriarchal, sexually uncontrollable and a potential rapist. In an imagination where ethnicity, gender and sexuality coincide, visual perception constitutes a cultural battlefield on which processes of orientalisation are put into work.

Our next example shows how practical orientalism is enacted in relation to tactile encounters in everyday life speech acts. The tactile apparatus of the human body is often taken for granted as an essentially physical capability of the human body. Yet it is thoroughly cultivated. The skin mediates between our body and its environment and it does so in culturally specific ways. Touch, tactile receptivity and spatial orientation is not neutral from gender, age and cultural difference. It has been argued by some writers that the sensuous mediation between space and the body implies cultural difference with respect to phenomena such as crowding, performance in public space, interaction through touch etc (see for example Rodaway 1994, 57–60). In public practices and imaginations, such issues are part of the construction of the spaces of the Muslim/Arab Other as essentially different from western, modernised space, and thereby of the exclusion of immigrants from national (Danish) public space. Listen, for instance, to the opinions from residents in a small Danish town (hosting a refugee center):

They dominated it all, you know. If they ... then they would be a band, walking in the middle of the road. If a car appeared and was about to approach them and, kind of, tooted at them, because they would not stand back, then they went ... then they threatened at it ... and were absolutely mad. They had a behaviour that we can't use for anything at all. (Interview extract, our translation)

They walked around the town, you know, and then suddenly they stood there, like, looking through the windows and then, what the f... we were doing. And that is not really our mentality. (Interview extract, our translation)

My wife was about to go out to pick the raspberries, in our own raspberry ... then five Lebanese were f... crawling around in the bed. You see, they do not respect private property in the same way as we do in this country. (Interview extract, our translation)

In the three extracts the embodied behaviour of Muslim immigrants is represented as a transgression of norms and rules of 'this country'. The tactile spaces of the Other are seen as threatening and intruding; hence as disturbance legitimising the exclusion/disciplining of the intruder, whose erratic behaviour must be adapted to 'our mentality' and how 'we do in this country'. This process of orientalisation is however not restricted to the imposing of western, tactile geographies on Other. In urban space the immigrant Other may turn into an alien intruder imposing his (male) animalistic order on the marginalised people in the city, as this quotation from an interviewee in Copenhagen suggests:

> ... and there you see that these 'second generation immigrants', they don't like them [socially marginalized persons of Danish origin – authors comment]. So they spite them, and some controversies come up. Especially the particular group of alcoholics and drug addicts is a threatened species ... by the second-generation immigrants. Because they don't like them. And they clearly think, that then can just hit them and kick them and do whatever you want to them. (Interview extract, our translation)

Here, the threatening behaviour of the immigrant Other is converted into an 'ecological' narrative, in which the disordered and potentially violent space of the 'second generation immigrants' is imposed on the 'native' alcoholics and drug addicts. The argument from above is reversed into a dismal fantasy about the appalling regime of Oriental space that might emerge if not kept under surveillance and control. Both examples show how differences between Oriental and Danish/western space and behaviour are constructed as dichotomous stereotypes related through an unavoidable struggle.

Concluding Remarks

Through the notion of 'practising fear', we have tried in this chapter to ground the discussion of fear that has penetrated academic and popular discourses post-2001. That is, we have tried to challenge the dominating hierarchical model that sees fear as a generalised emotion trickling down from overall forces of politics and media into everyday life. Instead, we have argued for a dual process also emphasising local and intercorporeal constructions of emotions/fear. Our starting point has been Said's notion of Orientalism as a concept which opens up, but does not in itself develop, the everyday construction of fear. To achieve this, we pursue a theoretical understanding of emotion that is grounded in everyday practices and encounters between different bodies. On this background, examples from a Danish case are used to show how boundaries between 'them' and 'us' are redrawn and enacted through small acts, corporeal attitudes and distinguishing comments. Our point is the existence of a general moodedness of all bodily encounters and the way in which encounters with O/other bodies (re)produce difference and antagonistic emotions. Imaginations of Other bodies do not just precede the bodily encounters of incorporation or expulsion; Otherness is also produced in and through these encounters. Geopolitics relies on embodied practices and everyday experiences.

Bibliography

Ahmed, S. (2000), *Strange Encounters. Embodied Others in Post-coloniality* (London and New York: Routledge).

Anderson, B. (2006), 'Becoming and Being Hopeful: Towards a theory of affect', *Environment and Planning D: Society and Space* 24:5, 733–52.

Billig, M. (1995), *Banal Nationalism* (London: Sage).

Bourke, J. (2003), 'Fear and Anxiety: Writing about emotion in modern history', *History Workshop Journal* 55, 111–34.

Bourdieu, P. (1977), *Outline of a Theory of Practice* (Cambridge: Cambridge University Press).

Bourdieu, P. (1990), *The Logic of Practice* (Cambridge: Polity Press).

Bourdieu, P. (1994), *Distinction, A Social Critique of the Judgment of Taste* (London: Routledge).

Fanon, F. (1986): *Black Skin, White Masks* (London: Pluto).

Gregory, D. (2004), *The Colonial Present* (Blackwell: Oxford).

Grosz, E. (1994), *Volatile Bodies. Toward a Corporeal Feminism* (Bloomington, IN and Indianapolis: Indiana University Press).

Haldrup, M., Koefoed, L. and Simonsen, K, (2006), 'Practical Orientalism. Bodies, Everydaylife and Constructions of Otherness', *Geografiska Annaler B* 88B, 173–84.

Herzfeld, M. (1997), *Social Poetics in the Nation-State* (New York/London: Routledge).

Irigaray, L. (1984), *Etique de la difference sexuelle* (Paris: Minuit).

Koefoed, L. (2006), 'Glokale nationalismer. Globalisering, hverdagsliv og fortællinger om dansk identitet', unpublished PhD thesis, Department of Environmental, Social and Spatial Change, Roskilde University, Denmark.

Massumi, B. (2002), *Parables for the Virtual: Movement, affect and sensation* (Durham, NC and London: Duke University Press).

Massumi, B. (2005), 'Fear (the Spectrum Said)', *Positions* 13:1, 31–49.

Merleau-Ponty, M. (1962), *Phenomenology of Perception* (London: Routledge and Kegan Paul).

Merleau-Ponty, M. (1968), *The Visible and the Invisible* (Evanstone, IL: Northwestern University Press).

Nielsen, E.H. and Simonsen, K. (2003), 'Scalling from "Below": Strategies and urban spaces', *European Planning Studies* 11:8, December.

Ó Tuathail, G. (2003), '"Just Out Looking for a Fight": American affect and the invasion of Iraq', *Antipode* 35, 856–70.

Robins, K. (1995), 'Collective Emotions and Urban Culture', in P. Healy, S. Davoudi, S. Graham and A. Madani-Pour (eds), *Managing Cities. The New Urban Context* (Chichester: John Wiley and Sons).

Rodaway, P. (1994), *Sensuous Geographies. Body, sense and place* (London and New York: Routledge).

Said, E.W. (1995), *Orientalism. Western Conceptions of the Orient* (London: Penguin Books).

Said, E.W. (1997), *Covering Islam. How the Media and the Experts Determine how we See the Rest of the World* (New York: Vintage Books).

Said, E.W. (2004), 'Orientalism Once More', *Development and Change* 35:5, 869–79.

Seigworth, G.J. (2000), 'Banality for Cultural Studies', *Cultural Studies* 14:2, 227–68.

Simonsen, K. (2005), *Byens mange ansigter – konstruktion af byen i praksis og fortælling* (Copenhagen: Roskilde Universitetsforlag).

Thomsen, M. (2000), 'Luder og Madonna igen', *Information*, 14 June.

Young, I.M. (1990), *Throwing Like a Girl and Other Essays in Feminist Philosophy and Social Theory* (Bloomington, IN: Indiana University Press).

Chapter 10

Neither Relaxed nor Comfortable: The Affective Regulation of Migrant Belonging in Australia

Greg Noble and Scott Poynting

Spaces of National (Un)Belonging

Australians like to consider themselves relaxed and comfortable, an easy-going and tolerant people. Indeed, we had a Prime Minister since 1996 to 2007 – John Howard – who prided himself on preserving these qualities (Howard 1997). This picture of Australian life is, of course, selective. As in other nations, it has become commonplace to recognise a pervasive culture of fear shaped by international, national and local factors. Mounting evidence of this anxiety is found in media and academic surveys which show Australians are more fearful, and in regards to more things (Mann 2006). These anxieties have been given a racial hue, centred around the 'Arab Other', the pre-eminent folk devil of our times, articulated through panics over 'Lebanese crime', 'race rape' and the perceived threat of terrorism (Poynting et al. 2004). Much attention has been given to thinking about this culture of fear but in abstract terms, with little research into the experiences of those concerned, and with a focus on the manipulation of (largely 'white') fears (Aly and Balnaves 2005) which forgets about the objects of those fears. Yet these circumstances have produced an increasing incidence of racism directed towards people of Arab and Muslim background; circumstances which constitute an altogether different experience of fear depending on who, and where, you are. This chapter, drawing on research into experiences of vilification amongst Arab and Muslim Australians, suggests that it is necessary to shift from a generalised conception of a 'culture of fear' to specific experiences of threat to understand the regulation of belonging for migrant groups as an affective process which shapes their ability to feel 'at home'.

Social inclusion is not a singular process, especially in societies that are economically, socially and culturally complex, because migrants inhabit various sites of integration. Their entry into social life is marked by 'differential exclusions' through which they are incorporated into some spheres of life, such as the labour market, but not so well in others, such as political participation and social networks, which entail different forms and degrees of power (Castles 1999, 4;

Young 1990). This has produced an increasing focus on explorations of cultural citizenship and the varying spaces of belonging (Dunn 2001a).

Hage (1998), drawing on Bourdieu, reconceptualises questions of national and ethnic identity by arguing that, rather than seeing the nation as an imagined community, it is a field in which citizens deploy their various resources to manage what he calls the 'national space'. The symbolic power of national belonging – what Hage dubs 'whiteness' – derives from the 'national capital' citizens accumulate. Ethnic identity is a generally negative form of symbolic capital within the field of whiteness. The capacity to position yourself as a 'manager' of the national space is, however, unevenly distributed, depending on access to forms of capital. Exploring the example of the tearing of the hijab, Hage argues that racism is best understood as a nationalist practice which attempts to define the nation, the proper inhabitants of the national space and legitimate forms of conduct within that space. In the context of debates about 'Australian values', citizenship tests and the 'unacceptable' aspects of Islam (Howard 2006), Hage's analysis seems particularly productive. Despite his discussion of the removal of the hijab, however, Hage has not pursued far enough the relation between everyday actions of civil society and national belonging.

Essed's analysis of 'everyday racism' focuses on the processes of marginalisation which punctuate the lives of migrants: the overemphasis on ethnic difference, the attributions of incompetence, humiliation, rudeness and patronising behaviour (1991, 160–72). To counter the false separation between individual and institutional racism, Essed uses the experiences of black women in the labour market, housing and education, to suggest how everyday encounters reproduce larger structures of domination (1991, 39). Belonging, and not belonging, are, of course, not simply cognitive processes of identification, but are highly charged, *affective* relations of attachment to and exclusion from particular places. As Ahmed (2004) notes, emotions such as hate and fear, as well as pride, bind us to nations. Taken together, these insights suggest that we need to explore the links between migrant belonging and processes of inclusion and exclusion in terms of the affective dimensions within and across social domains, and in terms of the relations between 'local' and national space.

Living with Racism

As part of a project conducted by the Human Rights and Equal Opportunities Commission (HREOC 2004), we completed a study of experiences of racial vilification amongst Arab and Muslim Australians in New South Wales and Victoria in 2003. Just as in the period during the 1991 Gulf War (HREOC 1991), the terrorist attacks in the United States on 11 September 2001 and other international and domestic events unleashed a spate of racially-based attacks on people of Arab and Muslim background (*Daily Telegraph* 2001, 13; HREOC 2004). These were not isolated, but part of long-term anxieties in Australia (Dunn 2001b) that have spiralled into panics around 'ethnic gangs', refugees and terrorism (Poynting et al. 2004).

The project entailed a survey of 186 people contacted through organisations in Sydney and Melbourne within Arabic-speaking and Muslim communities. The questionnaire focused on experiences of racism since 11 September 2001. It was followed by 34 interviews. The interviewees ranged from 17 to 57, and represented all socio-economic levels and major religious groups (Poynting and Noble 2004).

While the survey was not a representative sample of Arab and Muslim communities, it did reflect a significant number of citizens who have experienced vilification. The survey showed incidents from minor occurrences of abuse to institutional discrimination, media stereotyping, property attacks, and sexual and physical assault. Incidents occurred in a range of sites – the street, malls, the media, public transport, government offices, educational institutions, work and entertainment. Muslims were more likely to recount racism than Christians. Women were more likely to be victims than men, but perpetrators were more likely to be male. Almost three-quarters of respondents identified culprits as Anglo-Australian. Almost all saw their cultural or religious difference as the target – defined by dress, language or general appearance as Arab, Muslim or 'Middle Eastern', echoing Hopkins' (2004) research on experiences of exclusion amongst young Muslims in Scotland. These forms of visual identification set them apart from Anglo-Australians. Only a small number of participants reported incidents, however, claiming that their complaints wouldn't be taken seriously (Poynting and Noble 2004).

The Little Things of Racism

Experiences of vilification ranged from incivility – behaviours that are perceived as rude and insulting – to outright violence or discrimination. A typical incident was recounted, just after 11 September 2001, by Karimah, an 18-year-old college student, born in Australia of parents of Lebanese origin:

> I recall being in my brother's car at a petrol station with my sister-in-law … There were a group of boys that were saying 'oh that's Osama bin Laden's family, terrorists,' and comments like that. [They were] about 20ish, … they were maybe drunk … mostly of Australian background …, they just laughed and walked off … in the news was Osama bin Laden this and Osama bin Laden that … if you were Muslim, you were associated with Osama bin Laden, and if you were associated with Osama bin Laden you were a terrorist.

This kind of event was frequently recounted as evidence of the harassment that Australians of Arab and Muslim background receive. Several things make it typical: it was perpetrated by a group of young 'Australian' males, directed in a public place at a woman they do not know; it was linked to terrorism; it was unplanned; and it was relatively banal. Nevertheless, the frequency with which such encounters occurred was evidence of the ongoing experiences of these Australians. She also recounted other, 'little things' which 'happen quite often', such as at college one day: 'a group of guys in a car were driving past, and they stopped and started making comments [shouting] "terrorist," and swearing and then they drove off … making gestures … raising their finger … it was very disturbing, I was shocked.' Karimah didn't report either occurrence because, 'you just have to let it pass'.

While she dismisses these, Karimah recognises, as did others, that they relate to widespread anxieties, and that there are a lot of Australians who 'fear … other people'. Nermin, a 22-year-old trainee teacher, born in Australia to Turkish migrants, told this story of a man on a train:

> He was reading a newspaper, … and I could see what he was reading – 'Muslims, terrorists, bombing, attacks.'. … he saw my face … and the look on his face, his mouth dropped with fear. It was like 'oh my God, I'm reading about them here, and this is how vicious and violent they can be, and oh my God, there's one standing in front of me now'. I'll never forget the look on his face … he just froze.

It would be a mistake to assume Nermin wields the power here; she and her family have to work out ways of managing such situations given the stories they hear about Muslim girls being attacked. Her parents decided she was not safe to walk alone at night, and she tends to have her fiancée 'everywhere I go'.

Sometimes the encounter was more sustained, and less easy to dismiss. Jamila, a 26-year-old Muslim born in Australia of an Indonesian father and Singaporean mother, has a small child and studies part-time at university. One incident occurred when she was travelling by train to work at a call centre:

> It was the day after a *Sixty Minutes* report on the rape by the Lebanese men … so it was a bit fresh on everyone's mind that Muslims were 'evil'. These two men were talking about that report … they were saying things like, 'oh these Mussos they think they can do whatever they want to our women, … how would they like it if we went and raped a whole lot of Muslim women?' … and they'd glance at me … I said to them, 'What do you mean by 'our' people?' … well, they just kept taunting … 'How would you like it if we were to rape you guys?' … I just kept my cool … what was upsetting to me was the fact that there was about twenty other people on the carriage, and I was the only Muslim woman on the carriage, yet not one person said, 'Hang on a minute, that's out of line, mate' … there were sexual connotations, … innuendo in what they were saying to me. I felt a bit scared.

This was a private conversation but, Jamila felt, was intended for her and the whole carriage, 'like an announcement' that carried an implied, sexual threat. She came away 'scared', 'angry' and 'distraught'. When she arrived at work she 'burst into tears. I'd held it, I was putting on a tough front in the train, and then when I got to work … The minute I saw my supervisor I lost it, I just started crying, I was so upset'.

In contrast to what many would see as minor experiences of abuse, several recounted experiences which they believed demonstrated racism within particular social institutions. Zahra, a 24-year-old salesperson born in Australia of Lebanese Shiite parents, talked about how her younger brother was held by police during protests against the Iraq war: 'I was upset because ... had my brother been white he would not have been held unlawfully for that many hours.' When one of her colleagues overheard her complaining about what had happened, this had repercussions: 'The harassment I received from work ... was bloody endless.'

Ali, a 40-year-old Sunni who arrived from Lebanon when he was 21 and runs an information technology business, described a visit from the Australian federal police and the Australian Security and Intelligence Organisation (ASIO) just after 11 September, and was interviewed about whether he'd known in advance about the terrorist attacks. Ali felt it was an 'accusation' deriving from his earlier involvement in a youth group; a period when he was also approached by ASIO. He saw himself as 'a normal citizen', but these visits were meant 'to frighten us' and he believed he had 'been put under surveillance' and was being treated as 'a suspect' even though they had no evidence. While it did not lead to any legal problems, it 'affected me a lot', upsetting his 'life in the area'. A number of interviewees complained of profiling by police and security services and some made the point that these are the same police to whom racist attacks are to be reported.

Hamzeh, a 20-year-old Australian-born security guard of Lebanese background, was pulled over by three police cars while driving to prayers. They directed him by loudspeaker to get out of the car, and subjected him and the car to a search for 40 minutes. One officer had his hand on his gun the whole time. 'He was really, really arrogant. "Why are you here, why are you wearing that beard, where are you going?" I go, "I'm going to the mosque". He goes to me, "what the fuck are you going to do there?"' Hamzeh said it was fruitless to report it: 'complain to who? Go down to the police station and tell them that one of your officers was speaking to me in such a manner?'

In contrast, other interviewees talked of experiences within their personal realm. Heba, a 24-year-old Orthodox Christian student born in Lebanon, told of the response from a friend's mother when she told of her volunteer work with refugees.

> She just said 'oh no, why are you working with the boat people?', and she was really shocked about it, and that such a centre even existed to help them, because they should all be jailed or something. The amounts of times she said 'They're going to bomb us' ... You could really see the fear factor, and she had no concept of them being just human beings. It was so obvious that in her eyes they were these monsters who have just come here to bomb Australia ... I was really shocked and disappointed ... She started becoming very distrusting of me ...

Heba didn't want to 'offend' her friend's mother so she just avoids her. She also explained that her nickname at work is 'little terrorist' – her colleagues mean it in a 'joking way', and she wouldn't be 'comfortable' complaining to her boss. Yet it rankled. Her manager had once admitted that she 'hates Muslims ... she wanted them wiped off the planet', so she just kept quiet.

The Affective Regulation of Migrant Belonging

Several themes emerge from these stories. The first is the pervasive and 'ordinary' nature of these experiences, routine events that occur in a variety of social spaces. As Phillips and Smith (2003) point out, commonplace incivility is often seen as evidence of social fragmentation. However, the forms of incivility at work here suggest that it can be a rather more aggressive attempt to regulate cultural difference and sustain homogeneity.

The second is the way these experiences occur across a wide array of social sites – on the street and public transport, at home, in shopping centres and places of leisure, at work and school, and in government and private offices. Many of them may be arbitrary and fleeting, but they represent a pattern of incivility, harassment and abuse within the lives of interviewees. Combined with the sustained experiences at work and in local neighbourhoods, these represent extensive processes of exclusion: there are few sites which offer relief from the threat of vilification.

The third is the way these actions suggest a complex relation between local situation and national belonging. These local actions are done in the name of larger categories of identity – marking ethnic difference in contrast to national community. Similarly, as we saw in Heba's narrative, there is a slippage between interpersonal relations and national issues of security. Further, the interviewees see these actions as validated by other citizens and social institutions, especially those of the state and media.

The fourth is that these actions are highly charged, *affective* performances of exclusion. There is strong pattern of hatred, fear (even when the event is dismissed as trivial), disappointment, sadness, anger and resignation. The emotional dimensions of national belonging are rarely foregrounded in social analysis, but it is necessary to recognise these dimensions to comprehend the force of these processes. Indeed, they amount to an affective regulation of migrant belonging, policing the recognition of ethnic difference in terms of the symbolic capital of national belonging. Of course, national belonging is also shaped by gender and class (Poynting and Noble 2004), but we focus on ethnicity here.

As a pervasive experience of everyday life, the forms of vilification we have described function as a constant reminder of immigrants' not belonging. A common story is being told to 'go home'. Khaled (a 25-year-old Bangladeshi IT consultant) and his friends, for example, were subjected to racist abuse and sprayed with beer by a group of young men at the cricket when they tried to find a place for prayers: 'The F word was said a few times, also ... "Go home; you're not welcome here."' Such abuse embodies the pressures of exclusion for those migrants whose difference shapes their existence as citizens. These spaces of incivility become landscapes of exclusion because they define not just what but who is acceptable. Racial vilification, by its nature, emphasises cultural difference as a form of not belonging. Alya (a 40-year-old Egyptian Muslim) encapsulates this when she talks about encounters that produce this: 'Incidents, like "go on, get a move on ... in this country we do things like this", "you don't belong in this country, go home"; it's just knowing that people will judge you for things that are totally outside of your control, and again not feeling like I belong to this land that I call my home.' She described herself as feeling 'alien': 'I felt like I stood out. Before September 11, I felt fairly invisible, just a person going around doing their own thing.' After that, she felt 'people were looking at me'. Here invisibility is felt not as being ignored, but as 'fitting' comfortably in the public spaces of belonging. This diminution of social freedoms is part, however, of a wider, *felt* experience of disenfranchisement.

This involves an affective economy, an ensemble of emotions which link us to particular groups and places, or deny us that link. What Ahmed (2004, 62) calls the 'affective politics of fear' is central to this ensemble of emotions. She points out that fear shrinks space, restricting mobility. This very specific sense of fear is fundamental to our localised sense of freedom: it grants some the freedom to move and denies it to others (2004, 64 and 67–70). The affective dimensions of use of local space, then, links directly to larger questions of citizenship and belonging.

This *cultural* citizenship – or its denial – is shaped by inclusion within or exclusion from local as well as nationally significant public spaces (Rogers 1999, 249). As Heba remarked, reflecting on her daily experiences, 'The saddest part is that the Arab community on a general level, in Australia, no longer feels Australian'. The resigned belief that many racist experiences aren't worth reporting, together with the expectation that little would be done anyway, suggests that, in the current context, the organisations whose task it is to police vilification are seen as complicit in the experience of racism. This applies not just to institutions of law enforcement but also to organisations that defend citizens against discrimination. In other words, the state is seen as part of the problem. It doesn't help that governments are seen to be unwilling to police one of the social sites described as contributing to racism – the media.

Yet the significant point here is the intimate link between the personal experiences of public space and the larger categories of national belonging: the simultaneity of 'scale' (see Hopkins and Smith, this volume). For Jamila, for example, it was not worth reporting harassment on a train to station staff: 'They wouldn't do anything.' It reflected a larger problem: 'I don't feel like I'll be represented properly if I was to go to the state government office or a federal government office to complain about something that happened against me. I don't think they would really care.' She experiences a direct and affective relation between the local injuries of race she suffers and the lack of 'care' exhibited by the nation's authorities.

'We Let Go Our Rights'

Hage's (1998, 45) analysis of the management of national space focuses on the act of managing the 'ethnic object' as a mode of inhabiting the nation, rather than the experience of being managed. In these stories we see what Hage refers to as the 'caging of ethnic wills', whereby the 'ethnic' incorporates their subordination (1998, 113–15). Both violent forms of racism and mundane incidents of incivility produce a visceral sensation of marginalisation, where one's worth as a human being is at stake: the feeling of not counting. As Ali says: 'I felt that I am an Australian at a level lower than the other, I am not an Australian regular citizen.' The 'feeling of counting for others' (Bourdieu 2000, 240) is a crucial aspect of any coexistence, but has particular consequences for those accommodating themselves to a new nation.

In both the resigned acceptance of the 'little things' of racism there lies both the normalisation of the state of threat, and the internalisation of the process of management which underlines the disenfranchisement from civic life. As Shaden, a 19-year-old Muslim university student born in Egypt, says of her experience of young male drivers abusing her, 'it's only a small incident, it's no big deal … It's something I'm used to … It's something common, normal, I've become accustomed to it'. Similarly, Heba claims, 'That fear, I've sort of forgotten about it, for the sake of getting on', but she feels the pressure of 'having to justify yourself all the time'. Rokshana (a 26-year-old sales assistant born in Afghanistan), describing discrimination at a job interview because she wore the hijab, said that 'when you encounter that so many times you can't be bothered to fight the whole world'. Jamila's supervisor, a 'non-practising' Muslim woman of Lebanese background, 'hushed' her after her experience, 'as if to say, "Don't make a big deal, don't worry about it"': 'It's best to keep quiet, … like my supervisor said, because in the end I get over it.'

As a consequence, many interviewees engaged in forms of self-monitoring, altering their behaviour to 'fit' the circumstances. Khaled was considering changing his name, so he could not be identified as Muslim when he applied for jobs. Several others admitted that they stayed at home more often; some had given up their regular walks or going to shopping centres and many avoided public transport. A few talked of being careful about what they said or wore. One schoolgirl was so terrified of going out that she amassed an enormous number of sick days, and eventually had to go to counselling. Jamila's incident contributed to her decision to throw in her job and concentrate on looking after her daughter, what she described as a 'small sacrifice … because without sacrifice there's no ease'.

Perhaps most telling is Ali's description of his experience 'humiliating' him and affecting his work and dealings with others:

> … whoever ask us any question, I would be frightened to say anything, or express my opinion… you cannot discuss. I started feeling that … someone is following me, on the phone, on everything. My life changed … At home I'm scared that one day they'd come … break things and scare children, scare women.

He believed that, after the bombings in Bali in 2002, ASIO kept watch on his house. He felt that the 'police wanted to diminish our right and wouldn't treat us as Australians': 'our rights are not protected here.' As a result, he says, they stopped going even to the shops:

We're not comfortable to go ... anywhere... we're not comfortable in our own home. We're not comfortable outside. We can't go shopping ... One's whole life became troubled ... how to live like this? ... We don't deal with anyone at all. We don't want to get close to anyone and vice versa. We kept a distance from all people.

Conclusion

As the comments of interviewees attest, the capacity to be relaxed and comfortable is distributed unevenly in Australia. The forms of mundane and violent racism they suffer contribute to wider experiences of exclusion. The devalorisation of ethnic identity means that it is rendered a liability in the field of national belonging. As Rokshana said:

It made me feel very disillusioned, very sad, very upset, that they couldn't see past [the hijab] ... It made me feel very insecure, as if I'm not wanted in Australia, as an outsider ... Maybe I wouldn't get a fair chance in any organisation that I went to and that I had to fight for everything that comes in to my life ... it makes you feel like a stranger in a strange land.

The focus on everyday life here requires that we think of national belonging less as 'imagined community' and more as the ordinary practices of an affectively charged social existence framed as nation-ed (Noble 2002). Hage's (1998, 53) conception of what he calls 'practical nationality' as a form of symbolic capital that garners recognition of one's national belonging underlines the ways many migrants are made to feel *less* national, made uncomfortable in the neighbourhood and the national space simultaneously (Noble 2005).

Two years after this study was conducted, racially-motivated riots on Cronulla beach in Sydney's south demonstrated how violent the affective regulation of belonging can be. Five thousand 'white' Australians, displaying flags, tattoos and signifiers of anglo-Australianness (like cricket gear), turned out to protest what they saw as unacceptable behaviour by Lebanese louts. These actions expressed an urgent desire to control local and national identity and to exclude those who were seen not to belong. Signs asserting 'Shire Pride' (referring to the Sutherland Shire in which Cronulla sits) sat alongside those proclaiming 'Aussie Pride' (Poynting 2006). As 'revenge attacks' were undertaken by young men of Arab and Muslim background over subsequent evenings, lines in the sand were drawn between 'Aussies' and 'Lebs', the included and excluded. One year after the riots, families of Middle Eastern background have stopped visiting Cronulla.

This pervasive landscape of fear and incivility fundamentally alters the social opportunities for Australian Arabs and Muslims to function as citizens. It is not simply that people of Arab or Muslim background experience abuse in their lives, but that these practices serve to disenfranchise them from full participation in spaces of local and national belonging.

Bibliography

Ahmed, S. (2004), *The Cultural Politics of Emotion* (Edinburgh: Edinburgh University Press).

Aly, A. and Balknaves, M. (2005), 'The Atmos*fear* of Terror', *M/C Journal* 8:6, <http://journal.media-culture.org.au/0512/04-alybalnaves.php>, accessed 5 November 2006.

Bourdieu, P. (2000), *Pascalian Meditations* (Cambridge: Polity).

Castles, S. (1999), 'How Nation-States Respond to Immigration and Ethnic Diversity', in S. Vertovec and R. Cohen (eds), *Migration and Social Cohesion* (Cheltenham: Edward Elgar).

Daily Telegraph (2001), 'More Abuse for Muslims', 26 November, 13.

Dunn, K. (2001a), 'The Cultural Geographies of Citizenship in Australia', *Geography Bulletin* 33:1, 4–8.

Dunn, K. (2001b), 'Representations of Islam in the Politics of Mosque Development in Sydney', *Tijdschrift voor Economische en Sociale Geografie* 92:3, 291–308.

Essed, P. (1991), *Understanding Everyday Racism* (Newbury Park, CA: Sage).

Hage, G. (1998), *White Nation* (Sydney: Pluto Press).

Hopkins, P. (2004), 'Young Muslim Men in Scotland: Inclusions and Exclusions', *Children's Geographies* 2:2, 257–72.

Howard, J. (1997), 'Speech to Paterson', Newcastle, 16 July, <http://www.pm.gov.au/news/speeches/1997/pattdins.html>, accessed 11 September 2006.

Howard, J. (2006), 'Diversity, but Not at the Expense of Identity', *Sydney Morning Herald*, 15 September, 3.

Human Rights and Equal Opportunities Commission (1991), *Racist Violence: Report of the national inquiry into racist violence in Australia* (Canberra: Australian Government Publishing Service).

Human Rights and Equal Opportunities Commission (2004), *Isma Project* (Canberra: Australian Government Publishing Service).

Mann, S. (2006), 'Poll Finds Gloom Over Terror', *The Age*, 11 September, <http://www.thegae.com.au/articles/2006/09/10/1157826813759.html>, accessed 11 September, 2006.

Noble, G. (2002), 'Comfortable and Relaxed: Furnishing the Home and Nation', *Continuum* 16:1, 53-66.

Noble, G. (2005), 'The Discomfort of Strangers: Racism, incivility and ontological security in a relaxed and comfortable nation', *Journal of Intercultural Studies* 26:1, 107–20.

Phillips, T. and Smith, P. (2003), 'Everyday Incivility: Towards a benchmark', *The Sociological Review* 51:1, 85–108.

Poynting, S. (2006), 'What Caused the Cronulla Riot?', *Race and Class* 48:1, 85–92.

Poynting, P. and Noble, G. (2004), *Living With Racism: The experience and reporting by Arab and Muslim Australians of discrimination, abuse and violence since 11 September 2001* (Sydney: Human Rights and Equal Opportunities Commission), <http://www.humanrights.gov.au/racial_discrimination/ism/research/index.html>, accessed 21 August 2006.

Poynting, S. Noble, G., Tabar, P. and Collins, J. (2004), *Bin Laden in the Suburbs: Criminalising the Arab Other* (Sydney: Institute of Criminology/Federation Press).

Rogers, A. (1999), 'The Spaces of Multiculturalism and Citizenship', in S. Vertovec and R. Cohen (eds), *Migration and Social Cohesion* (Cheltenham: Edward Elgar).

Young, I.M. (1990), *Justice and the Politics of Difference* (Princeton, NJ: Princeton University Press).

Chapter 11

Youth and the Geopolitics of Risk after 11 September 2001

Kathrin Hörschelmann

Introduction

What constitutes 'the political' has been conceived primarily in terms of the actions of the state in international relations theory and geopolitics (England 2003; Cox and Low 2003; Marston 2003; Dowler and Sharpe 2001; Smith 2004). Although the often severe effects of geopolitical events such as interstate war on civilians and children in particular are recognised (Thorne 2003; Carlton-Ford et al. 2000), the power of state actors to instigate, manipulate and regulate international conflicts has led to a conceptual emphasis on elite discourses and actions, supplemented today by work on popular media (Sharpe 1996; Dodds 1996; 2000; 2005; Dittmer 2005). The primacy accorded to the state as geopolitical agent is notable even in critical geopolitics, where it is seen 'as a producer, administrator and ruler of space' and geopolitics as 'world space as organized by the state' (Dalby and Ó Tuathail 1996, 452; also see Mann 1993; Shapiro 1994). Although power is recognised here as not simply 'a matter of elite control or state rule but a matter also of contested localities where rule is resisted, thwarted and subverted by social movements' (Dalby and Ó Tuathail 1996, 453; also see Routledge 1996), we find few analyses that bring such an understanding squarely into the heart of critical geopolitics, moving beyond a 'resistance' model to theorise the complex involvement of agents at a range of scales, bringing 'the everyday fully into [political geography's] analyses' (Kofman 2003, 622). Feminist political theory has long engaged with these questions and shown that the gendered spheres of the 'private' and 'public' are intricately connected through cycles of social reproduction (Enloe 1989; Peterson 1992; Marston 2003; Staeheli and Kofman 2004). In political geography, such a perspective is only gradually leading to a revision of 'the political'.

In the cases that form the basis of this chapter, neglecting the voices of those seemingly on the sidelines of international conflict reinforces a sense of political disenfranchisement that can lead to a further decline in political interest or, on the contrary, to more radical responses. The focus of this chapter is on perceptions of risk after the World Trade Centre (WTC) attacks of 11 September 2001 of students between 16 and 18 years of age, most of them South Asian, in the British city of Bradford. For those students with hybrid locations in diasporic communities, attachment to people and places in different parts of the world has meant that the effects of these events have been felt strongly in both a direct and mediated way (also see Werbner 2002a and b; 2004; Sivanandan 2006; Hopkins 2007). While the political rhetoric of western pro-war governments and media has portrayed the attacks of 11 September 2001 as primarily a threat to democratic values and securities in the west, thus particularising the effects of this most global event (Smith 2001; Ang 2002), our research begins to show its plural consequences as individuals are increasingly placed in-between intersecting scales, social relations and political commitments. For disaporic groups, the personal and the local are intricately articulated with the political and supra-local, as Philo and Smith (2003) argue for children and young people more generally, especially as they share connections with friends and relatives across geographical distances, care for others on the basis of religious or ethnic affiliation, or are themselves the targets of increased abuse after 11 September.

In the west, ethnic minorities have been at the receiving end of increased racist sentiments that have been fuelled by debates about Islamic fundamentalism and terrorism (Sivanandan 2006; Hefner 2002; see also Hopkins and Smith; and Noble and Poynting in this volume). Their everyday lives have become more precarious and 'risky' due to the associations drawn in popular discourses, and supported by some political factions, between terrorism and Islam (van der Keer 2004; Ang 2002). Pnina Werbner argues that in the UK, the combination of moral panic about Islam invoked by irresponsible political declarations of some members of the Labour government and much of the popular media together with new laws and security measures have provoked a rising sense of alienation among South Asian Muslims:

> Above all, Asians and Muslims felt stigmatised as never before, associated with terror and subject to constant surveillance and suspicion. Young Asians moved around in groups. Women stayed home. Men avoided going out in the evenings. Businessmen suspected that customers were avoiding their firms. There was resentment as well as fear, a feeling of being perceived as unwanted outsiders. (Werbner 2004, 464)

The examples presented in this chapter show, however, that young people's fears about increased racism and potential terrorist attacks were secondary to their concerns about the effects of terrorism and of military conflict on others in distant places. Their interpretations of political responses to 11 September 2001 also show an ability to critique and subvert political discourses rarely recognised in debates on youth political agency and even in research on popular geopolitics. They point to the need to reconceptualise young people's political interests, as highlighted by authors such as Philo and Smith (2003), O'Toole (2003), Buckingham (2000), Furlong and Cartmel (1997) and Bhavnani (1991). Though many of our participants described themselves as 'not interested in politics' and thus mirrored the statistical finding that young people are 'not strongly represented in conventional political parties and political debates' (Wallace 2003, 243), a high number (15 of 25) of both male and female interviewees explained that they were either very (9) or somewhat (6) interested in political issues relevant to them (see also Kovacheva 1995; Wallace and Kovacheva 1998; and Machacek 2000) and argued that young people's apparent 'apathy' towards politics is related to their inability to vote and to affect change as well as to a sense of incompetence compared with adults. The political response to anti-war protests in Britain is likely to have reinforced this sense of ineffectiveness and of not being listened to, potentially radicalising some and increasing the disengagement of others (see also Hesse and Sayyid 2002; Such et al. 2005). The widespread participation of young people in these protests and the highly engaged debates that we witnessed in our focus group discussions, however, also indicate that what is perceived to be 'relevant' is not always what is most immediate or 'local', as current debates on citizenship might suggest (Bynner et al. 1997; Roche 2003; Cockburn 1998). Young people may not perceive these forms of engagement as 'political', since they go beyond conventional party politics (Bhavnani 1991; O'Toole 2003). This has been recognised by Buckingham, who calls for a broadening of definitions of politics beyond the formal operations of party politics (2000). For Philo and Smith (2003) such a broader definition would demand greater focus 'on connections between the micro and the macro', since 'it is very much in transitions from the one to the other – transitions with a clear change of spatial scale and orientation built in – that many of the most interesting questions for a political geography of children and young people will reside (even in these times of alleged post-modern apathy)' (111).

The interviews analysed in this chapter were conducted by Dr Lisa ElRefaie (Cardiff University) and myself as focus group discussions with students from both vocational (NVQ) and higher education colleges (A-Levels) in the British, west Yorkshire city of Bradford in July and November 2005. They formed the first and second phase of a research project funded by the British Academy on young people's understandings of political cartoons and their interpretations of geopolitical events. Twenty-five students were interviewed during these first two research phases, both individually in in-depth, qualitative interviews and in focus groups. In this chapter, I focus on the group discussions, where views on terrorism and the wars in Afghanistan and Iraq were debated. We recruited 12 female and 13 male students of mixed ethnic and religious backgrounds. Eight boys and five girls identified as British-South Asian Muslim, two girls and four boys as white Christian, one girl and one boy as British-Indian Hindu, one girl as Bangladeshi Hindu, one girl as English-Asian without religion, one girl as British-Indian Sikh and one girl as black Christian. Six of the students were from a vocational college, six from a further education college and 13 from an A-Level course (university access qualification) at a state school. Students were not recruited for their particular interest in politics. In letters to teachers and a flyer for students we explained that an interest in politics was not necessary to participation, but it is likely that politically engaged students volunteered more than others and that teachers had an influence on the selection of participants. Thus, it is not possible to conclude from the small sample interviewed here that similar levels of political interest will be found more generally. More important than statistical averages, therefore, are the qualitative explanations that our participants gave for their interest in politics (or lack of it).

In the following sections, students' perceptions of risk since the WTC attacks in 2001 are analysed, distinguishing between risks for themselves, for related others and for others in distant places. This section includes a discussion of broader risks than those associated with terrorism and war. Students' explanations for the causes of risks are also briefly summarised, before concluding with some thoughts on the political inclusion and exclusion of young people.

Whose Risks?

The Terrorist Threat

The question of terrorist threats to western populations and 'values' has dominated much political and media discourse in North America and Europe since 11 September 2001. We therefore expected that our participants would talk at length about their perceptions of global risks and terrorism in the group discussions. Yet, they rarely expressed concern about it and instead showed much scepticism about the political motives for producing fear about terrorism. Thus, Said argued that 'they make terrorism a big issue to frighten people' (group 3), while in group 4, participants discussed the negative consequences of anti-terrorist legislation for civil liberties:

> There is new terror laws in Britain isn't it? Normally, you are suspected and arrested. You have the right to a lawyer, you have a right to, they read you your rights. But under the new terror law, if they suspect you are a terrorist they just put you in gaol without anything and after four years they say, oh, sorry. (Group 4)

In response to the question whether 11 September had any effects on their own lives, the young South Asians in this group answered in unison that it had resulted in 'scary' consequences and that discrimination and ethnic segregation had increased, showing how this global event and its interpretation by UK politicians and media had changed the context of their own daily interactions. Being part of an ethnic minority themselves, they felt more threatened by the increase in racism than by possible terrorist attacks. The students recounted stories of discrimination that they had heard on the news or from friends and relatives, thus going beyond personal experience:

Ismail:	I don't know about the rest of you but I live in a predominantly white area and I got funny looks all the time.
Vandana:	Yeah, I know it happened.
Ismail:	It is scary. I mean, I have lived practically all my life in there since I was about four and it was pretty scary that the people you have grown up with and their parents won't let their kids play football with you on the street and that. People were like, we are not allowed out, we are not allowed out. That is when it hits you.
Vandana:	Discrimination happens.
Fatima:	Because of that.
Vandana:	You start to think, are we next? (Group 4)

Muslim students felt particularly vulnerable to discrimination and racist attacks. Thus, in group 2, Ishmael explained that he felt insecure and had started to panic about being identified and attacked as a Muslim, while Sumita expressed concern about the possibilities of Muslims to get jobs and progress in their careers due to discrimination. A similar discussion arose in group 3, where Asif, a male Muslim student with British Pakistani identity and Zara, a female English/Asian student without religious affiliation, discussed the increase of racist discrimination experienced by Muslims and black people in America since the WTC attacks. They worried about a rise in British National Party (BNP) support in Britain and the connections made between ordinary Muslims and terrorists:

I: Do you think that is something happening in Britain, racial issues?
Asif: Yes, I think because they obviously found some people with Al Qaeda from here so I think it is going to happen more here. The BNP rolls through as well. Like all these parties like the BNP.
Zara: That is one of the main effects I think on Britain, more of a racial divide. People use it as a form of racism. Now it is, back to your own country, you terrorist, and things like that. Just because you have got brown skin doesn't mean to say you are associated like you know you are not part of Al Qaeda just because you wear traditional Asian clothes [...] Kids in school, in my sister's school after that there was a lot of tension and things. People were saying a lot of stuff. I think it was an argument that went round the school, oh this kid, his dad was a terrorist or something just because they had seen him wearing the traditional clothes. (Group 3)

For Sumita, who lives in the nearby town of Keighley, racist discrimination is nothing new and the terrorist fear mainly reinforces existing prejudices, as white people in the area had never been interested in getting to know people from immigrant groups:

This just seems like an excuse. Oh my god, we never got to know them. They could be linked to this. People of the same colour, the same religion, they are typecasting in everybody just because of what they have seen on TV and that and because of that like racist parties like the BNP are getting in. They shouldn't be allowed to stand, never mind get in power. (Group 2)

Independent of their ethnic and religious background, our interviewees shared some concerns about terrorist attacks, especially on planes and public transport. The most concrete concerns were raised by participants of group 1, who we interviewed after the London bombings in 2005. The two Muslim and four white British students talked at length about risks at train stations and the need to watch out for people carrying backpacks. They called for tighter security and more police controls:

Zwain: You have to be more careful where you are going, watch your back every time. Because you can't trust no-one with a back pack. (Group 1)

Carol, a white English student, made exactly the connection between terrorists and immigrants critiqued by students in the other three groups:

I:	Do you think there is anything the government can do to reduce terrorism? Is there anything that they could do?
Carol:	They should stop letting all these immigrants in. All asylum seekers they are all coming from different places for asylum or coming in illegal and Britain are letting them in and then they get everything like money and all that ... Let everybody in, it is just stupid. (Group 1)

Although they did not openly disagree with her, the two Muslim students developed a more differentiated view, explaining that there were reasons such as persecution and military conflict that would justify asylum.

Britain's support for military intervention in Iraq was seen by most participants as a risk factor. For Zara in group 3, the terrorist danger had increased due to British involvement in the wars:

Zara:	I think I am more worried about any wars starting up and any repercussions of the war that could affect Britain. You know, terrorists coming over here to try and blow things up, trying to get revenge on Britain. Helping America, and I don't understand why we were involved. (Group 3)

She strongly felt that American politics had impacts well beyond the US and the regions in which it had intervened. In particular, Zara worried about those who had relatives in Iraq, such as the families of British soldiers.

This question of effects on the British families of soldiers in Iraq was not purely academic. Carol (group 1) had several friends in the army, one of whom had just returned from Iraq. The fact that soldiers are frequently recruited at a young age makes clear that young people are more strongly politically engaged and with greater consequences for their own lives than is commonly acknowledged. To what extent such involvement constitutes political agency, however, is open to debate:

I:	Do you know anyone that has been called up?
Carol:	I have got quite a few friends who have been to Iraq. There is a lass the same age of me, 18, she has just finished in Iraq. Been there for a year I think. Now she is being sent to Germany and she was in a tank and something happened and toppled over when she was in it and she got injured. (Group 1)

The impacts of American politics, including presidential elections, on other countries were also clearly identified by group 4. Although one participant raised the hope that because of its role as an ally of the powerful US, Britain was less likely to be attacked, other students expressed concern that the country could become embroiled in a conflict with Saudi Arabia or that it might lose American support and itself become attacked by the US military.

Fatima:	How do we know one day America is not going to bomb us?
Said:	Exactly. […]
Fatima:	Might be Britain next.
Vandana:	For his empire.
Fatima:	Britain standing against America that is small. (Group 4)

Risks to Others

Despite these concerns for their own safety, participants worried far more about the consequences of war for related and unrelated *others* in Afghanistan and Iraq, however. For some, these concerns were based on diasporic connections to relatives in these or nearby countries, while for others the overriding reason was a strong sense of injustice as innocent people lost their lives in the conflicts.

For Asif, a student from an Afghan family who had been born in Britain but maintained strong connections to Afghanistan, which he continued to see as his home country, the military intervention there had direct consequences. He was the only participant who embraced the military action there completely, although he still maintained an anti-war position in relation to the conflict in Iraq:

> I am from Afghanistan, so I am connected from there […] I was against the war in Iraq, but the war in Afghanistan […] I can remember the years of the Taliban, it looked really bleak, really bleak. But now it is looking better. I was there two years ago and it was much better. […] It has actually changed my life because it is my country and if my country has got better it is obviously going to change my life. (Group 3)

Thus, for Asif the international political events that followed the WTC attack were far from removed from his personal life and taking an interest in them was not a voluntary affair, as is often implied in discussions of postmodern, apathetic youth culture. Even the migration of his family to the UK and thus the context in which he had grown up was related to the political situation in Afghanistan, which in turn had been significantly influenced by foreign powers such as Russia and the USA over the last two to three decades (and Britain previously).

Such direct connections were described by no other participants, who also rarely discussed Afghanistan and instead concentrated mostly on the war in Iraq. They overwhelmingly opposed the latter and pointed to the high human cost of the conflict as one of the main reasons for their resentment. While we noted few differences in responses by gender, it was the girls in all groups who most strongly opposed the war on grounds of inhumanity and the killing of innocent victims:

Sumita:	I mean, I think the whole approach was wrong, going in and bombing people all through the night, that is just horrible, when you think of all the kids and it, I think it was wrong. I think they could have gone in a different way. I mean the war in Iraq, how many people did they kill? Saying it was an accident, still people did die. (Group 2)
Fatima:	But the main thing is, innocent people are dying.

Vandana: Why doesn't George W Bush go to war, why doesn't he be a soldier and die? How would his family feel? [...]
Fatima: When an American dies or one American soldier dies they have a whole silence for it.
Vandana: They tell it all over the media. They broadcast it everywhere. What about the millions of people he is killing himself? (Group 4)

Contrary to the simplistic logic of 'friends' and 'enemies' applied by the US government to separate those 'for us' from those 'against us' participants in all groups, independent of their ethnic background, shared a sense of horror and shock about the victims of the WTC attacks. They recounted not only the moment when they found out about the attacks, but also tried to understand how they might have reacted in the same situation and what it must have felt like to be trapped in the WTC or the planes:

Zara: I remember where I was when it happened and it is just so strange seeing all the news reports afterwards. It was more disturbing when you saw the families and looking for people. They would say, my brother was in there and that is where it kind of really started hitting home, even though we are not in America and stuff like that you kind of felt you could just feel really bad for them. You had like empathy more than sympathy because you felt it for them.
Asif: ... like a shock what has happened. (Group 3)

Other Risks

Despite these concerns for both the victims of terrorist attacks and the casualties of war in Iraq, our participants declined to see Islamic terrorism as the most important issue in current world politics. Thus, although the WTC attacks and the London bombings had clearly left an imprint on their understandings of world historical events, they questioned the extent to which this justified ignorance of other problems and subverted the rhetoric of anti-terrorism by a) questioning what terrorism is and to what extent the actions of the US and UK government could be equally described, b) critiquing the focus on Iraq, and c) asking which issues were intentionally or incidentally sidelined by the current preoccupation with terrorism. The students developed a broad perspective on risks and whose lives were currently most endangered. Since the interviews with groups 2 to 4 coincided with the G8 meeting in Edinburgh and the Live8 concert, poverty and Global South debt ranked as number one issues that politicians from rich countries ought to aim to resolve. The influence that this much mediatised event had on participants' political views shows some of the limits of young people's ability to develop autonomous opinions. Just as with adults, recognising their political interests should not lead us to ignore the discursive contexts within which they are formed.

In addition to world poverty, participants raised concerns about climate change, other dictatorial states and the Israel-Palestine question. The Middle-

Eastern crisis was a particular concern for Muslim students, showing that this issue remains central to how they view western geopolitics:

Ishmael:	[Bush] also has to change the situation of Palestine and Israel. That is a really, really big issue. Number two, number one on the list.
Sumita:	That is more important than the war in Iraq. That is not resolved. […]
I:	What moral principles would you like to see in politics?
Ishmael:	Well, equality with the rich and poor. There is serious inequality, justice you know, peace. (Group 2)

Power, Profit and the Causes of War

None of the participants drew a direct connection between terrorism and global inequality, but some critiqued the powerful position of corporations that they saw as a major reason for the continuation of unfair trading conditions as well as for the US-led military intervention in Iraq. For most, oil interests were the major motivation for war in Iraq, seeing the US, UK and even European governments as an arm of the oil industry:

I:	What do you think actually led to the Iraq war? Why did it happen?
Fatima:	It was oil …
Tanita:	Yeah, I think.
Fatima:	… It was basically economy. I mean America is richest and just wants more and more.
Hussein:	It's power.
Fatima:	And Iraq is rich in oil big time. Just to get that, it was Weapons of Mass Destruction, at the end of the day they never found any. Made up things just to cover the oil thing up […]
Hussein:	[Bush] wants to go down in the books as a hero. He wants to go down in history.
Fatima:	The way I see him is like a dictator, like we said before Hitler, yeah.
Tanita:	Hitler was doing the same thing as well. He wants an empire at the end of the day. (Group 4)

As in this quote, students referred to an extension of America's imperial position and to the personalities of power-seeking politicians as other reasons for the war. Only to a minor extent did they accept the rationale of removing a dictatorship, tackling terrorism and preventing the use of WMDs by a 'rogue state'. Indeed, they felt betrayed by government propaganda about WMDs and bemoaned the unilateralism of US and UK foreign policies that undermined the UN, an institution which most of our participants regarded as more democratic and significant:

Zara:	… if America is saying this country is doing something wrong then they go through the UN which is what they did with Iraq I think. But then the UN said look, they are not a threat, and then obviously America went around them which is wrong. […] … they didn't really have any

	grounds when they went in there, people were saying they didn't have any grounds for thinking that Iraq had WMD because of like something that happened with Saddam years before and then it became, did they actually find any WMD?
Asif:	No. That's the important bit.
Zara:	That's the things and they kind of destroyed everything, killed a lot of people. They found Saddam hiding in a hole.
Asif:	Unless they put him there. (Group 3)
Ishmael:	… when it comes to politics, the UN and stuff they have actually got to do something, they don't really do much. I kind of like the UN and cos they are at heart a good organisation.
Sumita:	People don't listen to them. George Bush didn't listen to them. They can't really do anything.
Ishmael:	… he is the most powerful man and he can do what he wants. Does make you angry though. (Group 2)

Politics and Agency

This sense of betrayal and the UK government's reluctance to engage with the anti-war protesters engendered a sense of disempowerment in the students, who questioned the democratic legitimacy of their government's actions:

I:	What do you think of Britain's role in the conflict?
Sumita:	It was pointless. I don't think Britain should have even gone to war and they didn't give good enough reasons to go to war and they said they had nuclear weapons but none were found and you know, I don't think they should have gone at all. (Group 2)
Carol:	Tony Blair just put us into it because George Bush told him and Tony Blair was all for it because they want their countries to be friendly with one another. So they, that is why we were all involved. [...]
Mustafa:	They should have paid attention to it all over the world, especially Britain and the protests. (Group 1)

A similar sense of powerlessness was notable from participants' discussion of their own political interests and the lacking engagement of many young people. They referred to the limited experience and knowledge of young people, to their position as non-voters and to the fact that politicians seemed disinterested in their views as an explanation for the so-called youth apathy. The overriding feeling was one of not being able to achieve any real changes, especially in relation to the 'big issues', such as Global South poverty:

Said:	I hate to say this but we are like chatting about Tony Blair and George Bush, but to be honest with you, we are never going to get to say that to them. [...]
Hussein:	Why don't you go to the big meeting in Scotland?

Said:	I am going.
Fatima:	Which meeting are you going to?
Said:	The summit.
Hussein:	The G8 one. [...]
Said:	We could all sit around talking, talking all night, but whether anything is done with the information we give and we learn from each other, that is a different thing, isn't it? Realistically is George Bush going to hear what we are saying?
Vandana:	No.
Taymur:	I very much doubt it.
Vandana:	And even if he did he wouldn't do anything. (Group 4)

I:	Did any of you take part in the protests?
Carol:	Wish I had been involved.
John:	There is no point anyway. (Group 1)

In their majority, the young people we interviewed felt that their political intervention was either ignored, ridiculed or ineffective and as such might have reinforced their belief in the pointlessness of becoming politically engaged. Judging by the anger expressed by some, however, it is also possible that individuals seek more radical action to make their opinions heard. The recommendation by our interviewees to politicians to counteract this as well as the lack of political interest was to lower the voting age and to make a concerted effort to consult with them about issues across a range of scales, starting with school councils and continuing with the recently established Youth Parliaments.

Conclusion

Fears over racist attacks and rising discrimination are one concern identified as a consequence of the terrorist attacks of 11 September by the students we interviewed in Bradford in June 2005. Their sense of risk extends, however, well beyond the confines of their own immediate contexts. Far from showing 'compassion fatigue' (Hoskins 2004; Moeller 1999), in focus group discussions and in-depth interviews they expressed feelings of empathy and connectedness with those who have suffered in terrorist attacks as well as with those whose lives have been and continue to be at risk due to military conflict in Afghanistan and Iraq. In some cases, the students still had relatives and friends in these or in neighbouring countries, while in other cases the sense of connectedness arose from a shared sense of oppression and powerlessness, especially in the face of American military might, and a general perception of people's blameless involvement in the conflicts. The students were highly critical of the suffering inflicted upon civilians, whom they saw as innocent, and they rejected sharply the contention that it is western securities which are most in need of protection. Instead, they pointed at a range of other important global issues that endangered the lives of people around the world. Influenced by media coverage of the Live8 event, our interviewees identified Global South poverty as the most important issue that they wanted to see urgently resolved. They challenged the perception of risks as a new and western phenomenon. Their wide-spread empathies also clearly ran counter the simplistic logic of being 'either for or against us', whoever that 'us' might be. Instead of focusing on terrorism as the main reason for war in Afghanistan and Iraq, most interviewees constructed a political-economic argument. They saw corporate interests as primarily responsible for the conflicts in Afghanistan and Iraq. Interviewees also critiqued American imperialist ambitions, personified by the figure of George Bush, and the British allied position.

Most worrying were the conclusions drawn by our participants about the in-effectiveness of their political engagement, especially given the lack of success of the anti-war movement. They were frustrated and angry that 'nobody ever listens to us. Why don't they listen to us?' (Vandana, group 4). While current debates on citizenship have been focused particularly on the scale of the local and the national, our case study shows the insufficiency of such an approach to address the hybrid positioning of young people from diasporic communities. It also points to the need to recognise the relevance of global political issues for young people, both because their everyday lives are directly affected by them and because they feel connected to and even responsible for others (Campbell and Shapiro 1999) in a globalising world.

Bibliography

Ang, I. (2002), 'After '911': Defending the global city', *Ethnicities* 2:2, 160–62.

Bhavnani, K.-K. (1991), *Talking Politics. A Psychological Framing for Views from Youth in Britain* (Cambridge: Cambridge University Press and Paris: Editions de la Maison des Sciences de l'Homme).

Buckingham, D. (2000), *The Making of Citizens: Young people, news and politics* (London: Routledge).

Bynner, J., Chrisholm, L. and Furlong, A. (eds) (1997), *Youth, Citizenship and Social Change in a European Context* (Aldershot: Ashgate).

Campbell, D. and Shapiro, M. J. (eds) (1999), *Moral Spaces. Rethinking Ethics and World Politics* (Minneapolis, MN: University of Minnesota Press).

Carlton-Ford, A., Hamill, A. and Houston, P. (2000), 'War and Children's Mortality', *Childhood* 7:4, 401–19.

Cockburn, T. (1998), 'Children and Citizenship in Britain', *Childhood* 5:1, 99–117.

Cox, K. and Low, M. (2003), 'Political Geography in Question', *Political Geography* 22, 599–602.

Dalby, S. and Ó Tuathail, G. (1996), The Critical Geopolitics Constellation: Problematizing fusions of geographical knowledge and power', editorial introduction, *Political Geography* 15:6/7, 451–6.

Dittmer, J. (2005), 'Captain America's Empire: Reflections on identity, popular culture, and post-9/11 geopolitics', *Annals of the Association of American Geographers* 95:3, 626–43.

Dodds, K. (1996), 'The 1982 Falklands War and a Critical Geopolitical Eye: Steve Bell and the If ... cartoons', *Political Geography* 15:6/7, 571–92.

Dodds, K. (2000), *Geopolitics in a Changing World* (London: Prentice Hall).

Dodds, K. (2005), *Global Geopolitics. A Critical Introduction* (London: Prentice Hall).

Dowler, L. and Sharpe, J. (2001), 'A Feminist Geopolitics?', *Space and Polity* 5:3, 165–76.

England, K. (2003), 'Towards a Feminist Political Geography?', *Political Geography* 22, 611–16.

Enloe, C. (1989), *Bananas, Beaches and Bases: Making feminist sense of international politics* (Berkeley, CA: University of California Press).

Furlong, A. and Cartmel, F. (1997), *Young People and Social Change* (Buckingham and Philadelphia, PA: Open University Press).

Hefner, R. (2002), '11 September and the Struggle for Islam', *Ethnicities* 2:2, 144–146.

Hesse, B. and Sayyid, S. (2002), 'The "War" Against Terrorism/The "War" for Cynical Reason', *Ethnicities* 2:2, 149–54.

Hopkins, P. (2007), 'Global Events, National Politics, Local Lives', *Environment and Planning A* 39:5, 1119–33.

Hoskins, A. (2004), 'Television and the Collapse of Memory', *Time and Society* 13:1, 109–27.

Kofman, E. (2003), 'Future Directions in Political Geography', *Political Geography* 22, 621–24.

Kovacheva, S. (1995), 'Student Political Culture in Transition: The case of Bulgaria', in CYRCE (Circle for Youth Research Cooperation in Europe) (ed.), *The Puzzle of Integration. European Yearbook on Youth Policy and Research*, Vol. 1 (Berlin and New York: De Gruyter).

Machacek, L. (2000), 'Youth and the Creation of Civil Society in Slovakia', in H. Helve and C. Wallace (eds), *Youth, Citizenship and Empowerment* (Basingstoke: Ashgate Gower).

Mann, M. (1993), *The Sources of Political Power*, Vol. 2 (Cambridge: Cambridge University Press).

Marston, S. (2003), 'Political Geography in Question', *Political Geography* 22, 633–6.

Moeller, S.D. (1999), *Compassion Fatigue: How the media sell disease, famine, war and death* (London: Routledge).

O'Toole, T. (2003), 'Engaging with Young People's Conceptions of the Political', *Children's Geographies* 1:1, 71–90.

Peterson, S. (ed.) (1992), *Gendered States: Feminist (re)visions of International Relations Theory* (Boulder, CO: Lynne Rienner).

Philo, C. and Smith, F. (2003), 'Guest Editorial: Political Geographies of Children and Young People', *Space and Polity* 7:2, 99–115.

Roche, J. (2003), 'Children: Rights, participation and citizenship', *Childhood* 6:4, 475–93.

Routledge, P. (1996), 'Critical Geopolitics and Terrains of Resistance', *Political Geography* 15:6/7, 509–31.

Shapiro, M. (1994), 'Moral Geographies and the Ethics of Post-Sovereignty', *Public Culture* 6, 479–502.

Sharpe, J. (1996), 'Hegemony, Popular Culture and Geopolitics: The *Reader's Digest* and the construction of danger', *Political Geography* 15:6/7, 557–70.

Sivanandan, A. (2006), 'Race, Terror and Civil Society', *Race and Class* 47:3, 1–8.

Smith, N. (2001), 'Scales of Terror and the Resort to Geography: September 11, October 7', *Environment and Planning D: Society and Space* 19, 631–7.

Smith, S. (2004), 'Singing Our World into Existence: International Relations Theory and September 11', *International Studies Quarterly* 48, 499–515.

Staeheli, L.A. and Kofman, E. (2004), 'Mapping Gender, Making Politics: Toward feminist political geographies', in L. Staeheli, E. Kofman and L. J. Peake (eds), *Mapping Women, Making Politics. Feminist Perspectives on Political Geography* (London: Routledge).

Such, E., Walker, O. and Walker, R. (2005), 'Anti-War Children. Representation of Youth Protests Against the Second Iraq War in the British National Press', *Childhood* 12:3, 301–26.

Thorne, B. (2003), 'Children and the 2003 War in Iraq', editorial, *Childhood* 10:3, 259–63.

Van der Keer, P. (2004), 'South Asian Islam in Britain', *Ethnicities* 4:1, 135–46.

Wallace, C. (2003), 'Introduction: Youth and politics', *Journal of Youth Studies* 6:3, 243–5.

Wallace, C. and Kovacheva, S. (1998), *Youth in Society. The construction and deconstruction of youth in East and West Europe* (London: Macmillan).

Werbner, P. (2002a), *Imagined Disaporas among Manchester Muslims: The public performance of transnational identity politics* (Oxford and Santa Fe, NM: James Currey and School of American Research).

Werbner, P. (2002b), 'Reproducing the Multicultural Nation', editorial, *Anthropology Today*, 18:2, 3–4.

Werbner, P. (2004), 'The Predicament of Diaspora and Millenial Islam. Reflections on September 11, 2001', *Ethnicities* 4:4, 451–76.

SECTION 4

Regulating Fear

The three chapters that follow provide a foil to Section 3, which focused on the ways fear is encountered and made sense of. Henk van Houtum and Roos Pijpers, Nadia Abu Zhara and Peter Shirlow all begin their analyses of fear by mapping out political contexts in the European Union, Israel/Palestine and Northern Ireland respectively. Their chapters go on to emphasise the ways that everyday lives have political form themselves, and are present in, interwoven with and often resistant to the complex sets of national and international politics which each chapter disentangles. In that sense, this section adds in innovative ways to existing work around the geopolitics of fear which tends to presume, downplay or even ignore the significance of people's everyday lives and local spaces.

Van Houtum and Pijpers examine the geopolitical landscape of the European Union, and turn to fear and desire to understand the growing wish to police borders and protect against immigration. Ultimately contradictory, the 'wall of conservative solidification' that is erected is 'fierce and terrifying in its sometimes deathly consequence', yet also helps to 'sustain our easiness and comfort' by ignoring certain illegal workers. Moving between scales of analysis, they draw parallels with gated communities where individuals fence themselves off, desiring separation from socially and economically different people and places. Like that of gated communities, the protection which EU immigration policies seem to provide is illusory, tending to increase rather than dissipate fears. This, van Houtum and Pijpers argue, is political expedient in other ways too.

Abu Zhara offers a powerful account of the security situation in Israel/Palestine. She focuses on the use and abuse of identity documentation which, she argues, simultaneously represents deprivation and entitlement. In the Israeli context, identity cards and the threat of their confiscation are used to closely regulate the movements of Palestinians. As the empirical material makes clear, this threat is often employed without any grounds, and along with 'stop and search' has become part of everyday discrimination, harassment and abuse that many Palestinians encounter. Abu Zhara offers her illustration of the ways in which identity cards become entangled with a politics of fear as a warning to other places which are considering introducing them.

Shirlow's account of segregation based on ethnosectarian tensions and fear shows clearly how political processes and conflicts become written on the ground, and this spatialisation, alongside their historicisation, embeds them securely. His research maps out the social and emotional geographies of those in Catholic, Protestant and mixed communities. While officially there has been a cessation of most paramilitary violence, it is the case that hostility, abuse, and the very small actions and movements with which people exclude and avoid each other continue apace. Again, national and local spaces become politicised in many different ways, literally and more subtly, obviously and more quietly, publicly and privately; and the role of emotions in holding this process together – but also, importantly, in resisting it – are clear from his respondents' accounts.

Chapter 12

On Strawberry Fields and Cherry Picking: Fear and Desire in the Bordering and Immigration Politics of the European Union

Henk van Houtum and Roos Pijpers[1]

Living is easy with eyes closed
Misunderstanding all you see.
Nothing is real and nothing to get hungabout.
Strawberry fields forever.

> The Beatles (1967)

Introduction

Over time, but especially since the opening of the Internal Market, the European Union has 'modernised' its immigration policy, specifically focusing on containing asylum migration, fighting irregular/illegal migration, and extending European migration policy onto countries of origin and transit. Development aid is increasingly tied to agreements obligating these so-called 'third countries' to take back irregular migrants, and non-EU states are increasingly being encouraged to control emigration more firmly. Furthermore, all non-EU states on the edges of Europe are financially sponsored to reinforce their border controls. This renewed border regime has led to an increased closing, fortifying and policing of the external borders of the European Union.

In sharp contrast with this policy of closure for immigrants from outside the European Union however, borders are selectively opened up for (mostly) high-skilled labour forces from third countries in order to bypass temporary as well as structural labour shortages in the member states. This need for more economic immigration in the immediate future, a direct consequence of Europe's ageing labour forces, is increasingly outspoken (European Commission 2000; 2003; 2005). The internal liberalisation of cross-border labour mobility and moral equality for

---

1   This chapter is a reworked version of an article published in *Antipode* in 2007: Van Houtum and Pijpers (2007) 'The European Union as a Gated Community: The Two-faced border and immigration regime of the EU', *Antipode* 39: 2, 291–309.

'all' EU-citizens (and a happy few non-EU nationals) on the European internal market is thus combined with the tightening of control at the new external borders, as well as transitory measures to regulate freedom of movement of the Union's newest inhabitants. These two manifestations of European migration policy (the simultaneous attraction of economically required and rejection of allegedly market-redundant immigrants) are inherently contrasting and difficult to manage and sustain in combination.

This chapter argues that borders as 'spatial manifestations' (following Falah and Newman 1995) of ambivalent migration policy express an 'ensemble' or assemblage of fear and are strategically selective to sift and sort the feared and the fearful. A key theme in managing this assemblage of fear in relation to an increasingly paradoxical, bifurcated EU migration policy is protection. Although the term protection is a telling metaphor for restrictive immigration policies, it is by no means new (see for instance Hiebert 2003; Engelen 2003; Jordan and Düvell 2003); however, a more systematic and critical use of the concept starting from its original economic interpretation could well prove insightful in explaining why and how the European Union protects itself against unwanted immigration, and in setting out what really is protected on the inside when these unwanted immigrants are kept on the outside. To this end, the chapter starts by drawing a parallel between the economic protection against free mobility of goods and restrictive measures against (free) migration. There are obvious limitations to such a comparison in terms of economic theory and political reality, but working with the lens of (selective) protection as a means of managing and manipulating fear, leads us to propose an alternative to the well-known, yet flawed Fortress Europe metaphor. Our argument is that the border-management of the European Union and particularly its Internal Market project resembles that of a gated community. In a gated community, a lifestyle of easiness and comfort is both created and protected at high material costs. It is argued that whereas harsh realities of a hostile world outside may evaporate in gated communities, they continue to haunt the desires and dreams of those inside. Fear of immigrants for that matter, we argue, will not dissolve through protection.

Guest Labour and Security Traumas: The Politically Invoked Foundation of Protection

Issues of immigration and minority integration have topped political agendas and media headlines in all of the member states of the European Union in recent years. Restrictive measures against immigration and asylum have become 'deeply political' (Hiebert 2003, 189). Just as protectionism in the realm of foreign trade is by definition connected to domestic sectoral policies (for example, in the field of agriculture), there exists 'elective affinities' between immigration policy and policies of integration and labour market (Engelen 2003, 504). In one of her earlier writings on global capitalism, Saskia Sassen phrases this intrinsically political nature of an ideologically economic border as follows:

National boundaries do not act as barriers so much as mechanisms reproducing the system through the international division of labor ... Border enforcement is a mechanism facilitating the extraction of cheap labor by assigning criminal status to a segment of the working class – illegal immigrants. Foreign workers undermine a nation's working class when the state renders foreigners socially and politically powerless. At the same time, border enforcement meets the demands of organised labor in the labor-receiving country insofar as it presumes to protect native workers. Yet selective enforcement of policies can circumvent general border policies and protect the interests of economic sectors relying on immigrant labor. (Sassen 1988, 36–7)

Although debates on the pros and cons of global labour mobility have in a way become subordinate to what Huysmans and others have called a securitisation of migration issues (Huysmans 2000), both discourses are linked through the concept of guest labour trauma, introduced by Dutch sociologist Engbersen (2003) for the case of the Netherlands. The idea here is that dissatisfaction with the socio-economic integration of immigrants from Turkey and Morocco, who were supposed to return home again but stayed, is now contributing to the new conservatism in immigration policy. The existence of a guest labour trauma is nowhere more clearly visible than in the transitional labour market entry restrictions imposed by the majority of 'old' member states (imaginable as a cordon sanitaire) upon low-rated labourers from new member states. They were feared to come in masses and stay, too. The guest labour trauma, hence, points to a fear of becoming overwhelmed by strangers; of becoming, as the Germans say, *überfremdet*. However, recent research in the Netherlands has shown that one of the direct consequences of the transitional arrangements is that specialised labour market intermediaries, subcontractors and legal advisory firms actually profit from, gain a rent from, the transitional border closing through the application of all kinds of circumvention strategies in order to recruit scarce low-skilled labour from new member states (Ter Beek et al. 2005).

Within the framework of neoclassical economic trade theory, such rent-seeking behaviour is the predictable reaction to a protection wall against presumed harmful effects of free trade. This harm consists of 'loss of welfare'. Free trade (and free labour mobility) would cause a welfare transfer from the importing country to exporting countries – to the detriment of the national economy and its producers. States issue protective measures to shield its firms, particularly those in newly emerged, 'infant' industries, from harsh export competition (Krugman and Obstfeld 1997). Neoclassical economic trade theory demonstrates that protectionism in the form of tariff walls and quota, rather than free trade, is inefficient in terms of welfare distribution effects, at least from a macro-perspective. It is for this reason, using the same dominant economic theory as an argument, that the European Union in 1988 launched the institutionalisation of an Internal Market, featuring the four freedoms of labour, capital, services and goods. Drawing on Ricardo's and Heckscher-Olin's seminal ideas about the (re)allocation of production processes according to comparative advantage with regard to production factors, the various protection models show that in many cases, certainly for small economies which are unable to influence world prices, loss will exceed gain (Krugman and Obstfeld 1997). Tellingly, however, this ideology and conviction was easily put aside when freedom of labour for citizens of new member states was at stake.

The dissatisfaction with immigrant integration mentioned above has now, at least in the Netherlands, contributed to a dominant rhetoric that strongly critiques the alleged 'anything goes' character of migration policies in the past. As a result, current political forces have expressed a key interest in controlling the numbers of 'redundant' and allegedly difficult to integrate 'non-western' immigrants/refugees in order to preserve social cohesion and protect national labour markets within the European borders. The result is a policy that is so much focused on competence of assimilation, that the migration motives of those who want to enter the EU are being categorised into a mere binominal 'good or bad', with the consequence of being in or out. The World Trade Centre attacks on 11 September 2001 have only strengthened the perceived inevitability of constructing a restrictive (common) labour and asylum immigration policy, which is being reinforced by anxieties post-11 September (and since the 2004 Madrid bombings) over security and global terrorism. The European Commission has composed a so-called 'black list', consisting of a total of 132 states whose inhabitants require a visa for entrance into EU space (Council Regulation 539/2001). The criteria used for a state to be put on this list relate to the perceived possibility of illegal residence after entering EU-space and the perceived influence on public security. This example serves to demonstrate that there is a remarkable inconsistency in the logic of the member states of the European Union when it concerns the opening of national borders of the labour market among those who are inside the club, and the forceful restriction and protection against a free flow of migration for those outside the club and even for new members.

Borders as Spatial Manifestations of Fear

In order to understand the persistence of (in theory) economically inefficient political protection walls against unsolicited migration, the analysis of the borders of the European Union should encompass the politically expressed societal traumas with regard to (labour) migration. For, we believe that the persistent desire to control, to manage the opening and closure of borders, could be considered as the outcome of fear (Falah and Newman 1995). Below, we will be more explicit in specifying who is fearful, and who encourages and communicates fears. We first want to zoom in to outline what we consider as fear. For us, fear is the emotion of being confronted with negation of the own world, of deletion, of emptiness. Fear reveals the 'nothing' and therefore has no object (Heidegger 1970, 33–4; Lacan 2004). This nothingness is overwhelming in the sense of the lack of space for oneself, a lack of the realisation of one's own desires. According to Lacan (2004), when 'le manque vient a manquer', when this lack is lacking, when there is too much presence at too close a range, then there is fear. It is this nothing that tightens, oppresses (angustia) the (national) Self and the (material) resources of the (national) Self: 'Es ist einem unheimlich' (one becomes uneasy, not at home). The nationally constructed and imagined Self and the national (material) resources of the Self represent the footing for the Self. When the nothing threatens to replace this (national) Self, the threat that the difference between the inside and outside becomes blurred and one becomes a nobody amongst everybody, one of the most used strategies counterbalancing it will be a distance creation, a rebordering, a strengthening of the imagined unity of the (national) Self, of the border around the (national) Self and the (material) resources that support it. A border is therefore saying: keep your distance. As a result, an object is created to symbolise, objectify and to name the threatening revealing of the emptiness ('vide': Lacan 2004). The fear is given a name, that is the Other. Analytically, then, this existential fear expresses itself in two ways; one, the protection and conservation of the national identity, and two, the protection of gained resources, jobs or incomes or access to social funds.

It is these two articulations as the outcome of the existential fear of the nothing that are high on the current political agenda in the various member states. In the last ten years or so, politicians and media have often played out the card of appealing to the existential fear of mankind mentioned above, that is the fear of being overwhelmed by nothingness. Typical terms that have been used in these parliamentary and media debates are flows, hordes, masses, streams, or even 'tsunami', implying anything from 'tens/hundreds of thousands' to 'millions' of people. Fear of immigrants across the European Union however is generally not grounded in a thorough awareness of migration developments throughout the world; there is no real acknowledgement that despite the often used rhetoric, the EU is only 'receiving' a tiny fraction of the total population of refugees or people on the move. As subsequent Eurobarometer reports have demonstrated, advocates as well as opponents to the 2004 eastward enlargement shared the opinion that the EU-accession of Poland and other countries would negatively affect their home country employment situation.[2] Highly topical in this respect is the potential EU-membership of Turkey which is instigating a great deal of populist geopolitical talk about what 'Europeanness' is, and whether Turkey and the Turks are 'European' (enough) to enter (Kramsch et al. 2004). In this way, perceptual difference is reproduced and sustained between 'us Europeans' and 'them, non-Europeans' (van Houtum 2003).

Apparently, in the present make-up of the European Union, a pressing desire exists for confronting the normal with the deviant and the self with the Other, a desire that is so strong that it might even run against the potential economic benefit that could be gained from a free flow of labour with the economy of the Other. The Other is feared and 'utilised' to compare with, associate with, or to oppose and to protect oneself against (see also Derrida 1973; Luhmann 1985).

---

2   Eurobarometer public opinion surveys are conducted each spring and autumn by the European Commission, consisting of identical sets of questions submitted to representative samples of the population aged 15 years and over in each member state. The November 2002 edition shows that no less than 31 per cent of respondents who are 'for' enlargement expect unemployment numbers to worsen after EU-accession. Sixty-one per cent of respondents 'against' enlargement share this view.

For it is only in the awareness of imaginative Others that social identity can be reproduced to be a relevant and contingent source of meaning and experience (Jenkins 1996). This dominant and negative conception of social identity resonates with Bauman's argument that 'each order has its disorder and each purity its own dirties' and Sibley's well-known notion of 'purification of space' (Bauman 1997; Sibley 1995). By definition therefore, a border deconstructs a difference (the outside in and/or the inside out) but creates a difference (a new outside) at the same time. The function of (b)ordering is precisely that: the making of a divisive order in an assumed chaos, an illuminated, enlightened island in a world of darkness. The fear that is being produced, then, is a fear of chaos and dark imag(in)ed by slumps, conflict zones and environmental devastation. As it defines a border between normality and deviance, such defining, making and exclusion of the Other is, as Sibley calls it, a 'colonisation' of social life (Sibley 1995). What is beyond the border is justified to be neglected and to be indifferent about (van Houtum and van Naerssen 2002). In that sense, (b)ordering and (b)othering go hand in hand.

A spatial imaginative bordering process accordingly rests upon the redefinition of friends as natives (Bauman 1990), among whom common assets of knowledge and wealth are constructed and distributed (Giddens 1984). To strangers, residential rights are granted only if such an extension of rights is desirable (though desirability is often disguised as 'feasibility') (Bauman 1990). The identity of strangers is therefore usually not a choice of themselves (see also Bradley 1997) they are excluded on the basis of their other or absent nationality (country of birth, colour, creed or culture: see Urry 2000) and must adjust to the new one if they wish to be included. Each society then, as Bauman famously argued, 'produces its own kind of strangers' (Bauman 1997,17). Depending on the circumstances in individual member states, currently in the European Union, this desire has found new socio-political outlets and performances, thereby often creating a new, normative vocabulary.

In the present case, it could be argued that the pressing and even disciplining discourse on the need to 'communify', expressed in terms like 'common market', 'internal market', 'a borderless Europe' and 'the need for European citizenship', has invoked a certain state of an 'abnormality', portrayed by people living outside the EU and non-EU refugees seeking shelter inside the Union, only increased after the events of 11 September. The consequence is an increased anxiety and fear of the Other, or in the words of Sibley, a moral panic, which in his view concerns 'contested spaces, liminal zones which hostile communities intend on eliminating by appropriating such spaces for themselves and excluding the offending other' (Sibley 1995, 39). Attempting to make such a categorical difference between EU and non-EU citizens, yet also wishing to stay politically correct, there has been a constant search to appropriately define and term the non-insiders, the people from outside. Many terms are used, such as strangers, aliens, foreigners, newcomers, fortune seekers and in the Dutch context 'allochtonen',[3] to name but a few.

---

3   'Allochtonen' is old Greek for people born 'elsewhere', literally 'out of other soil'.

Common in this name-giving development is that migrants from outside the EU who previously were a subject of social protection, now themselves have become subjected to protectionist measures in the name of security (Huysmans 2000).

At the same time, it is important to realise that politicians at the national and EU levels must not be imagined as mainly reacting to fears of the Other in constructing border and immigration policies. On the contrary, some also rekindle fear. Fear, for some at least, is the means to an end, in this case security. In the words of Falah and Newman:

> Leaders are successful in uniting the people around security matters more than any other issue – essentially because the appeal to national security is related directly to the issue of protection against a dangerous enemy and involves the physical survival of ones family, friends and nation. The national threat is translated to reality at the micrological level. (Falah and Newman 1995, 694)

Consequently, the inhabitants of the 'chaos' surrounding the insulating Union are the politically invoked new barbarians from a world outside who are undesired and hence denied access. As a result, the securitisation and militarisation of the external border has been drastically sharpened in recent years, even to the point where attempts to remain unseen or escape from the hunt and chase by border guards leads to the death of would-be immigrants. The defensive policy of the European Union is apparently willing to go as far as making the external border literally a 'deadline' by criminalising the lives of those who are trying to find work or shelter in the European Union. Hideously, their deaths are implicitly seen as the 'collateral damage' of a combat against illegal migration. Estimates of 'death at the border' differ, but many would agree that it is now between five or six thousand (Sassen 2002).[4] There may not be consensus over who is to blame for these deaths, but the fact remains that these people died awaiting entrance of the European Union: they died in the 'waiting room'. This draws attention to the idea that the immigration policy of the European Union presently is in the embrace of fear. This fear is largely instigated from below and strongly resonates at the European level: in the individual member states there exists a strong political will to retain national sovereignty over immigration and asylum issues. So, despite the large number of policy proposals that has been released in recent years, the European Union certainly is not in control in this policy field, a position which turned for the worse since the recent stagnation of the European Constitution's ratification process. Meanwhile, those who manage to survive the game of Russian roulette at the border enter a dense web of national and supranational immigration policies which very much lacks clarity and consistency. It is no wonder, then, that the European Union resembles a fortress to many. Neither is it surprising that many others regard the EU as a maze or sieve, identifying practices of venue shopping across the internal borders and failing fortification efforts along the external borders due to lack of funds, equipment and competence. In either

---

4   Hence, the fear is as sizeable among those who wish to enter the EU illegally, for it can mean their death.

case, unwelcoming and even 'hostile visualisations' of closure abound (Kramsch et al. 2004, 23).[5]

Borders as Spatial Manifestations of Success

However, we would argue that the idea of Fortress Europe, besides its all too dramatic ring and its geographic incorrectness (referring to the borders of the European Union), is also increasingly untenable. The foregoing measures against unsolicited redundancy and the images of people dying at the gates of the EU, both of which fit the idea of a fortress, sharply contrast with acquisition policies with regard to economically desirable, scarce forms of labour. The often populist fears and measures against unsolicited redundancy and people being stopped at the borders of the EU are increasingly being countered by various (business) pressures to open up the border partially, temporarily, phased or fully. A crucial issue here is the *selective* allowance of labour immigration into the European Union. Many (western) European nations are increasingly coping with shortages of specific (academic) knowledge or skills or an ageing active work force. Persistent shortages of knowledge and skills cause economic demand for foreign experts in possession of such knowledge to be made explicit in numbers of visa, work and residence permits granted to migrant workers from outside the Union. By all means taking on the form of an intra-EU competition for knowledge, there now are Green Cards (Germany), accelerated work permit procedures (Great Britain), quota systems (Italy), and even a speed-office (The Netherlands) enabling foreign employees to bypass immigration bureaucracy. Top managers, engineers, PhD-students and talented soccer players from global south countries all can be strategically and arbitrarily selected by non-state actors such as large firms, universities and specialised employment agencies. In the case of new EU member states, nurses and seasonal workers in agriculture or construction are occasionally granted access as well under the auspices of bilateral agreements. What is happening here is a race for the fittest migrants. In contrast with the 'anti-redundancy' and 'anti-burden' politics applying to the many, a few are seen as valuable 'assets', who are most welcome on the European Internal Market in order to gain or sustain competitive advantage.

Hence, increasingly, the borders of the EU represent a bifurcated spatial manifestation of a desire for purity and success and a fear of the reverse. This bifurcation could, according to Bauman, be taken as a metaphor for a newly emerging stratification:

---

5   Another horrific illustration of how images of wealth are radiated is the story of an illegal immigrant from North-Africa, who died on the shores of Italy when trying to enter EU-space. Upon being asked his motives for migrating by a television crew, this man's family answered that he was so intrigued by the glamorous Italian entertainment shows he watched on TV he went to get his share of 'glamour'.

... it is now the 'access to global mobility' which has been raised to the topmost rank among the stratifying factors. It also reveals the global dimension of all privilege and deprivation, however local. Some of us enjoy the new freedom of movement sans papiers. Some others are not allowed to stay put for the same reason. (Bauman 1998, 88)

A recent report (Green Paper, 12 January 2005) produced by the European Commission is indeed hinting, although still circumspectly, in the direction of a system of fast-track migration and US-style Green Cards for the European Union as a whole (the so-called Blue Card system). In defence of such a system, Franco Frattini, the new EU Justice and Security Commissioner argued in an interview with the Financial Times, that 'for the first time Europe is facing not a threat but a possible opportunity to manage in a coherent manner the important phenomenon that is economic migration. We need a new strategy.' So, those who fall in the category 'high competence to assimilate' or 'high potential for an added value to a country' will be subject of economic need, instead of fear. Moreover, the European Commission has expressed a trust in what is called *replacement immigration* (immigrant labour replacing ageing domestic labour forces) in the nearby future in its strategy paper 'On a Community Immigration Policy' (European Commission 2000). In 2003, the Commission explicitly spoke of an economic and demographic 'challenge' alongside the challenge of immigrant and minority integration in the Union (European Commission 2003). In the 2005 Green Paper 'On an EU approach to managing economic migration', the Commission proposes the use of an 'economic needs test' by the member states and hints to extending official entry procedures to 'not necessarily only highly qualified' immigrants (European Commission 2005, 5). Negotiated and still imprecise, it is unclear how strategic the proposals towards 'communification' raised in these strategy papers really are; testing the needs of the moment, and introducing seasonal quota in some sectors only, reflects the whimsicality by which (groups of) immigrants are granted and/or denied access by the member states' national migration policies at present.

In such selectively protective surroundings as the European Internal Market, the protection wall that is the economic border becomes a source of creativity and innovation: it is a stimulus for rent seekers to find or cross the edges of law in order to let low-rated workers in, yet it also serves as decisive location factor for the highly skilled and mobile. Favell and Hansen provocatively argue that market-driven selectivity is here to stay. Non-state actors irrevocably become a major determinant of migration flows in the European Union and on its internal market. In their view, 'normative' Fortress Europe is quite open in 'positivist' reality for economic migrants through legal and illegal rent-seeking activities (Favell and Hansen 2002). States can only marginally protect themselves against transboundary, networked practices of human trafficking and unlawful subcontracting as they are, by definition, bounded by national jurisdiction (see also Jordan and Düvell 2003). Slavoj Žižek in this respect foresees a *de-politicisation* of European politics, wherein a consensus about the need to strive for economic success, efficiency and efficacy that goes beyond ideological differences reduces the role of European migration policy to a mere administrative one, defining and installing procedures and networks of passage (Žižek 2002; see also van Houtum and van Naerssen 2002).

The EU as a Gated Community: Protecting 'Easy Living' in the EU

So, what is left of the Fortress Europe rhetoric when selective access of economically desirable immigrants is considered? To understand and better grasp why the border is closed for an overwhelming majority yet open for some, we have to ask ourselves what exactly we are trying to protect in the European Union. We would say that these paradoxical border policies are means to the same end, that is to protect the own internal comfort zone, the space of *Heimlichkeit* (the feeling of being at ease, at home) (see also Houtum 2003). Protection principally concerns *comfort*, which is an interpretation and extension of the concept of *easiness*.[6] Thus, the interpretation of the national border is the degree of distance creation, of protection of the national entity, of 'our national interest'. The latter interest is an issue of appropriating and justifying comfort. The chances for strangers to be allowed to play a role in the national arena are higher when estimated national wealth and employment effects of them entering are net-positive and/or when s/he is perceived as easy and safely to be assimilated in the national society, hence when the Other is not overwhelming or replacing us. The protection of the national interest and identity (to be amongst 'one's own'), and of amounts of money and/or (the growth of) gained wealth is hence a form of collective self-interest of the community of human beings who call each other 'member' of the club that is the European Union (Ugur 1995; Hiebert 2003). Club membership offers a lifestyle of easiness, securing the members' comfortable position on the Internal Market because job competitors are denied access and otherwise redundant outsiders are channelled through or turned a blind eye to in order to do low-rated yet desperately needed work.

Hence, we would argue, that much more than a fortress, the European Union is beginning to look like a *Gated Community* through its protectionist and selective immigration policies (see also Walters 2004). A gated community, a defended neighbourhood, is a form of real estate development increasingly found in countries with large internal income differences such as Mexico and Brazil but also in the United States and the United Kingdom (see also Blakely and Snyder 1997). Historically, secured and gated communities were built in the United States to protect family estates and to contain the leisure world of retirees (Low 2001). The gated community phenomenon then spread to resorts and country clubs, and finally to middle-class suburban developments (Low 2001). Now the common purpose of gated communities is the creation of a space in which the nation's affluent wall and gate themselves off from the rest of society in an enclave, primarily driven by fear of crime and the need to be amongst 'ourselves', hence protecting welfare and security. Gated communities hence physically restrain

---

6   'Comfortare' in Latin means 'to strengthen', 'to ease'.

access to their gated territory, and therefore offer an assumed greater level of control over a territory and over those who enter it. The newly created spaces are often 'militarised' through the use of cameras, guards, surveillance systems, and other security devices. According to Davis, the panopticon-like screening fits in the larger societal trend of social control and militarisation of public spaces (Davis 1992). In an excellent recent empirical overview, Blandy et al. (2003) adopted the following definition of gated communities:

> Walled or fenced housing developments to which public access is restricted, often guarded using CCTV[7] and/or security personnel, and usually characterised by legal agreements (tenancy or leasehold) which tie the residents to a common code of conduct (Blandy et al. 2003, 2).

Hence, gated communities express a clear-cut form of socio-spatial insolidarity, of the purification of space, by shutting the gates for the 'outside' world under the flag of privacy, control, comfort and security. A gated community is made to produce and reproduce segregation and to pronounce and maintain social homogeneity and wealth inequality. Non-members, usually the non-white (Davis [1990] even defines the gates of the community as a 'White Wall') and non-rich, are excluded from these spatially bordered contractual associations. Membership is paid for and non-members are labelled guests. It does not come as a surprise then, that the identity of its members is marketed as a life-style, as a status that you buy. In a way, the gated community represents a commercialisation of fear of the outside darkness. The gates of the gated community are not only a result of the desire to produce a space for the outsider, the stranger, but even more so a purified, enlightened space for the insider.

One of the world's most widely boasted gated communities is Palm Island. This artificially constructed island (designed in the shape of a palm tree) is located just offshore of the city of Dubai, providing a haven of luxury to those able to afford its exclusive villas and apartments (Palm Island's website speaks of 'a unique island experience', www.palmsales.ca, accessed March 7, 2005). Strawberry fields-like gated unities like Palm Island are remarkably similar to the European Union's Internal Market ideology in terms of its accommodation of wealth and its resistant, antagonistic and hostile practices to the mobile Other, especially the deprived, such as fugitives, gypsies, migrants, vagrants, and travellers (Urry 2000).

Much like a gated community, the European Union promises 'easy living', portraying shiny, happy (white) people who comfortably relax on beaches and bikes (see the cover pages of two information booklets in Plates 12.1 and 12.2). Private parties play an important and increasing role in deciding who enters; politics defines preconditions and facilitates. Like a gated community, the European Union is constructed to control, monitor and manage its external borders and thereby safeguard those who are in from those who are out. The EU too has retreated itself behind heavily guarded gates. The politically invoked

---

7   'CCTV' stands for 'closed circuit television'.

Plate 12.1   Representing Strawberry Fields: Palm Island

Source: information leaflet for Palm Island (www.palmsales.ca, 2005).

Europe on the move

It's a better life

How the EU's single market benefits you

European Commission

Plate 12.2   Representing Strawberry Fields: the single market

Source: *The Internal Market* (European Commission, 2002).

hysteria about assumed hordes of migrants overwhelming our soils by opinion leaders in various western European countries, as well as the shock of the events of 11 September, has certainly added to the militarisation of these gates. And much like a gated community, new members of the European club are sought after if they are attractive enough to the internal market, others are stopped at the gates. Another group of people, unidentified and largely invisible yet of considerable size, slips through the maze, sometimes with the help of human traffickers, sometimes with the help of legal rent-seekers: they are the ones who clean, cater and pick strawberries, sustaining the easy living of its inhabitants.

Notwithstanding a recognition that selective admission and exclusion are at the core of communal independence, normative stands on territorial (b)ordering and (b)othering abound. Walzer (1983), for instance, provocatively states that the rule of citizens over non-citizens and members over strangers is 'an act of tyranny'. Seyla Benhabib, following Derrida's essay on hospitality in her plea for 'interactive universalism', is with him on this point (Benhabib 1996; see also Derrida 1998). For, she asks, what is the ethical difference between the right to leave a democratic country, since in democratic societies citizens are not prisoners, and the right for others to enter? Jordan and Düvell (2003) propose a 'cosmopolitan economic membership': new forms of 'global economic nomadism' demand a redefinition of citizenship beyond national borders, involving communal duties for those who have access and rights for those who remain outside. Similarly, liberal philosopher Will Kymlicka (2001) argues that borders are 'a source of embarrassment for liberals of all stripes, at least if these boundaries prevent individuals from moving freely, and living, working and voting in whatever part of the globe they see fit' (2001, 249; see also Carens 1987 and Veit Bader 1997). 'Any political theory', he continues, 'which has nothing to say about these questions is seriously flawed. Moreover, the result, intentional or unintentional, is to tacitly support the conservative view that existing boundaries and restrictive membership are sacrosanct' (2001, 253).

We would argue that a key precondition for the development of any such (geo)political theory is a profound understanding of why and how borders as mechanisms of protection are inextricably linked to strategically rekindled and mediated fears, and conversely, why these fears cannot be reduced by the (selective) drawing of borders. On the contrary: protection makes fears even stronger, as is convincingly demonstrated for the case of gated communities by the Blandy review and similar work by Wilson-Doenges. Residents of high-income gated communities are not safer in reality, for actual crime rates do not differ. Moreover, fear of 'outsiders' is higher and, strikingly, 'sense of community' in terms of social engagement is significantly lower in gated communities (Wilson-Doenges 2000; Blandy et al. 2003, 3). Apparently so, the more borders are closed, the more unknown or untruthful subjects beyond or inside one's (knowledge) domain are undesired and subject to suspicion. Hence, with a gated community false perceptions of security are gained (bought) but social bonds are lost. Because of the constitutive and increasing fear of these Others, the twisting and turning of the window of reality that is easy life protection is a vicious circle which is perpetual and unbounded, yet not priceless. The price is paid by the excluded

Other, and by the self-confined, protected but really un-free insiders. Protection, hence, is inefficient and ineffective, a conclusion very much in accordance with the one drawn by neoclassical economic trade theory when the quantitative notion of 'welfare' is extended into a quality-inclusive 'well-being'.

Conclusion: Strawberry Fields Forever?

Looking at the present European geopolitical landscape, it can be ascertained that notwithstanding the post-modern calls for and local celebrations of heterotopia, the making and marking of borders and thereby processes of social exclusion have not dissolved. The European Union is writing a new landscape of walls. A wall of conservative solidification is being erected that is fierce and terrifying in its sometimes deathly consequence, yet also contains neoliberal mazes and conscious blindness for specific (illegal) labour forces that help to sustain our easiness and comfort. This neoconservative (b)ordering practice increasingly fits the description of a gated community, reinforcing a conservative protectionist logic to the disadvantage of local and individual attempts to transgress the gated containment. Whilst the EU certainly should not be seen as hermetically sealed, as it indeed allows for selective entry, the notion of gated communities speaks to what this bordering practice also does to those inside and their ever present generalised anxiety and desire for comfort protection. It is a kind of security-obsessed strawberry fields-politics inside and cherry-picking outside the European Union, which we think is highly questionable from both global economic welfare and a normative point of view, as it sustains and reproduces global inequality and segregation materially as well as symbolically. The gated community of the European Union is a kind of neverneverland, as the dream of purity and easiness is never-ending. The (national) self is never ready, never complete, never one, hence the desire to be one is perpetual. Maybe the lesson is that we have to live with 'le manque' (the lack) (Lacan 2004) of not being a completed and full (national) Self. From that lack the Other can be engaged with trust, for s/he is not a category and s/he is also facing a lack of not being fulfilled, not being one. In doing so, and returning to the Beatles melody of strawberry fields, maybe, we could find a way to live and dream with our eyes open.

Bibliography

Bader, V.M. (1997), 'Fairly Open Borders', in V.M. Bader (ed.), *Citizenship and Exclusion* (Houndsmills: Macmillan), 28–62.

Bauman, Z. (1990), 'Modernity and Ambivalence', in M. Featherstone (ed.), *Global Culture: Nationalism, globalization and modernity, A Theory, Culture and Society Special Issue* (London: SAGE Publications).

Bauman, Z. (1997), *Postmodernity and its Discontents* (Cambridge: Polity Press).

Bauman, Z. (1998), *Globalisation. The Human Consequences* (Oxford: Polity Press).

Benhabib, S. (1996), 'Toward a Deliberative Model of Democratic Legitimacy', in S. Benhabib (ed.), *Democracy and Difference: Contesting the Boundaries of the Political* (Princeton, NJ: Princeton University Press).

Blakely, E. and Snyder, M. (1997), *Fortress America* (Washington, DC: Brookings Institute).

Blandy, S., Lister, D., Atkinson, R. and Flint, J. (2003), *Gated Communities: A systematic review of the research evidence*, Summary, ESRC Centre for Neighbourhood Research.

Bradley, H. (1997), *Fractured Identities: Changing patterns of inequality* (Cambridge: Polity Press).

Carens, J.H. (1987), 'Aliens and Citizens: The case for open borders', *Review of Politics* 49, 251–73.

Davis, M. (1990), *City of Quartz: Excavating the future of Los Angeles* (New York: Verso).

Davis, M. (1992), 'Fortress Los Angeles: The militarization of urban space', in M. Sorkin (ed.), *Variations on a Theme Park* (New York: Noonday Press).

Derrida, J. (1973), *Différance, Speech and Phenomena and other Essays on Husserl's Theory of Signs*, trans. David B. Allison (Evanston, IL: Northwestern University Press).

Derrida, J. (1998), "Hospitality, Justice and Responsibility: A dialogue with Jacques Derrida", in R. Kearney and M. Dooley (eds), *Questioning Ethics: Contemporary debates in philosophy* (London: Routledge).

Engelen, E. (2003), 'How to Combine Openness and Protection? Citizenship Rights, Migration, and Welfare Regimes', *Politics and Society* 31:4, 503–36.

Engbersen, G. (2003), 'Vlijt zonder Inhoud', *De Volkskrant.*

European Commission (2000), *On a Community Immigration Policy* (Brussels: CEC).

European Commission (2003), *On Immigration, Integration and Employment* (Brussels: CEC).

European Commission (2005), *Green Paper on an EU Approach to Managing Economic Migration* (Brussels: CEC).

Falah, G. and Newman, D. (1995), 'The Spatial Manifestation of Threat – Israelis and Palestinians Seek a Good Border', *Political Geography* 14:8, 689–706.

Favell, A. and Hansen, R. (2002), 'Markets against Politics: Migration, EU enlargement and the idea of Europe', *Journal of Ethnic and Migration Studies* 28:4, 581–601.

Giddens, A. (1984), *The Constitution of Society: Outline of the theory of structuration* (Cambridge: Polity Press).

Heidegger, M., (1970), *Wat is metafysica?* (Tielt-Utrecht: Lannoo).

Hiebert, D. (2003), 'A Borderless World: Dream or Nightmare?', *ACME* 2:2, 188–93.

Huysmans, J. (2000), 'The European Union and the Securitization of Migration', *Journal of Common Market Studies* 38:5, 751–77.

Jenkins, R. (1996), *Social Identity* (London: Routledge).

Jordan, B. and Düvell, F. (2003), *Migration: The boundaries of equality and justice* (Cambridge: Polity Press).

Kramsch, O., Pijpers, R., Plug, R. and van Houtum, H. (2004), *Research on the Policy of the European Commission towards the Re-bordering of the European Union* (Radboud University Nijmegen: Department of Human Geography and Spatial Planning).

Krugman, P. and Obstfeld, M. (1997), *International Economics: Theory and policy* (New York: Addison Wesley).

Kymlicka, W. (2001), *Politics in the Vernacular: Nationalism, multiculturalism and citizenship* (Oxford: Oxford University Press).

Lacan, J., (2004), *L' angoisse (Le seminaire, livre X)* (Paris: Seuil).

Low, S., (2001), 'The Edge and the Center: Gated communities and the discourse of urban fear', *American Anthropologist* 103:1, 45–58.

Luhmann, N. (1985), *Soziale Systeme, Grundriss einer Algemeiner Theorie*, 2 (Frankfurt am Main: Auflage Frankfurt am Main).

Sassen, S. (1988), *The Mobility of Labor and Capital: A study in international investment and labor flow* (Cambridge: Cambridge University Press).

Sassen, S. (2002), 'Is this the Way to Go? Handling Immigration in a Global Era', *Eurozine*.

Sibley, D. (1995), *Geographies of Exclusion: Society and Difference in the West* (London: Routledge).

Ter Beek, H., Mevissen, J., Mur, J. and Pool, C. (2005), *Poolshoogte: Onderzoek naar Juridische Constructies en Kostenvoordelen bij het Inzetten van Poolse Arbeidskrachten in Drie Sectoren* (Den Haag: Raad voor Werk en Inkomen).

Ugur, M. (1995), 'Freedom of Movement vs. Exclusion: a reinterpretation of the "insider"–"outsider" divide in the European Union', *International Migration Review* 29:4, 964–99.

Urry, J. (2000), *The Global Media and Cosmopolitanism* (Lancaster University: Department of Sociology).

Van Houtum, H. (2003), 'Borders of Comfort: Ambivalences in spatial economic bordering processes in and by the European Union', *Regional and Federal Studies* 12, 37–58.

Van Houtum, H. and van Naerssen, T. (2002), 'Bordering, Ordering and Othering', *Tijdschrift voor Economische en Sociale Geografie* 93:2, 125–36.

Walters, W. (2004), 'The Frontiers of the European Union: A geostrategic perspective', *Geopolitics* 9:3, 674–98.

Walzer, M. (1983), *Spheres of Justice* (New York: Basic Books).

Wilson-Doenges, G. (2000), 'An Exploration of Sense of Community and Fear of Crime in Gated Communities', *Environment and Behavior* 32:5, 597–611.

Chapter 13

Identity Cards and Coercion in Palestine

Nadia Abu Zhara

What is the best piece of advice you have received?
From my mother: don't talk too much, don't work so hard. But I have never managed either!

What items do you always carry with you?
A USB mass-storage device, which has scans of my family's official papers. I used to sleep with it next to me in bed during the invasions and bombings of 2002 in fear of displacement.

Associate Professor Rita Giacaman, interviewed in the *Lancet*, 2004 (364: 2089).

'Official papers' or identity documents (IDs) are widely accepted as vital anywhere. But a series of circumstances in Palestine make it an extreme case, a place where identity documents are so important, that their confiscation represents one of the most powerful threats possible. This chapter will present some theoretical interpretations of identity documents to date, as well as empirical material from observations and testimonies, and focus on one aspect that emerges from these: the power of IDs to coerce. It argues that in this setting, IDs are entangled with a politics of fear, in which political and everyday concerns are tied together.

The literature on identity documentation has emphasised its dual nature, whereby IDs can lead to deprivation or entitlement. Aiwa Ong drew attention to the entitlements granted through identity documentation in her concept of 'flexible citizenship' whereby individuals could access multiple markets and thus accumulate capital gains. Her work on IDs as entitlements has been cited by researchers looking at other situations, such as Matt Sparke's study of the NAFTA region, and Julie Chu's study of a Chinese village. Sparke (2006, 30) describes the travel documents that enable 'the kinetic elites of the NEXUS [expedited Canada-US border-crossing] lane ... to buy for themselves at least a little of the borderless world fantasy-life'. Chu's article, *Card Me When I'm Dead* (2007), is about the use of US Green Cards to avoid state-mandated cremation in China. While the two articles are strikingly different, they both emphasise the duality of identity documentation, which can be used for deprivation or entitlement. Sparke contrasts jet-setting 'Gulfstream citizenship'[1] with the US transport of

---

1 An extension of Don Mitchell's (2005) phrase of 'SUV citizenship'.

chained and beaten captives[2] in Gulfstream jets. Chu contrasts state deprivation of villagers' freedom to choose their own form of funeral rites, against the regaining of this entitlement through a US Green Card. In both situations, identity documentation simultaneously represents deprivation and entitlement.

To reconcile this seeming contradiction, the entitlements of IDs need to be considered from a historical perspective. Focusing on the passport, John Torpey writes:

> Only under conditions of pure freedom to come and go, irrespective of who or what a person is, would a passport constitute nothing but a restriction. Once the genie of the state's authority to identify persons and authorize their movements is out of the bottle, it is hard to get him back in. (Torpey, 2000, 35)

From this perspective, even entitlements are representative of wider restrictions. Once the system is in place, people require identity documentation and therefore seek it. Prior to this, however, IDs are an imposition on human freedom. This explains the dichotomy of IDs in the present. Although 'Gulfstream citizens' are beneficiaries, Sparke's and Chu's analyses show how they remain subjects, and how their participation in the system perpetuates its hierarchical and unequal nature. Control of one's own movement or burial – or any other aspect of life – can be removed as an automatic right, and then granted at the discretion of a state (or states). IDs are enforced through government benefits, financial institutions, employment or accommodation agreements, renting cars or equipment, and 'myriad small ways, such as entry to official buildings' (Davies 1996). In a process described as 'function creep', identity cards 'develop a broader usage over time, than was originally envisioned for them' (Davies 1996). As one opponent to IDs in the UK stated simply, 'once the wretched things are in circulation it becomes impossible to live daily life without one' (Angus Gulliver, quoted in BBC 2004).

The example of Palestine illustrates the ways in which entitlements can be amalgamated into a single document – the identity card – and then withheld arbitrarily to enable coercion. The process of this amalgamation, and its combination with 'stop and search' practices, unfolded gradually. In 1967, Israel introduced identity cards for Palestinians in the West Bank and Gaza Strip, following the Occupation of these zones by the Israeli military. From 1948 until the Occupation of 1967, these Palestinians were living under foreign rule: the West Bank controlled by Jordan and the Gaza Strip by Egypt. Most of those in the West Bank held Jordanian passports (though these were downgraded to the status of travel documents in 1988), but the Gazans remained without passports, possessing only travel documents and identity cards. From 1967 and especially from 1988, the Israeli system of identification and monitoring prevailed. Ironically, when the Palestinian Authority began issuing identity cards and travel documents in 1994, they used the same personal identification numbers allocated by Israel, thereby reinforcing the Israeli formula.

---

2   Like Canadian Maher Arar.

Through a series of Israeli military orders 'legislating' everything from taxation to land management, the *hawiyyeh*, or identity card, became Palestinians' single most important document. The ID is required to 'register' one's personal affairs with the state: to establish or effect residency, health, marriage, educational achievements, tax payments, construction, commercial transactions, employment, and countless other details. The ID acts not only as an external passport but crucially as an internal travel permit limiting and circumscribing movement.

Legitimised with reference to population registration, the creation of ID cards is a strict monopoly, and replacement of cards is difficult. If an ID were to be produced without Israeli legitimation, 'the minute an Israeli soldier at a checkpoint or border crossing checked such a card, he would discover that its holder does not appear in Israel's computers, and treat the card as invalid' (Hass 2005).

This chapter explores the way this 'politics of ID' works, drawing attention in particular to its entanglement with a politics of fear. IDs are part of the materiality of coercion and control, but equally, fear of being stripped of an ID opens those who are already tagged and targeted to other kinds of coercion. The data resources used to illustrate this argument are drawn from participant observation in intervals over a seven-year period, and from in-depth interviews during the latter intervals. Interview excerpts are also drawn from testimonies documented and published by human rights groups.

(Im)mobility

The significance of ID cards becomes evident in the context of mobility restrictions. The Israeli army has prescribed particular geographical zones for Palestinians, from which they require permission to leave. For instance, males living in Nablus aged 16–36 are forbidden from leaving Nablus – they must spend these 20 years in their town, on pain of detention; similar restrictions apply to Gaza and other Palestinian urban areas. Detention in Palestine is the punishment for those who move beyond these confines; but any person who assists them is equally vulnerable. A driver in Jerusalem with a passenger holding a West Bank ID, for instance, would be sentenced to one to six months in prison, confiscation of the automobile, and a fine of close to US$2,000 (Jum'a, interview) (this is despite the fact that East Jerusalem is part of the West Bank). This is a punitive amount in a context where the unemployment rate sometimes reaches over 50 per cent and poverty has skyrocketed due to movement restrictions, land confiscations, suspension of international aid, house demolitions, and other aspects of military occupation.[3]

Employers are also detained for the movements of their employees. A typical case of such a detention was in June of 2004, where an elderly baker was tortured

---

3   In 2005, Israel's gross national income (GNI) per capita was US$18,620, compared to US$1,120 in the West Bank and Gaza (World Bank 2005, 2–4). The following year, 2006, GNI in the West Bank and Gaza fell by 30 per cenet due to continued mobility restrictions (on people and goods) and Israel withholding Palestinian taxes (World Bank 2006, 10).

Plate 13.1   Identity information on a soldier's laptop

Source: Machsom Watch 2006.

(spending three days in the 'seat', a small, slanted chair to which the person being tortured is tied), sentenced to six months in prison, and placed in solitary confinement (Safa, interview). His crime was to employ a man from the 'West Bank' in his 'Jerusalem' bakery (Israel illegally occupies East Jerusalem and declares it as separate from the remaining West Bank, contrary to international legal rulings and United Nations resolutions).

Palestinians must carry their ID at all times, and an Israeli soldier may check the ID of any Palestinian, anywhere, at any time. Testimonies from soldiers in al-Khalil describe this in more detail:

> Someone comes and throws a remark which he shouldn't, like, 'What do you want from me?' which is legitimate in his opinion, and even in my opinion, that person lives there, you know ... It's a street where they're allowed to pass, and a soldier comes and stops him and checks him and searches him and his kids are there and his family is there, and it's humiliating for him, and there's a stage when you just don't care anymore, old man, not old man, you check them all .... (Quoted in Shaul 2004)

While the system is often described as 'arbitrary', this soldier's testimony expresses how comprehensive it becomes. Disrespect for all people, including the elderly, disabled, and very young, effects a kind of 'saturation', instilling the importance of always carrying an ID.[4]

Plate 13.2   ID and checkpoints

Source: photograph taken by Neta Efroni, 16 March 2006.

---

4   Thanks to Susan J. Smith for this point.

The penalty for not carrying an ID is a year's imprisonment; soldiers administer additional punishment at their discretion.

> If you are caught they might beat you up (if you don't have the right papers), maybe imprison you. Maybe they arrest you for two hours and then they would release you. There was a young man, a friend from Masha, they broke his hand.
>
> Many people were caught that would sell vegetables in Kufr Qassem. They were forced to eat hot chilli, maybe half a kilo, or a full kilo of hot chillies. Forced to eat onion, no bread nothing, just plain onion. One, two, three – it didn't matter. They would even feed potatoes to the people. They (Israelis) would take off all their clothes and tell them to leave. (Shalabi, interview)

The irony of this experience is that the people of Masha are refugees from Kufr Qassem, and the two areas are effectively one village, split into two. Palestinians – through IDs – are made 'illegal' on the very land they own.

Plate 13.3 Dispossessed

Source: photograph taken by Neta Efroni, 6 August 2006.

Coercion

While movement restrictions and dispossession are sufficient cause to rule the ID system illegal (as was done by the International Court of Justice in 2004; see ICJ 2004, 136), an additional concern is the issue of coercion. Because identity cards must be carried at all times and must be presented on request to any soldier, they are used 'to control the population by, *inter alia*, coercing people to carry out orders on threat of confiscation of the card, controlling the population growth of the West Bank and Gaza Strip, restricting the movement of Palestinians into, out of, and within the Occupied Territories, and harassing persons for unsubstantiated reasons of security' (Al-Haq 1989, 323–4).

Initially, it was primarily men who were prone to have their ID cards confiscated. However, 'in the vast majority of families, since it is the men who are the breadwinners, the confiscation of their identity cards poses a potential threat to the whole family' (Al-Haq 1989, 336). Confiscation can be threatened to force a family member of a person alleged to have committed an 'offence' (against a military order) to surrender to the authorities, or make outstanding tax or health insurance payments, for example, on the person's behalf (ibid.). From 1987 onward, Palestinians boycotted paying taxes as a method of disengagement from the military government; ID confiscation was the threat used to force individuals and their family members to comply with military occupation (ibid.).

Confiscation is also used to force Palestinians to police other Palestinians; examples are almost bizarre: four elderly residents of the Gaza Strip were compelled to cut down fruit trees allegedly used as cover for stone-throwers; a 19-year old in Tulkarem was asked to guard a main street from stone throwers from 7:00 p.m. until 1:00 a.m .... he refused and lost his ID; soldiers frequently forced Palestinians to remove barricades or flags, extinguish burning tyres, or paint over nationalist graffiti; one person, ordered to remove tin-cans hanging from high-tension electricity wires, died as a result of electrocution (ibid.).

Often, confiscation is merely for harassment.

Bishara 'Issa Elias Kheir, 24, a resident of Beit Sahour in the Bethlehem district, was stopped at a military checkpoint. His identity card was confiscated by a soldier who told him that he was wanted by the authorities. Another military jeep arrived. An officer stepped out, checked the identity card, and told the soldier that Mr. Kheir was not wanted. The first soldier then tore up Mr. Kheir's identity card, saying to the officer that this would cause problems for Mr. Kheir. Mr. Kheir was subsequently blindfolded, handcuffed, and beaten; he was then transferred to the military government compound in Bethlehem, where he was detained for five days. (Al-Haq 1989, 327)

Wissam Tayem (recorded on video in Plate 13.4) was asked by an Israeli officer at a checkpoint in Nablus to 'play something sad', while soldiers laughed at him (McGreal 2004).

This conjured more attention among Israelis than other recorded incidents in the same time period, such as 'the recording of an Israeli officer pumping the body of a 13-year-old girl (Iman al-Hams) full of bullets and then saying he would have shot her even if she had been three years old', and 'pictures in an Israeli newspaper of ultra-orthodox soldiers mocking Palestinian corpses by impaling a man's head on a pole and sticking a cigarette in his mouth' (ibid.). British journalist Chris McGreal explains:

The matter of the violin touched on something deeper about the way Israelis see themselves, and their conflict with the Palestinians ... [an article in] Yedioth Ahronoth

Plate 13.4   Playing the violin

Source: Photograph taken by Horit Herman-Peled; video shown at http://www.horit.
com/violin.htm.

newspaper [suggested] that the soldiers responsible should be put on trial 'not for
abusing Arabs but for disgracing the Holocaust'. (McGreal 2004)

The coercion that takes place through IDs is downplayed in this and other
ways. It has become so commonplace, even Palestinians say 'it's normal':

> Yes, they told me to clean the street. Many times; three or four times. People don't talk
> about it because it's normal. They would tell someone to count his melons. He would
> have to take them all out of the truck, and then put them all back in again. They would
> tell people to insult their grandfathers, who were walking with them. They would tell
> people to dance – especially people with beards. My friend had a beard and I didn't. I
> was 13 or 14 years old. They asked him, 'Do you like Khomeini?' And he said no. He
> wasn't lying. The soldier said, 'If you don't dance, I won't give you the ID'. He started
> dancing and he got the ID back. (John, interview)

Seen from the perspective of the individual, identity documentation (and
other surveillance) is in large part about the created inequality of power – given
to some and taken from others – that enables coercion. This does indeed begin

with discrimination: both supporters and opponents of IDs agree that the card will act as a classifier, between those to be harassed and those to be left alone.

> All discrimination is based on one of two conditions: situational or sectoral. Situational discrimination targets people in unusual circumstances, i.e. walking at night, visiting certain areas, attending certain functions or activities, or behaving in an abnormal fashion. Sectoral discrimination targets people having certain characteristics i.e. blacks, youths, skinheads, motorcycle riders or the homeless. ID cards containing religious or ethnic information make it possible to carry this discrimination a step further. (Davies 1996)

Yet coercion is not only about overt, institutionalised discrimination, nor is it solely about indirect discrimination, where institutional gaps leave opportunities for discrimination.[5] Instead, coercion is about the heightened powers, on the one hand, given to those in a position to discriminate, and the severity of the consequences, on the other hand, for those discriminated against. Thus, not only are discriminatory practices enabled through identity documentation (as is the common argument against surveillance), but also their consequences are magnified.

Specifically, identity cards link David Lyon's (2003) 'social sorting' to a system that extends into people's lives and on which they are, to some extent, dependent. As shown below, the example of identity cards issued by the Israeli government, to Palestinians in the West Bank, illustrates the degree of dependence on identity documentation that can be engineered through pseudo-legislation and a harsh system of enforcement. The inequalities created ensure a system that is both inherently discriminatory and allows for further, non-institutionalised discrimination. But the true influence of the created inequalities is the opening of opportunities for coercion. Thus, discrimination is not merely a matter, for instance, of commercial advertising or differential opportunities; the inequalities created also allow for coercion, which is something far more personalised, humiliating and violent.

Nazih Damiri (not shown in Plate 13.5) is a 27-year-old shepherd in a village near the town of Tulkarem, in the northern West Bank. For ten years, he took his flock out at 6:00 a.m. every day, and returned them home in the afternoon. One Thursday, in June of 2003, he walked the flock to a gate (that the Israeli army had erected to prohibit Palestinian farmers from reaching their land), along with his brother and cousin, where they were confronted by a Border Police jeep ....[6]

> Two male border police officers were in the jeep, and they let the flock pass through the gate. They also let my brother pass, and told him to continue walking. One of the border policemen demanded my ID card and started to check it.

---

5   For instance, referring to a bill that prohibited student visas to people from Iran, Iraq, Sudan, Libya, Syria, Cuba, and North Korea, except for those passing a 'security' check, Schildkraut (2002, 250) writes, 'this bill does not call attention to a particular ethnic group, but creates the potential for ethnicity-based policy *implementation* and institutes new restrictions based on one's country of origin [emphasis in original]'.

6   Testimony taken and translated by B'tselem: The Israeli Information Center for Human Rights in the Occupied Territories.

Plate 13.5   At the gate

Source: Gustaf Hansson 2004.

I had a donkey with me and was holding him by a rope.

The officer who was sitting next to the driver asked me if I had ever been in jail. He spoke very good Arabic. I told him that I had never been in jail.

After the policeman checked my ID, he took the rope from my hand and tied it to the front of the jeep. Then he told my cousin to unleash the donkey's saddle. He unleashed it. Then he told him to put the saddle on the ground.

Then he told me to wear the saddle. I put it on my shoulders, and my cousin tied it on me, like the policeman told him to do. Then the policeman told me to walk to the greenhouses not far away and to come back. I did that several times.

Then he ordered me to sit on the donkey. He bound my hands with the rope that was tied to the donkey. After I sat on the donkey, he told me to ride toward the greenhouses and to come back.

He still had my ID card.

He had me do it three times. The first time, my hands were tied. Then he untied my hands. The saddle remained tied on my back. Then he told me to ride to the nearby grove.

I asked him about my ID card.

He told me that we hadn't finished, and that he would be behind me. He and the other policeman followed me in the jeep. When we reached the grove, he tied the donkey to a tree and told me to fuck it. He repeated his demand a couple of times.

He also told me to lift up the tail of the donkey and tie it around my head. I told him that the tail was too short, and that I wasn't able to do it.

Up until this point, Nazih's emphasis is on the ID card. It is only after this that Nazih mentions the threat of weapons.

> He stood facing me and aimed his weapon at me. The other policeman was in the jeep, watching what was going on.
>
> I stood behind the donkey, took out my penis, and told him 'enough'. He said, 'I'll tell you when it is enough'. I was frightened to death, and I couldn't get an erection, so I couldn't do anything. He made me continue, and I pretended that I was doing what he wanted me to do.
>
> I tried to look over at them, but the policeman yelled at me and told me not to look, and that if I did, he would shoot me. This went on for about 30 minutes, before he told me to stop.

In the end though, it is the return of the ID card that marks the end of the day's coercion.

> He tightened the saddle on my back and gave me back my ID card.
>
> Then he told me, 'Ride over to the flock, fuck them, and I'll chase you'. I rode away, the saddle still on me, and he watched me go.
>
> After I got some distance away from them, I untied the saddle and walked over to my brother ... and told him what happened.
>
> My cousin and lots of other people saw what happened to me. I have not gone [back there] since then. I am afraid that I'll come across border policemen again.

Black Lists and Detention

> By pressing a key on a computer terminal, any civil administration official can gain access to name-lists of 'positives' and 'hostiles', and decide on the fate of their applications, from car licensing to water quotas, import permits and travel documents. 'Black Lists' have for a long time been an important element of the 'reward and punishment' system. (Benvenisti 1987, 35)

In 1989, Israel introduced green IDs for former detainees. Prior to this, certain residents were identified as 'security' risks by marking their identity cards with special signs (Al Haq 1989, 328). However this was the first time separate and easily distinguishable cards had marked out a group of former detainees. And of course, it enables harassment. One case among many documented by human rights group involved a man who, with his wife and son in the car, was stopped on his way from the doctor's to the pharmacy, and asked for his identity card:

> When I handed it to him, I saw the excitement on their faces and heard one of them saying, in Hebrew, 'Yarok! Yarok!' which means green. (Ibid., 329)

He was then taken to an isolated location, beaten and kicked for about seven minutes; his ID was returned and he was told to leave (ibid.). Green IDs were nevertheless most noted for their impact on geographical mobility. The former prisoners were the test case for a system of movement restrictions that, following the Oslo Agreements in the early 1990s, came to apply to every Palestinian in the area (this has also been noted by Kelly 2006).

Markings on ID cards are not unique to Israel. Indonesia has 'special punchings for those in the sub-series 'subversives' and 'traitors' (Anderson 1991, 185). Yet these markings have been given relatively little attention in academic work, mentioned in footnotes if mentioned at all. Perhaps this is because the advent of databases has enabled 'marking' to be hidden from those who are marked. In Israel, the Population Registry serves this purpose. Israeli authorities develop and use lists of individuals they want to detain, and those persons are subject to immediate arrest (Cook et al. 2004). Palestinians do not know the lists; new versions are issued frequently. Writing about the approximately ten percent of prisoners under the age of 18, researchers from Defence for Children International describe how it begins, 'If arrested, the children are not informed of the reason and are often forced to stand or kneel blindfolded with their hands tied behind them as they wait for transportation to an interrogation centre ...' (ibid., 55).

Palestinians who entered Jerusalem or Israel without a permit, or during a period when all permits had been invalidated, were fined and/or imprisoned. In a five-year period, 1991–1996, over 112,000 workers were imprisoned, spending more than 224,000 days in prison (Elzein et al. 1997, 7). In the same period, workers paid over US $16,800,000 in fines (ibid.). By the late 1990s, Palestinian workers in Israel were mostly replaced by immigrants from Eastern Europe and Southeast Asia (Rosenhek 2006, 2).

Nowhere in the world have so many been detained as punishment for moving within their own country, except in South Africa.[7] In South Africa, from 1916 until 1981, 17.5 million people were detained for contravening pass law regulations (Savage 1984, cited in Giliomee and Schlemmer 1985, 1). In 1983 alone, 262,904 were prosecuted and 142,067 convicted for reference book and influx control offences (Giliomee and Schlemmer 1985, 1). While these numbers are not matched elsewhere, detentions and other abuses have been documented in other countries:

> French police have been accused of overzealous use of the ID card against blacks, and particularly against Algerians. Greek authorities have been accused of using data on religious affiliation on its national card to discriminate against people who are not Greek Orthodox. (Davies 1996)

Indeed, detention and abuse are to be found 'in virtually all countries':

> A Privacy International survey of ID cards found claims of police abuse by way of the cards in virtually all countries. Most involved people being arbitrarily detained after failure to produce their card. Others involved beatings of juveniles or minorities. There were even instances of wholesale discrimination on the basis of data set out on the cards. (Davies 1996)

---

7   Records are not available for China and the former Soviet Union, both also known for internal movement restrictions (see Torpey 1997).

Plate 13.6   Arrest at checkpoints

Source: Photograph taken by Machsom Watch, April 22 2004; see Machsom Watch
2006).

In Palestine, the Israeli incarceration system relies on identity cards. On arrest,
adults and children are asked for their IDs, which are confiscated (Cook et al.
2004, 53, 55, 62). During one mass arrest, a detainee explained:

> Once we got there, the soldiers split us into groups, forcing the guys who were between
> 15 and 20 years old into one corner, separated from the rest. Some of the younger ones
> were too young to have ID, but the soldiers did not care. (ibid., 60)

Adults and children are 'not charged with any particular crime, and they
have no legal recourse … Israel isolates the prisoners from the outside world,
and there is no way to monitor what Israel is doing inside the detention centres'
(ibid., 61). Children are ineligible to receive ID cards before the age of 16 and
must be registered on a parent's ID. They are thus more vulnerable when detained,
because all systems are linked to the Population Registry.

> Families are rarely told where their children are being detained… Since many detained
> children are under 16 and have not yet received their ID cards, they often are not
> properly registered in the military's files …. (Ibid., 63)

If lawyers wish to visit their clients in Israeli prisons, they must send their own
ID cards and permits to the prison 48 hours before the visit, which makes visiting

difficult, and in an emergency, impossible (ibid., 99). Sometimes Palestinians are killed before anyone knows their whereabouts, such as 17-year-old Murad 'Awaisa in March and an 18-year old in December of 2002 (ibid., 63).

Following mass arrests in 2002 and 2003, many prisoners were released without their identity cards.

> Palestinians arrested and then freed during the Israeli military invasions that began on 29 March 2002 faced further danger on their release, because most of the West Bank was under direct re-occupation, and the population under total curfew. In many cases prisoners were released on to the streets in areas several hours' drive away from their homes. They were forced to seek shelter during the curfews, when anyone leaving their homes risked being shot by Israeli soldiers. The military did not give discharged prisoners documents showing that they had been released, and failed to return many confiscated ID cards. Consequently these released detainees risked not only being shot, but also being re-arrested if Israeli soldiers stopped them. (Cook et al. 2004, 58)

Mass arrests have taken place since 1999, but were further enabled by a military order in April 2002, allowing for 18-day detention of Palestinians not suspected of any offence (Cook, Hanieh and Kay 2004). In two phases between 27 February and 20 May 2002, about 8,500 Palestinians were arrested in the West Bank (ibid.). Mass arrests also continued afterward: on 2 April 2003, all males aged between 15 and 40 in Tulkarem refugee camp were ordered to a girls' schoolyard. After detention, the one to two thousand Palestinian detainees were expelled.

> [We were told] we could go anywhere as long as it was not back to our homes in the Tulkarem camp.
> [I thought] I might never be able to go back home again, nor see my family or my brother who is ten years old. (Ibid., 61)

Israeli arrest raids and military operations took place daily in 2005; by the end of the year, the IDF had carried out over 2,000 incursions into Palestinian population centres (HRW 2006). Israel holds over 8,000 political prisoners and over 600 'administrative detainees' (held without trial or charge) (ibid.).

Conclusion

> Anyone who brings up the 'if you're innocent, you have nothing to fear' argument has obviously led a very sheltered existence. (Alex Swanson, quoted in BBC 2004)

Most identity documents – such as birth certificates or passports – contain an element of entitlement: to residency, welfare assistance, health care, education, or mobility, to name but a few 'entitlements'. While identity documents can also represent restrictions on these entitlements, they are rarely discussed as negative additions to people's lives (Caplan, personal communication). Yet they are often instrumental in conscription, discrimination, and individual or group persecution (ibid.).

Identity documents work beyond the typically envisaged technologies of surveillance like cameras, online monitoring, and databases. They have the potential to combine the surveillance powers of all these mechanisms; they can both 'sort' people, *and* invade their personal privacy. Yet the power of identity documents extends beyond even this. What has largely escaped attention, even of most civil rights groups, is the potential of identity documents for *coercion*. If a single identity document is the sole key to a series of 'entitlements' – as mundane as entry to public buildings or as vital as health care and mobility – any person empowered to confiscate that document holds power over the document's bearer. If identity documents are combined with 'stop and search' powers for various authorities (police, security guards, etc.), the potential to 'sort' and 'know' a person is combined with the potential to coerce.

The examples in this chapter are few in comparison to the wider reality of identity documentation in the West Bank. They omit the numerous effects of indirect coercion: on employment, education, land ownership, the ability to live as a family or community, and countless other aspects of life. Furthermore, these examples cover only part of the issue of coercion. They focus mainly on the infrastructure of checkpoints and prisons, ranging from established 'terminals', to 'flying' checkpoints and makeshift prisons. Such a focus is not only narrower than the reality; it may also lead to these examples being discounted as unique: an infrastructure that could never be exported.

Yet coercion is broader than just checkpoints and prisons. The fear it engenders is felt in the middle of the night in one's own home, as soldiers enter and demand all the IDs in the house. It is felt when the ID must be requested for the first time from the Ministry of Interior – where Palestinians themselves must go to register, rather than soldiers or officials coming to them. It is felt when a building permit is denied, when families live in housing densities surpassing those in most of the world. Coercion – through IDs – is a topic with examples that multiply each passing day. Unfortunately, it is a topic unlikely to remain confined to isolated geographic locations. The principle that IDs have the potential to centralise control over individuals – into the hands of other individuals – is likely to find avid advocates in places outside the West Bank. It is hoped that it will also have its opponents.

Bibliography

Al-Haq (1989), *Nation under Siege* (Ramallah: Al-Haq).

Anderson, B. (1991), *Imagined Communities* (London: Verso).

BBC (2004), 'Should We Carry ID cards?' *Talking Point* (updated 30 April 2004), http://news.bbc.co.uk/1/hi/talking_point/3649577.stm, accessed 7 March 2007.

Benvenisti, M. (1987), *West Bank Database Annual Report* (Jerusalem: West Bank Database Project).

B'tselem (2003), 'Zeita: Border Police officer forces man from 'Attil to commit sexual act with donkey, June 2003' (no date listed for last update), http://www.btselem.org/English/Testimonies/20030626_Sexual_harassment_of_Naziya_Damiri_in_Zeita_Witness_Damiri.asp, accessed 7 March 2007.

Caplan, J. (2006), personal communication, 16 June, Oxford.

Chu, J.Y. (2007), 'Card Me When I'm Dead: Identification papers and the pursuit of the burial rights in Fuzhou, China', presentation at the Sixth Berlin Colloquium on Transnationalism, 14–19 February, Berlin.

Cook, C., Hanieh, A. and Kay, A. (2004), *Stolen Youth* (London: Pluto Press).

Davies, S. (1996), 'Identity Cards: Frequently asked questions' (updated 24 August 1996), http://www.privacy.org/pi/activities/idcard/idcard_faq.html#10, accessed 7 March 2007.

El-Najjar, H.A. (2002), 'News Photos' (no longer online), http://www.aljazeerah.info/Islam/Galleryofnewspictures/june_2002_news_photos.htm, accessed 24 June 2006).

Elzein, Sa'ed et al. (1997), *Palestinian Water Resources: A rapid interdisciplinary sector review and issues paper* (Ramallah: Democracy and Workers' Rights Center).

Giliomee, H. and Schlemmer, L. (eds) (1985), *Against the Fences: Poverty, passes and privilege in South Africa* (Cape Town: David Philip, Publisher).

Hansson, G. (2004), unpublished photograph taken in Masha, 4 July.

Hass, A. (2005), 'You Exist if the Israeli Computer Says So', *Ha'aretz*, 28 September.

Human Rights Watch (HRW) (2006), 'Israel/Occupied Palestinian Territories (OPT)', in *World Report 2006* (updated 31 December 2005), http://hrw.org/english/docs/2006/01/18/isrlpa12224.htm, accessed 7 March 2007.

International Court of Justice (ICJ) (2004), 'Legal Consequences of the Construction of a Wall in the Occupied Palestinian Territories', *ICJ Reports*.

John, telephone interview, 7 March 2007, Oxford [name changed].

Jum'a, J., interview, 26 June 2004, Jerusalem.

Kelly, T. (2006), 'Documented Lives: Fear and the uncertainties of law during the second Palestinian Intifada'. *Journal of the Royal Anthropological Institute* 12, 89–107.

Lancet (2004), 'Rita Giacaman', *The Lancet* 364:9451, 2089.

Lyon, D. (ed.) (2003), *Surveillance as Social Sorting: Privacy, risk and digital discrimination* (London: Routledge).

Machsom Watch (2006), 'Pictures' (no date listed for last update), http://www.machsomwatch.org/eng/pictures.asp?link=pix&lang=eng, accessed 7 March 2007.

McFarland, S.G. (2005), 'On the eve of war: Authoritarianism, social dominance, and American students' attitudes toward attacking Iraq'. *Personality and Social Psychology Bulletin* 31:3, 360-367.

McGreal, C. (2004), 'Israel Shocked by Image of Soldiers Forcing Violinist to Play at Roadblock', *The Guardian*, 29 November.

Ong, A. (1999), *Flexible Citizenship: The cultural logics of transnationality* (Durham, NC: Duke University Press).

Rosenhek, Z. (2006), 'Incorporating Migrant Workers into the Israeli Labour Market?', Euro-Mediterranean Consortium for Applied Research on International Migration (CARIM) Analytical and Synthetic Notes – Political and Social Module.

Safa, interview, 26 June 2004, Jerusalem [name changed].

Sarah, interview, 27 June 2004, Jerusalem [name changed].

Savage, M. (1984), 'Pass Laws and the Disorganisation and Reorganisation of the African Population in South Africa', paper presented to the conference of the Carnegie Inquiry into Poverty and Development in Southern Africa, University of Cape Town, April.

Schildkraut, D.J. (2002), 'The More Things Change … American Identity and Mass and Elite Responses to 9/11', *Political Psychology* 23:3, 511–35.

Shalabi, N., interview, 7 August 2005, Masha, Palestine.

Shaul, Y., ed. (2004), *Breaking the Silence: Soldiers speak out about their service in Hebron*, http://www.shovrimshtika.org.

Sparke, M. (2006), 'A Neoliberal Nexus: Economy, security and the biopolitics of citizenship on the border', *Political Geography* 25:2, 151–80.

Thierer, A. (2001), 'National ID Cards: New technologies, same bad idea', *TechKnowledge Newsletter* 21 (updated 28 September 2001), http://www.cato.org/tech/tk/010928-tk.html, accessed 7 March 2007.

Torpey, J. (1997), 'Revolutions and Freedom of Movement: An analysis of passport controls in the French, Russian, and Chinese Revolutions', *Theory and Society* 26:6, 837–68.

Torpey, J. (2000), *The Invention of the Passport: Surveillance, citizenship and the state* (Cambridge: Cambridge University Press).

World Bank (2005), 'GNI Per Capita 2005, Atlas Method and PPP', http://siteresources.worldbank.org/DATASTATISTICS/Resources/GNIPC.pdf, accessed 7 March 2007.

World Bank (2006) 'West Bank and Gaza Update', http://siteresources.worldbank.org/INTWESTBANKGAZA/Resources/UpdateSept06Eng.pdf, accessed 7 March 2007.

Chapter 14

Ethno-sectarianism and the Construction of Fear in Belfast, Northern Ireland

Peter Shirlow

This chapter tackles the enduring relationship between fear, prejudice and residential segregation in Northern Ireland. It shows how segregation is both a response to and a factor in the reproduction of (and inertia in) the suspicion and hostility that divides Catholics and Protestants[1] in Belfast. It contains an account of the entanglement of ethno-sectarianism with fear, and an empirical overview of the most recent trends based on surveys reported in Shirlow and Murtagh (2006).

The steady deconstruction of enmity at party political level in Northern Ireland gives the impression of a society emerging from conflict. In reality, the hostility that exists between communities remains and there is evidence[2] that violent sectarian incidents have continued to rise in recent years. This chapter argues that the basis of enmity and territoriality remains largely undiminished and that fear and prejudice are both enduring edifices of ethno-sectarian practice. It is an account of the burden that remains embedded in the segregated spaces that are a legacy of Northern Ireland's distinctive sectarian history.

The complexity of ethno-sectarian[3] relationships is woven around the notion of an 'other' community that is to be feared. Such fears are linked to suspicion at best but can be the basis upon which violence is performed and mobilised. A common concern located within ethno-sectarian disputes is the fear of losing a predominant position, as demographic shifts or boundary changes lead to the

---

1   The conflict in Northern Ireland is not about religion but constitutional allegiance. However, the use of the terms Protestant and Catholics is employed as an explanation of the conflict and its many complexities, a full explication of which is beyond the remit of this chapter.

2   A presentation by the Police Service in Northern Ireland at Stormont Castle held in January 2007 stated that 'sectarian incidents are rising and have now risen for four years in a row. These incidents do not result in death but physical sectarian violence continues apace'.

3   Ethno-sectarianism is a form of racism within which labelling and group identities are based upon prejudice and stereotyping.

acquisition of an undesirable minority position.[4] In Northern Ireland the assault upon communities is tied to a combination of prejudice, harm and also fear of minoritisation at every spatial scale.

A folk memory that invokes previous harms brought upon an ethnic group by those they are opposed to can remain as a distant fear. However, when strain is placed upon ethnic relationships such memory can induce the performance of violence. Thus fear has the potential to motivate and to do so along the boundaries between culturally opposed peoples. But fear is also important in forging group togetherness.

Fear of the 'other' community is both a process of representing a group's fears and a way of purposefully denying the fears of the ethno-sectarian 'other' (Anderson and Shuttleworth 1998). This is not achieved by simply remaining silent with regard to the 'other' communities suffering, but by pro-actively denying that harm was caused by your community and/or to allege that if harm was caused that the violence used was 'legitimate'. Thus within an ethno-sectarian conflict, fear becomes established as an ordered, moral and self-righteous discourse (Shirlow and Murtagh 2006).

This chapter shows that fear is tied to other forms of anxiety and phobia. In the context of blaming the 'other' community the sense of being violated as opposed to having violated means that communities demand guilt and shame from the 'other' community. The refusal of the 'other' side to apologise furthers ethno-sectarian separation and deepens senses of hostility. Such social mistrust and the inability to control the attitude of those who are hostile to you, especially with regard to establishing 'truth', creates wider senses of doubt and furthers a lack of control that intensifies senses of insecurity (Shirlow 2001: 2003). Gold and Revill (2003, 21) have shown that as fear intensifies and as threat is experienced 'fear connects with debates concerning the rationality and irrationality of decision-making behaviour'.

The chapter also shows how fear and the perception of threat influences mobility and the cognition of safe and unsafe places among most residents living within highly segregated communities. It is established that those who fear most or who are definably prejudiced against the 'other' community are also those who aid the reproduction and celebration of place-centred notions of group loyalty. For such persons place is not merely a site of habituation and exchange but is consciously cast as a site of resistance and salutation. The promotion and protection of place is thus a 'rational' and 'cogent' part of an identity construction around essentialist ideas and viewpoints. Such people are purposeful spatial determinists who promote and sustain the need to demarcate community allegiance both cognitively and via territorial delineation.

However, and despite the presentation and explanation of fear, this chapter also pinpoints a virtually ignored section of the population – non-sectarians living within segregated and violated communities who do not eulogise place-centred renditions of fear and cultural separateness. The imagination of group loyalty and the experience of significant ethno-sectarian violence does not convert all

---

4   This is a particular problem within working class Protestant communities in Belfast that are in demographic decline.

residents of highly segregated communities to the allure of unquestioned ethnic allegiance. For this group, loyalty to place is less defined, and in many instances such allegiance is viewed by non-sectarians as misplaced and incongruous. Moreover, the desire to not submit to a place centred concept of identity is purposeful and ongoing.

In societies within which racism or ethno-sectarianism forms an extremist discourse, this not only highlights the failure of multiculturalism, but also stimulates the emotions of hate and loathing – feelings that are ultimately linked to notions of purity and impurity, that are themselves the basis of practised and performed 'otherness' (Shirlow and Murtagh 2006). Thus fear and low levels of interaction between separated communities are the outcome not merely of traumatic events, but also of competition between communities who utilise fear as a strategy that encourages difference. Fear is not only an ethno-sectarian experience but also part of a social process of categorisation.

The evidence on how sectarianised fears reduce mobility and inter-community contact illustrates how social practice still engenders different imaginings of community and the production of community-based forms of political identification and violent enactment. Work within the Northern Irish arena, which has evaluated the link between religious segregation, victimisation, security-consciousness and ultimately the impact of fear upon mobility, has remained underdeveloped.

The capacity to reduce the impact of place upon identity and belief is undermined by complex renditions of physical territory and cognitive territoriality. Segregation is more than a crude separation of peoples and the sundering of urban space. In effect it is the basis upon which loyalty and devotion remain committed to forms of identity that are reproduced through remaining disparate from oppositional places. The control of place permits the promotion of ethno-sectarian propaganda and the capacity to influence younger generations who have not experienced previously high levels of violence. Thus the experience and rationale of fear are communicated via inter-generational modes of prejudice and a biased promotion of community history.

The remainder of the chapter falls into two sections. First, it advances previous work on segregation in Belfast to show how entrenched residential separation and the social segregation that goes with this can be viewed as experiences which are practiced and understood. Second, it talks to a neglected community of interest – to the non-sectarians whose liminal locations cast light on the options and limitations for a less segregated Northern Irish future.

A Tradition of Segregation and Separation

Boal's seminal work (1969) on immobility between segregated communities was a crucial starting point regarding the link between divided place and avoidance strategies. In his latter work Boal (1976; 2000) conceptualised responses to conditions of ethnic-sectarian segregation and cultural decline in terms of a continuum of 'loyalty, voice and exit'. This work indicated that members of communities who felt isolated or threatened used existing order to reduce vulnerability and achieve security through joining their co-religionists. Boal's depiction also noted that threatened communities would voice their concerns in a number of ways such as campaigning, demonstrating or even through the use of violence to maintain boundaries between communities. Some, within Boal's framework, doggedly chose to remain and indicated their loyalty to place through a desire to remain defiant in the face of assault and threat. This body of work was important in that it explained the effect of violence upon general attitudes, but it was less forceful in explaining how the reproduction of residential segregation regulated violence, harm and fear via interlinked spatial devices (Burton 1978; Douglas and Shirlow 1998).

In addressing this lacunae in previous research, this chapter examines the relationship between ethno-sectarian segregation and fear through analysing the competing discourses of loss, victimhood and harm. The manner in which fear is practiced with regard to spatial mobility and territorial belonging is also examined through appreciating the meaning and practice of fear (Feldman 1991; Jarman 1998). In establishing the nature of attitudes and experiences of fear, we can not only explore the meaning of ethno-sectarian attitudes but highlight that those who promote the most vociferous and antagonistic attitudes are those most likely to also exhibit loyalty to their community.

Despite the location of these more positive voices, and the decline in deaths, the majority of residents in segregated communities remain opposed to the 'other' community in very significant and hostile ways. This suggests that the formation of place via segregation, ideological presentation and the experience of hate and loathing of the 'other' community remain as a dominant form of identity formation. Without doubt, place, and the experience of living in places that have been violated by violence, remain as significant factors in the construction of community.

The relationship between fear and residential segregation is contingent upon a series of relations such as the environments of everyday life, violence (both imagined and real) and political manipulation (Shirlow and Pain 2003). The presentation of fear, by certain political entrepreneurs, has been a central element in the construction of ethno-sectarian tradition within a range of urban environments. In some cases socially dominant groups (such as the Irish Republican Army and the Ulster Defence Force) aim to control the ownership and presentation of a community's fears, phobias and traumas in a desire to triumph particular political discourses and related practices.

The realities of politically motivated violence in Belfast are obvious. Between 1969 and 1999, around 1,400 people were killed and over 20,000 injured by paramilitary and state violence. Fear of being a victim of such attacks meant that many people living in the most violent arenas developed a comprehensive knowledge of 'safe' and 'unsafe places' (Burton 1978). Furthermore, mental maps created a process of awareness that was strengthened through the mobilisation of fear, victimhood and risk.

As Tables 14.1 and 14.2 show, the majority of people from a Catholic or Protestant community background live in places that are at least 81 per cent Catholic or Protestant. Just over two-thirds of Catholics (67.3 per cent) and 73 per cent or Protestants live in such places. A mere 10.7 per cent of Catholics and 7.0 per cent of Protestants live in places that are between 41–60 per cent Catholic or Protestant, those places that could be described as mixed. There is a near equal population split between these two populations within the city, a situation that reflects an increasing share of the population emanating from a Catholic community background. The level of segregation is now stabilising, but the growth in segregation in the 1970s and 1980s was linked to the sudden rise and sustainability of violence.

Table 14.1   Segregation in Belfast (by ward) by community background (Catholics)

% Catholic population share by level of segregation	Community *background* % of total Catholic population in band
0–20 Catholic	4.7
21–40 Catholic	3.6
41–60 Catholic	10.7
61–80 Catholic	13.8
81–90 Catholic	9.3
91–100 Catholic	58.0

Source: Census of Population, 2001.

Table 14.2   Segregation in Belfast (by ward) by community background (Protestants)

% Protestant population share by level of segregation bands	Community *background* % of total Protestant population in band
0–20 Protestant	3.4
21–40 Protestant	7.3
41–60 Protestant	7.0
61–80 Protestant	9.3
81–90 Protestant	28.4
91–100 Protestant	44.6

Source: Census of Population, 2001.

Segregation led to a form of urban space that de-territorialised inter-community connection and contact. As communities became more ethno-centric, the belief grew that the ethno-sectarian 'other' was intent upon harm and violent retribution. Violence furthered senses of distrust and impairment that were understood through an ongoing sense of anxiety and threat (Shirlow 2001). Fearfulness became strongly associated with senses of resentment and disbelief (Downey 2000).

Many people living in interface[5] areas have often defended physical separation by claiming that it provides them with a degree of security against attack from the 'other' side. Ironically, the 'protective' walls that were assembled to 'protect' communities were to become the sites within which frequent, persistent and recurrent, if often low-level, violence occurred. The impact of fear upon physical separation and thus mobility has meant that violence has subordinated many to a discourse of ethno-sectarian affiliation.

Such a high rate of violence within highly segregated places indicates the link between factors such as residential segregation, interfacing and also social class. It is not surprising that violence encouraged political and cultural retrenchment and the physical and cognitive re-mapping of the city. The reorganisation of space, due to violence, increased separation and re-emphasised the fundamentals of ethno-sectarian 'difference'. As Figure 14.1 shows, most people who died in conflict-related incidents were killed close to their home address. Nearly one-third of all victims were murdered within their homes or only a matter of metres away. Death within one's own community was commonplace, then, and furthered the idea that violence was based upon an assault upon community. Given the proximity of death to residence it is evident why conflict-related deaths are understood within discourses of group suffering. The proximity of so many deaths to home places forged strong and at times endurable notions of group-based losses, and in so doing diluted the capacity to see beyond violence as community-based assail. The parochial nature of violent enactment aided the overall process of territorial entrapment. It has also meant that the ability to build peace has been undermined by memory and the notion that although violence is declining that it is too soon to trust the 'other' community.

This community based experience and collectivisation of harm raised and still raises community consciousness. Suffering thus remains tied to the overall geography of political resistance and the ethno-sectarian manipulation of victimhood. The ability to consolidate identity, however loosely, remains dependent upon the capacity to govern the memory traces of conflict through a series of notions of belonging. The process of strategic management remains based upon convincing sections of each respective community that resistance to the 'other' community is a historical struggle, and that the residents of harmed places are the makers of a profound and more importantly 'legitimate' history.

The recent and significant growth in the erection of community-based memorials testifies to twin strategies of commemoration and the political commodification of landscapes of suffering and endurance. One of the primary reasons for the perpetuation of political discord is the controversy over victims, state collusion and the demand for apologies. The never-ceasing demand for enquires into deaths and the abuse of human rights is rarely, if indeed ever, based upon a shared inter-

---

5　　An interface is the boundary between segregated communities.

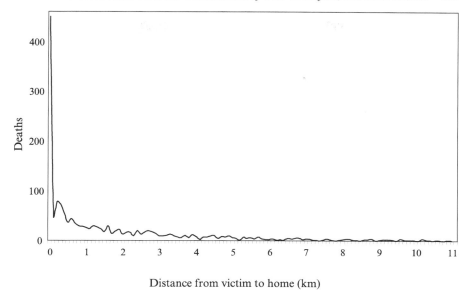

Figure 14.1 Distance between location of conflict-related fatalities and the victim's home in Belfast, 1966–2004

Source: Shirlow and Murtagh (2006, p. 112).

community request. For many, there remains a less complex and passionate series of relationships between memory and contested legitimacy. As eloquently argued by Aughey:

> … there existed a pervasive feeling of victimhood, real and imagined, that has been common to the cultures of unionism and nationalism. Emotionally, this condition served to displace responsibility on to others. Politically, it encouraged a helpless attitude of going with the flow, an acceptance that the history of destruction all around was indeed 'natural'. (Aughey 2005, 11)

As I discuss below, the decline in violence that followed the paramilitary ceasefires in 1994 has not led to greater mobility between communities. Evidently, the threat of low level violence and the memory of previous violence still undermine meaningful and positive shifts in community relations.

Immobility Entrenched?

This section is concerned with evidence on ethno-sectarian enclaving and the reproduction of ethno-sectarianised fears within Belfast contained in two surveys conducted in 2004. These surveys sought out individuals living within interface communities in Belfast. Data were collected on households and information on over 9000 individuals was included.[6] The surveys aimed to cast new light on the level of spatial interaction between interfaced Catholic and Protestant[7] communities, as well as exploring the nature of inter-community engagement/ disengagement. The discussion which follows juxtaposes the leaning to segregation found among the sectarians with the complex spatial ambivalences in the ideas of the non-sectarians. Most critically, I pay attention to those living in highly segregated communities who do not subscribe to an enduring ethno-sectarian 'logic'. This is important in that media depictions generally cast segregated communities as being wholly belligerent and beyond compromise and conflict transformation. For the non-sectarians, identity is important but is also shaped by experiences and discourses which understand that a unidimensional sense of place, harm and identity is overtly simplistic and politically sterile.

Given that each of the six pairs of communities surveyed in this study share similar socio-economic profiles and are adjacent, it would be expected that there would be a likeness between each in terms of public and private sector based usage. Yet levels of social, cultural and economic interaction between communities were low, and the reasons for these dissimilar mobility patterns are firmly attached to an emotional landscape of fear, intolerance and the experience of violence. Furthermore, the marking of territory with hostile imagery and graffiti is also important in terms of generating low levels of contact between these communities.

Most respondents felt relatively safe within their own community, but had reservations, at best, concerning entering areas dominated by the 'other' community. The lack of contact between communities was similar and no one group were disadvantaged more than any other. Enclaved communities, places that were surrounded by the 'other' community, suffered most and residents within them undertook wide-ranging journeys to access services. Larger and more homogenous communities, within which an extensive range of facilities are located, produced internalised mobility patterns.

In general it was found that only one in eight people worked in areas dominated by the 'other' community. Moreover, 78 per cent of respondents provided examples of at least three publicly funded facilities that they did not use because these services were located within areas dominated by the 'other' community. In enclaved communities, around 75 per cent of the survey respondents refused to use their closest health centre if it was located in a place dominated by the 'other' community.

Over half of all respondents (58 per cent) travel at least twice as far as they have to, usually into neutral areas or areas dominated by co-religionists, in order to locate two or more private sector based facilities. Eighty-two per cent of respondents whose nearest benefit office was located in the 'other' community's

---

6   The communities, with republican/nationalist places first, were Ardoyne/Upper Ardoyne, New Lodge/Tiger's Bay, Manor Street/Oldpark, Lenadoon/Suffolk, Whitewell/ White City and St. James'/Village.

7   The conflict in Northern Ireland is not over religion as it is a constitutional conflict. Religion acts as a boundary marker between British and Irish identity.

Table 14.3 Percentage share of those who do not use facilities in areas located in the other community, by age and reason

Age	Fear of the other community	Fear of my own community	Fear of both communities	Loyalty	Other
65+	45.6	20.2	20.2	8.5	5.5
45–64	49.6	16.2	14.2	13.5	6.5
25–44	64.6	9.4	9.2	8.8	8.0
16–24	75.8	8.4	6.2	5.6	4.0
Av.	58.9	13.5	12.4	9.1	6.0

Source: Shirlow and Murtagh (2006 p. 154).

territory used facilities located in areas dominated by their 'own' community, even though this meant undertaking significant journeys. Such disruptions to everyday living are alarming when it is considered that they impact upon other forms of social dislocation and deprivation within segregated areas. A mere 18 per cent or respondents undertook, on a weekly basis, consumption based activities in areas dominated by the 'other' community. It is generally assumed that fear of being attacked by the 'other' community is central in determining low levels of inter-community contact.

Nearly 60 per cent (58.9 per cent) of respondents who did not undertake shopping and other consumption activities in areas dominated by the 'other' community made this choice because of what they recognised as fear of either verbal or physical violence. Around 9 per cent stated that they would not undertake such journeys due to a desire not to spend money in areas dominated by the 'other' community, deeming this to be based upon 'loyalty' to their own community. Immobility, as shown in Table 14.3, is a much stronger determinant in the choice of facilities than loyalty to the home community.

Just over one in eight respondents would not undertake journeys into areas dominated by the other community due to fear of being ostracised by their own community. A similar number stated that fear of both the 'other' community and the 'home' community was also a motivating factor in their refusal to enter areas dominated by the 'other' community. Fear of 'my own community' was directly linked to the belief that entering areas dominated by the 'other' sectarian group would lead to individuals being 'punished' by members of their own group. As such, fear operates as both an inter- and intra-community based judgement. People aged over 65 were those least likely to perceive the 'other' community as a menacing spatial formation and were thus more likely to cross between segregated communities. On the other hand, for these older people, fear of 'my own community' or both communities was more palpable than it was among those aged 16–44. Relatedly, those aged between 16 and 44 were more likely than their older counterparts to acknowledge fear of the 'other community' as the primary reason for not crossing of ethno-sectarian boundaries.

The interviews conducted after the survey revealed a series of complex cultural and demographic positions. A group of non-sectarian respondents was composed of those who believed that the 'other' community was not a homogenous cabal and that their community had also been involved in transgressive sectarian behaviour. This group included around one in every five respondents. These people tended to have been in mixed relationships, or had an extensive social contact network with the 'other' community. They generally articulated the argument that any fear of the 'other' community that they had was tempered by their more experienced forms of cultural understanding in comparison with their neighbours. However, the desire to articulate a non-sectarian discourse is tempered by a fear of reprisal from within your own community. It was generally understood among most non-sectarians that to display frustration with the ethno-sectarianism of one's own community was injudicious, and could lead to being ostracised or even threatened. A male Protestant respondent (aged 45) who is involved in inter-community dialogue presented this fear as follows:

> People round here think I'm odd because I don't agree with them. They think because I am non-sectarian that I am disloyal at best or a Fenian [Catholic] lover at worst. I don't mind them thinking that but when you have children it affects them too and they get stereotyped by my actions and beliefs. So you learn to shut up. It's the same on the other side. They will undermine you in both communities if you challenge their legitimacy. So even if you have the ideas that are needed to build a new society you fear expressing them. People just don't like difference within their community, they find it uncomfortable.

Stronger, more sectarian attitudes were located among the majority. Their general failure to engage in cross-community activities was due to fear of attack by the 'other' community. For this group the experience of residential segregation was interpreted via a framework of exclusive and sectarian representations and 'traditions'. Sectarianism was not understood as a repressive relationship but as an articulatory process based upon experienced 'truths'. As stated by a male Protestant respondent aged 32:

> Look, if we share our community with them they will take over. That's what they want. Republicans want to drive us out. So when I say that we must stop them and use whatever force is needed for to do that then that's fine by me and others, right. This is our place and we defended this place agin [against] them ones. So I want to keep this place for Prods [Protestants]. They won't scare me I'm not afeard [afraid] of them, not one bit.

The following Catholic male aged 34 had a similar perspective:

> The conflict was about us standing up to their violence and hatred of us. So I don't see any change in them ins [them] concerning us. They hate us and we need to make sure that we respond by standing up to them. We aren't croppies [subservient] to them anymore and we need to keep reminding people in this district that they can try to make us afraid but we are always going to make sure that they know we are up for

anything they throw at us. We stand together against them and make sure they don't get one over on us.

Among those who promoted sectarian discourses, the materialisation of residential segregation into spatial constructs was imperative in order to functionalise and advance topographic conflict. One of the most pronounced factors that distanced the sectarian and non-sectarian group was the manner in which they eulogised the communities within which they lived. Sectarian group members discussed their community within utopian discourses of integrity, loyalty, kinship and impunity. In comparison, non-sectarians were more likely to denote that 'their' communities contained multiple forms of impurity, contravention and deviant behaviour. This sense of enduring belief in one's own community was expressed by one female Protestant aged 42:

They're [Catholics] scum. They are hateful scum. You couldn't trust them even if you reared them. You see them all the time with the hatred for us written all over their faces. People in here [this community] are good hard-working people who care about each other. You couldn't say that about them!

Similarly, from a Catholic female respondent aged 44:

Look at them [Protestants] in their cheap jewellery and their tracksuits. They are so fat and ugly and mean sorta [sort of] looking. You see in this district people are decent and look after the way they look and dress and the like. Them lot couldn't live the way we could. We are good people and that can't be said about that shower of shit up the road.

The interviews conducted among the sectarian group produced passionate sectarian narratives and the most pronounced sense that the 'other' community was abnormal, antagonistic and uncompromising. Fear, within this group, was explained through the framework of reproaching the contrary community. According to a respondent from a Republican community aged 22:

Look they want to hurt us ones all the time. They are out to get us. They want to keep us in fear and that's all there is to it. They make us feel afeared [afraid] all the time through chucking at us and spitting on us. They want us to bow down. So the way I sees [see] it they need to be put on the back step and learn to be afeared of us.

In comparison, the following was a common commentary among non-sectarians:

It's a Catch 22 situation. People are afraid of each other. But instead of saying let's stop scaring each other most people think if they think we will harm them they will keep their heads down. The more people think that their community is special and the other one isn't then you realise this country is going nowhere.

Other commentaries from within the non-sectarian group actively challenged the notion of inter-group solidarity and questioned the notion of community purity as imagined by the sectarian group. As explained by a Protestant female respondent aged 39:

> There are eegits [idiots] in both communities. See in this community there are people I want nothing to do with and I am sure it's the same on the other side. There is a saying you will know it is 'you can choose your friends but not your family'. I think it should be 'you can choose your friends and not your community'. The problem is people talk a lot of shit about community. I can tell you all the times my community has let me down. So there is a choice and I chose a life in which I choose who I like and don't like. I ain't going to like someone just because they're a Prod [Protestant], as that wouldn't make any sense to me.

A Catholic male respondent took this antipathy towards sections of one's own community further:

> People in this community go on about the IRA protected us and that. Let me tell you something, I am a republican but I hated the IRA as they was [were] nothing but bullies. Look at how many people in this community were harmed by them. As far as I always thought the IRA and the loyalist were against me because I wouldn't be a republican bigot or just because I am a Taig [Catholic]. See all that rubbish that's crap. See me I get on with my life and pick who I like and don't like according to my principles. I don't need a community that is brainwashed by lying about the past. I want people who are prepared to be honest to be my mates and friends. I suppose I'm odd and thank God for that.

Given the hostility that is directed towards those who are non-sectarian from members of their own community, it is evident that few arenas exist within which to articulate non-sectarian beliefs. Without doubt, paradigms of ethno-sectarian purity and impurity predicate social relations to such an extent, and with such power, that the capacity exists to silence the dialogue capable of challenging ethno-sectarian discourses. This implies that telling, violence and the reproduction of fear are based upon sectarianised relationships which aim to not only reproduce residential segregation but to also suppress any belief system which identifies ethno-sectarian purity as a socially constructed and imagined set of relationships. Preserving the capacity to control the propaganda of ethno-sectarian belonging is facilitated through spreading the myth that the 'other' community is to be feared. Ensuring that sectarianised places remain will continue to be achieved through endorsing the morality of cultural and political sectarianism.

Conclusion

Despite the cessation of most paramilitary violence in Northern Ireland, we are left with a situation where the historical creation of territorial division and rigid ethno-sectarian communities means that fear and mistrust still frame the desire to create communal separation. Without doubt, residential segregation still regulates ethno-sectarian animosity through complex spatial devices. More importantly, the capacity to reconstruct identity and political meaning is obviated by political actors who mobilise fear in order to strengthen unidimensional classifications of political belonging. Community based self-representation assumes the form of a mythic reiteration of purity and self-preservation. As such, the potential to create cross-community understandings of fear is, in terms of politics, marginalised by wider ethno-sectarian readings.

As the chapter has also shown, the construction of ethno-sectarian landscapes is influential, but does not convert everyone who lives in such places into accepting homogenous senses of belonging and affiliation. Many people who live in highly segregated communities do not subscribe to the unidimensional logic that their dreads and fears are sourced merely from elements that exist outside of their 'own' community. Yet this does not mean that such people are completely against the dominant political representations that exist within their own community. Instead, it could be argued that highly segregated communities contain diverse populations that either reject, partly reject/accept or accept symbolic representations and discursive hegemonies that are tied to ethno-sectarianised discourses.

In critiquing the immutability of ethno-sectarian boundaries it is argued that low levels of social interaction between ethno-sectarian communities does not necessarily mean that ethno-sectarian polarisation is as rigid as may be assumed. But intra-community heterogeneity lacks the capacity to de-territorialise Northern Irish society toward more agreed and agreeable forms of political ownership. Sadly, fear and mistrust undermine consensus-building and a more extensive understanding that harm has been caused not only within but more importantly between communities.

Bibliography

Anderson, J. and Shuttleworth, I. (1998), 'Sectarian Demography, Territoriality and Political Development in Northern Ireland', *Political Geography* 17:2, 187–208.

Aughey, A. (2005), *The Politics of Northern Ireland: Beyond the Belfast Agreement* (London: Routledge).

Boal, F. (1969), 'Territoriality on the Shankill-Falls Divide, Belfast', *Irish Geography* 6, 130–50.

Boal, F. (1976), 'Ethnic Residential Segregation', in D. Herbert and R. Johnston (eds), *Social Areas in Cities* (Chichester: Wiley).

Boal, F. (2000), *Ethnicity and Housing* (Aldershot: Avebury).

Burton, F. (1978), *The Politics of Legitimacy: Struggles in a Belfast community* (London: Routledge).

Douglas, N. and Shirlow, P. (1998), 'People in Conflict in Place: The case of Northern Ireland', *Political Geography* 17:2, 125–8.

Downey, D. (2000), *The Guilt of Today* (Athlone: Red Line Books).

Feldman, A. (1991), *Formations of Violence: The narrative of the body and political terror in Northern Ireland* (Chicago, IL: University of Chicago Press).

Gold, J. and Revill, G. (2003), 'Exploring Landscapes of Fear', *Capital and Class* 80, 27–50.

Jarman, N. (1998), *Material Conflicts: Parades and visual displays in Northern Ireland* (London: Berg Publishing).

Shirlow, P. (2001), 'The Geography of Fear in Belfast', *Peace Review* 43, 12–28.

Shirlow, P. (2003), 'Ethno-sectarianism and the Reproduction of Fear in Belfast', *Capital and Class* 80, 77–94.

Shirlow, P. and Murtagh, B. (2006), *Belfast: Segregation, violence and the city* (London: Pluto Press).

Shirlow, P. and Pain, R. (2003), 'The Geographies and Politics of Fear', *Capital and Class* 80, 15–26.

SECTION 5

Fear, Resistance and Hope

This collection has so far focused largely upon fear, yet any accounts of fear are partial if fear is all they recognise and make space for. As we suggested in Chapter 1, the winding route the book has taken to disrupt and reconfigure the commonly employed hierarchical scaffold of geopolitical and everyday fears has involved analysing politics, power, danger and damage, but also encountering hopes, dreams and the road to repair. Indeed, as we have argued, fear and hope are not two separate emotions (as emotions are never singular, in experience or constitution) but sides of the same coin. We do not encounter one without the other. Both hope and fear – or fear/hope as one powerful emotional force – are politically useful, and powerfully bound into the everyday as well as more formal politics of resistance. Both hope and fear connect and move between the assemblage represented in Figure 1.1b. And just as fear and hope speak through geopolitical discourses and events, they are implicated in the processes of speaking back to them.

In this section, the coin is slowly flipped, so that the glints from its more hopeful side which we have seen throughout the book so far become more central to its analysis. In common with Section 4, the chapters here move further away from the 'war on terror', though the lessons they bring from other fears in other settings have much to inform future analysis of that particular set of global fears.

The section begins with resistance: resistance to fear, and resistance to expert and authoritative accounts of how fear is and should be. Rachel Pain develops a grounded and materialist approach to understanding fears for children's safety, suggesting that this is of use in analysing recent terror fears in the west. Like Katz in Section 1, she draws parallels between fear discourses surrounding both. Pain is critical of any expert fear metanarratives, preferring to turn to those under the spotlight for their own detailed analyses. Just as the idea of 'paranoid parenting' fails to take account of the reality of many western children's lives, or the sharp social and material divisions between them, the notion that people in the west are widely and irrationally fearful of terror needs debunking. Along with Alexander (in Section 1), Pain finds children to be knowledgeable and capable experts on risk in the places where they live. This account problematises simple notions of the movement of fear from macro political structures to everyday landscapes.

In her innovative chapter, Sarah Wright tackles hope head on. In her research on farmer livelihoods, she finds hope a more revealing concept than fear that links directly to social change. In very oppressive situations, particularly the global south, hope is always present as a radical response to fear that galvanizes social action. Moreover, through the farmers' engagement in social action, their subjectivities were recast as creative and resilient. Hope, Wright argues, is generated through practice, in this case collective action.

Finally, in an inspiring contribution, Kye Askins maps out the possibilities for what she calls 'a transformative geopolitics'. Her focus is perceptions and use of the English national parks amongst people from Asian and African Caribbean backgrounds. Through this study, she addresses the pressing issue of dealing with difference which has simmered through the earlier parts of the book. Arguing (like Hopkins and Smith in Section 3) that most mainstream approaches have failed, she suggests that negotiating between and across bodily and spatial difference can move us towards a transformative politics of place and identity. Again, difficult encounters laden with a negative history also offer opportunities for more positive change. We take up these issues of resistance, hope and transformation again in our Afterword.

Chapter 15

Whose Fear Is It Anyway?
Resisting Terror Fear and Fear
for Children

Rachel Pain

This chapter explores the insights that critical scholarship on the fear of crime has to offer for understanding fear of terrorism. I begin by observing that at least three widely circulating metanarratives about fear are identifiable in the west since 11 September 2001, intersecting popular culture, governance and academic scholarship. One is that terrorists are using fear as a weapon against western societies which is as effective as bombing itself. After the London bombings of 7 July 2005, the media suggested that our fear of terrorism was widespread (though not without congratulating Britons on their resilience and stiff upper lip, in comparison with supposed mass hysteria after 11 September 2001). Another is that governments are promoting and manipulating fear in order to sanction domestic and foreign political priorities (see Cowen and Gilbert, and Megoran, in this volume). A third is that the victims of the 'war on terror' are marginalised groups outside or within the west.

The most dominant and politically practicable idea – deployed by both neoliberal governments and their critics – is that people in western societies are now widely fearful of terrorism. However, such metanarratives contain crucial assumptions, not only about the movement of fear from political acts and discourses to ordinary people, but also about who is affected most by fear, and where. These need to be countered, as fear metanarratives have disturbing political implications which have not been considered in the recent spate of attention from critical scholars. As critical research on fear of crime has long maintained, people's emotions are not simply reactive to events, or this easily open to contagion, because they are already situated in complex individual and collective histories, places and everyday experiences (see Davidson et al. 2005; Alexander in this volume).

The chapter illustrates the danger of over-simplifying the impact of the war on terror by drawing parallels between the new supposed terror fear and fear for children's outdoor safety. Stranger danger for children is a longer-standing western concern in which certain metanarratives of prevention and protection (such as 'paranoid parenting') also become privileged at the expense of textured understandings of emotions in the everyday lives of those who are marginalised.[1] I use recent research about risk and fear from children's perspectives to illustrate the difficulties inherent in making remote assumptions about the fears of others; and to promote the need to listen to the narratives, as well as recognise the resistances and actions, of those concerned. For both terror fear and fear for children, I suggest that caution must be exercised in the naming, knowing, placing and privileging of certain fears rather than others.

Whose Fear Is It Anyway?

I begin by questioning the current emphasis on the 'war on terror' in debates around fear, even though this 'war' is an increasingly central subject of academic as well as popular interest. This emphasis should be open to question rather than taken for granted for at least four reasons.

First, in practical terms, there is surprisingly little in-depth research suggesting how terrorist events affect fear among the wider population. Their impact is presumed rather than demonstrated. There is, to be sure, evidence of long-term trauma for those directly or closely affected, and there was evidence of short-term anxiety among those using public transport in London in 2005. But beyond the first few weeks after these incidents – and I am speaking here of western countries where terrorism is rare – how intensely people in general feel fearful as a result of terrorist incidents, how it affects the way we go about our everyday lives, and how serious it is in comparison with other everyday concerns is largely unknown.

Second, speculating about these fears is conceptually complex, as it assumes that we know how fear works at a collective level. While there are simple theories of transmission and more complex theories of affective contagion, the truth is we do not know how fear may have diffused socially and spatially after recent incidents. These questions also connect to the intent of those who spread fear – both the terrorists in their pronouncement that 'Britain is now burning with fear, terror and panic in its northern, southern, eastern and western quarters',[2] and the ways in which British, US and other governments have used the idea of fear to justify political actions at home and abroad in response to similar incidents (see Cowen and Gilbert in this volume; Robin 2004; Sparke 2007; Gregory and Pred 2007).

Third, the relationship between terror and fear is likely to be highly dependent on context; at a mundane level how safe and protected we generally feel, and at a more critical level what sort of global postcolonial relations we have with other

---

1   Katz (in this volume) also draws parallels between terror fear and parental fear. While she examines representational, commercial and policy forms of parental hypervigilance and homeland security anxieties, my focus here is on people's personal feelings and material experiences. This leads us to slightly different takes on the relationship between the state and the everyday.

2   From an internet statement of the Secret Organization of al-Qaeda in Europe, who claimed responsibility for the 7 July bombings.

nations and peoples (see Hopkins and Smith in this volume). Within Britain, there are socio-cultural gulfs between London and other regions which affect any scaling up of generalisation about how it might affect the wider population. And in particular places, the context and details of people's lives shape how they relate and respond to more visible incidents. As I will go on to argue in relation to children's fears, social marginality and social wellbeing are especially important axes here.

Fourthly, and following directly from this, discussions of fear and the 'war on terror' bring issues of positioning to the fore. Who can I, or anyone, speak for, given the complexities and gaps in knowledge listed above? Other chapters offer grounded insights into the significant fears of *specific* communities within western populations (see Hopkins and Smith on Muslim communities, and Noble and Poynting on migrants in this volume). For many of us, these are the 'new' global fears which seem most urgent, and as these authors emphasise, they are not so new.

These difficulties in evaluating terror fears reflect a wider theme of this chapter: that of problematising expert knowledges about fear. The way in which fear has rapidly been cast in academic and popular discourses since 2001 can be questioned. For example, the fact that metanarratives of fear are manufactured by state and media is useful for legitimising policy, and questioning this is a useful line of policy critique, but the assumption of homogenously and equally fearful masses should not be assumed. We need to pay more careful attention to *whose* fear it is that we are talking about.

Fear of Crime: What Does Critical Analysis Tell Us?

In contrast to terror fear, fear about children in public space have received a considerable amount of attention. While other risks to children's safety have been explored (Roberts et al. 1995; Hillman et al. 1990), most of the literature has concentrated on fear of crime. In criminal justice and community safety policy-making, young people are almost exclusively defined as the perpetrators not the victims of crime, but a robust body of critical literature now challenges the associated givens about fear within mainstream discourses, often grounded in sensitive local fieldwork. Recent accounts of parents' fears for their children (Tucker 2003; Valentine 1997) have been joined by investigations of children's own fears (Anderson et al. 1994; Maguire and Shirlow 2004; Pain 2006; Tucker 2003). Such work explores the contradictory position of children, who are viewed in western societies as both vulnerable and as troublesome, as victims and perpetrators of disorder and crime (Aitken 2001; Scott et al. 1998; Valentine 1996, 1997). Poverty, race, gender and geography profoundly affect everyday experiences. Young people variously labelled marginalised or excluded – for example those from black and minority ethnic backgrounds, those who are homeless, excluded from school, suffering mental health problems or living in deprived neighbourhoods – are more likely to be victims of crime than offenders, and to be fearful as well as feared (Aitken 2001; MacIntyre 2000; Muncie 2003; Pain and Francis 2004).

The parallels with terror fears are clear: while they tend to be represented in the popular media as though they are distributed across a flat earth, the hidden impacts of terror in the west are sharply unequal and unjust; they are largely felt by othered bodies associated with threat (see Haldrup et al. in this volume). As we have discussed (Pain and Smith in this volume), there are questions around how we name, place, know and privilege fear raised in the critical literature on fear of crime which are also highly relevant to the global fears which this book begins to disentangle. This disentangling requires interrogating and questioning *whose* fear we are talking about, and emphasising the accounts of those who feel and are affected by it.

Contested Fears for Children's Outdoor Safety

To illustrate these points, I first make a critique, and then go on to show how these problems might be addressed, by discussing recent debates about children's outdoor safety in the western world. Below, I discuss 'paranoid parenting' as a widespread metanarrative in western societies. I then ground this critique using research conducted with children in northeast England. The comparison to terror fear is relevant as the research examined children's everyday experiences and understandings of fear in relation to widespread discourses about danger and childhood. I was interested in examining fear discourses beyond public panics and media frenzies about strangers or paedophiles, to include expert knowledges of fear created by academic and other professional commentators. The research found that these expert knowledges contrast sharply with children's own knowledges and material experiences of fear, danger and harm.

'Paranoid Parenting' as a Metanarrative

While there is now much work across the social sciences on children, risk and fear, I want to take as an example of an expert discourse the work of Frank Furedi, author of *Culture of Fear* (2002) and *Paranoid Parenting* (2001). I have chosen this focus because of the wider resonance of his arguments, and the speed with which they were taken up in the popular media. The tone of his work is reflective of a wider body of social critique about parents worrying excessively and irrationally about their children in the UK and USA (see Bennett 2001; Ferguson 2001; Freely and Bright 2001). I suggest here that these are primarily accounts from the more privileged (middle-class professionals in the UK) reflecting on the lives of other more privileged families. The metanarrative or grand story of fear produced is neither representative, nor specific in its focus.

Furedi's emphases in his work are on the general shift towards a risk society (2002), and the specific rise in fear-based 'paranoid parenting' which he sees as extremely damaging to children (2001). For Furedi, the widespread discourse of 'children at risk' is largely made up of imaginary fears. Parents are now bombarded with advice about bringing up children, covering nutrition, health, sleeping, play, stimulation and development, and physical and emotional safety from a wide range of dangers. Furedi argues that much of the advice is contestable, contradictory or simply unnecessary and damaging. These fears are manufactured by the state, scientists, childcare experts and businesses with products to market (see Katz in this volume): the media is complicit, but gives shape to our existing fears rather than creating them from scratch. Some of the *Paranoid Parenting* argument is convincing and well founded. However, I focus here on the aspect of the book that sparked much of the press interest after its release, parents' fears about children's safety from abuse. Furedi premises his critique on the assumption of a disproportionately low 'real' risk of child abuse, and the foolishness of parents who keep their children inside or drive them everywhere in response. He discusses the dangers of what he sees as constant supervision:

> There is now a consensus that parents' concern with their children's safety has acquired obsessive proportions ... the main focus of this obsession is 'stranger-danger' – a fear that has haunted British parents since the 1980s ... the greatest casualty of the totalitarian regime of safety is the development of children's potential. Playing, imagining and even getting into trouble has contributed to the sense of adventure that has helped society to forge ahead. (Furedi 2001, xiv–xv)

While it is presented as a common sense critique of expert-led discourses of fear, however, Furedi's argument replicates the same problem. It comprises another reactionary metanarrative or fear story which is based on partial evidence, and barely at all on the perspectives or experiences of the parents or children involved. In other words, it runs up against the problems of naming, placing, privileging and knowing fear that we have outlined (see Pain and Smith in this volume). Its main limitations are as follows.

First, a key theme running throughout Furedi's work is that abuse is primarily a cultural construct which has become normalised within a broader culture of fear (Furedi 2002). This is highly problematic given key evidence about the extent and nature of child abuse which is omitted from his research. Fear, too, is presented as a culturally produced, rather than something which is partly informed by experience. Here as in other rationalist accounts, risk and fear tend to be dichotomised, with 'risk' presented as given, real and material, and fear as immaterial, imagined, fluid, a state of mind 'in here' which has little connection to what is actually happening 'out there'.

Second, there are limitations to the assessment of risk which underpin Furedi's arguments about the irrationality of fear for children's safety outdoors. The sources of data that he draws on are extremely unrepresentative, especially given that most risk to children is not reported to the police or to official surveys. He talks simply of 'the gap between adult perceptions and the reality of the risks faced by children' (2001, 5), drawing together survey evidence showing that parents view the risk of child abduction and murder by a stranger to be far higher than it actually is. A wealth of in-depth local evidence which suggests much higher levels of broader outdoor risk to children such as assault and sexual harassment (for example Anderson et al. 1994; Aye-Maung 1995; Brown 1995; Hartless et al. 1995; Loader et al. 1998; Mori 2001) is not mentioned at all. Moreover, there is little appreciation of the circular relationships between fear and risk. For example, death rates for child pedestrians are decreasing in the UK, but this does not mean the roads are safer; it reflects an increasingly unsafe environment for pedestrians and consequent restrictions on children's exposure (see Hillman et al. 1990).

Thirdly, Furedi fails to address the uneven nature of risk. Class, income, age, ability, race, ethnicity, gender and geography all have profound bearing on this debate. Furedi's account is of a white, middle-class suburban childhood to be found especially in certain parts of the UK (especially in the southeast), where children are shuttled by car between structured activities and have little independent contact with public space. This is a quite narrow slice of contemporary UK society, given that 25 per cent of households nationally do not even own a car. Even within the bracket he describes, there are wide differences in transport patterns, play spaces and opportunities, values and practices of parents and children.

Fourthly, parents' agency, and in particular their ability to ignore, evaluate or resist expert advice and cultural fear is seldom mentioned. They are presented as media dupes who absorb what they read uncritically and without reference to their own personal contexts and experience. In fact, parents are immersed in and actively form and sustain powerful non-expert cultures through their beliefs and practices. These are not independent of 'expert' views (Furedi does hint at some interplay here), but are longstanding, deeply embedded and affect parents' choices as much or more than the expert advice. Parents also have their own knowledges about risk which feed into these knowledges, from their own childhood experiences of danger (see Pain 1997) and from first and second hand experience of the neighbourhoods they live in (Pain 2006).

Lastly, and most importantly, children are almost completely absent from Furedi's argument. They are presented as fiercely contested at material and discursive levels, abused through attempts to protect them from abuse, but as essentially passive victims in the whole theatre with nothing to contribute in terms of expertise. Furedi is right that children have a 'formidable capacity for resilience' (2001, 25), by which he means their ability to survive unscathed any slight risks that may exist with public space. But children are also knowers, negotiaters, agents and experts in their own safety, who often have detailed local knowledge about risk, the extent of which is unknown to adults, and they wield considerable influence over their parent's assessments of and responses to risk.

'Paranoid parenting', then, is not only an expert criticising experts (an irony which we might nonetheless be sympathetic to), but replicates the distinction implicit in much official advice on child safety between experts and those in the know (professional adults) and non-experts and the ignorant (parents and children). The reality of fear is far more complex. While I do not question that paranoia about children's safety grips certain people in certain places (and is aggressively promoted by manufacturers; see Katz in this volume), we have been too quick to accept this metanarrative, and slow to find out what is going on for people in their localities. The idea of terror fears has found the same popular and academic resonance, without attention to grounded knowledge. As the critical literature on fear of crime informs us, a more pressing task than castigating or supporting the lifestyle choices of middle-class parents is to reveal what is going on for the more marginalised.

Listening to Children: Everyday Fears and Everyday Risks

The research reported here was carried out in Gateshead, a town of around 190,000 people in northeast England. The inner wards of the town, where the study was carried out, are some of the most economically and socially deprived in the UK. Children aged between 10 and 16 years were sampled from schools and exclusion units. Through discussion groups, self-completed questionnaires, and participatory diagramming, they were asked about their experiences of crime and sub-criminal behaviour, and the impacts of their own and their parents' fear of crime. The research was designed in a way which allowed children to define the categories and risks which the research then collected information on. Detailed data were gathered about the places in which incidents occurred to children, and the places to which children and parents attached their fears (for more details on the methodology see Pain 2006).

The research showed that children in this area still have strong independent relationships with public space, as is still the case in many other parts of the UK (see also Matthews et al. 1998; Skelton 2001). Unsupervised use of public space was widespread throughout the age bracket. Walking to school alone, and playing outside after school, were common, and some children had very wide spatial ranges, especially boys and older girls. Most of the children, especially those aged 12 and under, reported that there were some places their parents warned them not to go to, and some heeded these warnings. But a significant number of others disobeyed them, often being conservative with the truth about their movements or using mobile phones to mislead parents about their location (see Pain et al. 2005).

Most relevant for the argument put forward here is the findings on experiences of danger, which challenge the cornerstone of the 'paranoid parenting' thesis that children are exposed to negligible danger outdoors and therefore that parents' fears are groundless. Children reported experiencing and witnessing high levels of crime, harassment and disorder (Table 15.1), rates which are similar to those reported to comparable research elsewhere (Anderson et al. 1994; Brown 1995; Hartless et al. 1995). These reported experiences make it difficult to dismiss children's fears or those of their parents (Table 15.1) as groundless or even disproportionate. Some of these experiences of danger may be minor, trivial, part of growing up, real learning experiences: many others involved physical or psychological harm.

One of the key paradoxes in the debate over fear and children's safety is that parents' fears tend to revolve around public space (although not exclusively), whereas children are subject to much higher levels of abuse in private spaces (Morgan and Zedner 1992; Stanko 1990; Walklate 1989). Bullying has been recognised more recently as a key aspect of children's experiences of violence and fear outdoors (Percy-Smith and Matthews 2001), and it is common in this research (see Table 15.1). However, many other outdoor incidents involved adults rather than other children.

Table 15.1   Reported victimisation in the last 12 months, and children's and parents' fear*

	Boys (%)	Girls (%)
Property crime in last 12 months		
My bike was stolen	11	6
My home was broken into	7	6
Something was stolen from me on the street	8	3
Something was stolen from me at school	12	11
Something was stolen from me on the Metro**	2	1
Something was stolen from me somewhere else	3	3
Violent crime in last 12 months		
I was bullied	28	42
Someone threatened to hurt me	24	21
I was hit	27	17
I was beaten up	10	4
I was attacked/harassed because of my race/religion***	37	20
I was glassed/bottled	3	2
I was stabbed	3	0
Harassment in last 12 months		
I was followed	24	25
Someone tried to get me to go somewhere with them	6	6
Someone flashed at me	7	6
Total number of victimisations reported	**n=808**	**n=814**
Children's fear of crime		
Worry when out and about because of crime	35	58
Find some places scary	48	60
Avoid certain places to avoid crime	35	40
Parents' fear of crime		
Parents worry about my safety	95	99
Parents tell me to avoid certain places	55	43

*   Sample = 1069.
**   Light rail transit system.
*** Of children in ethnic minority groups.

The research also compared the locations where crimes and other incidents had taken place, with the locations which children said that they and their parents feared. There was considerable congruence; on the whole, the places that children feared the most were the same places where they or their friends had had experiences of violence or harm. For the places which parents worried about their children being in, the association is not quite as strong, but still demonstrates a reasonably good awareness of the local places in which children are at risk. The analysis emphasises the importance of the local specificity of parents' and children's fears (Pain 2006). It is crucial that these local experiences and knowledges are made visible before we make judgments about the rationality of different patterns of parenting.

Reconciling Fear Metanarratives and the Everyday

What does this analysis of children's fear suggest for the new issues of fear that are emerging in the twenty-first century? I have suggested that there are problems in the common naming, placing, privileging and knowing of fear for/of children, just as we suggested for terror fear (see Pain and Smith in this volume). In both cases, there are widely appealing popular metanarratives which are circulating, which academic work sometimes seems to reproduce uncritically. There are competing metanarratives about fear for children's safety, of which 'paranoid parenting' in response to a negligible risk of abuse is the most popular. There are various stories about fear being circulated in relation to the 'war on terror', of which the most popular is that people *are* scared, which terrorists and governments may seek to create, manipulate or capitalise on. What critical research on the fear of crime has emphasised, and the example of fear for children illustrates, is that fear is an emotional response more strongly rooted in lives, local topographies and daily experiences of insecurity than representations of distant threats. Research underway on fear of terrorism is beginning to reveal this point (Pain et al. 2007). Fear was not dropped on Britain after the 7 July 2005 bombings, either by terrorists or politicians, to spread inexorably outwards from London. We know it was already there, embedded in and focused on complex places and identities, and local as well as international histories of risk and threat (see Hopkins and Smith in this volume). There is a need for more grounded analyses which pay attention to these social and political differences in fear, and their situation (see Pain 2007), and to downplay spectacular metanarratives about terror fear or children's fears and look closely at the spatial politics of fear: and especially at where fear is most destructive.

In both cases, too, important questions remain about the movement of fear – a point which is germane to understanding how global and everyday scales, events and experiences are linked. Sometimes fear moves very directly, arising from material experiences of risk and harm to children and their communities as I have argued here, or from increased racist violence in response to terrorist events (see elsewhere in this volume). Such findings may downplay, though do not cause us to wholly dismiss, the effects of contrasting media representations of danger on the fears of the wider public. We know that neither fear for children or fear about terror is simply passed down to people remotely from outside their own situation: we may suspect that the movement of fear is not a movement from 'up above' filtered down to be taken up in the same form by those 'down below' – but we need to further explore these processes to make sense of them. As many other chapters in this volume have vividly illustrated, these binaries of global/geopolitical/discursive versus local/everyday/lived are artificial and misleading, though replicated in much academic work on the politics of fear. I have intentionally moved between them in this chapter, and between theoretical ideas and experiences on the ground. The task is to unpick them, to get a closer sense of the connectivity and shifting relations between them.

Most importantly, fear-provoking discourses – and the practices and materialities that accompany them – are interpreted, resisted and subverted by people in different ways. Accounts of fear must allow for this, seeing hope and resistance not just as a possible alternative to fear, but as always already a part of fear, a way of managing fear and making lives liveable and a means of protesting inequalities (see Askins, and Wright, in this volume). People define and redefine their identities and places in the face of fear and negative discourses. Children constantly practice strategies for dealing with their own fear and negotiating with the fears of their parents. Participatory work such as Cahill et al.'s (2004) with black and minority ethnic young women provides a powerful example of the transformation of fear and insecurity through research, into more positive action to challenge stereotypes about them and their neighbourhood in the face of global change. Work on terror fear might follow this lead.

Bibliography

Aitken, S.C. (2001), *Geographies of Young People: The morally contested spaces of identity* (London: Routledge).

Anderson, S., Kinsey, R., Loader, I. and Smith, C. (1994), *Cautionary Tales: Young people, crime and policing in Edinburgh* (Aldershot: Avebury).

Aye-Maung, N. (1995), *Young People, Victimization and the Police*, Home Office Research Study No. 140 (London: HMSO).

Bennett, C. (2001), 'Protective Parents, Yes. But Paranoid?', *The Guardian*, 8 February.

Brown, S. (1995), 'Crime and Safety in Whose 'Community'? Age, Everyday Life, and Problems for Youth Policy', *Youth and Policy* 48, 27–48.

Cahill, C., Arenas, E., Contreras, J., Jiang, N., Rios-Moore, I. and Threatts, T. (2004), 'Speaking Back: Voices of young urban women of color. Using participatory action research to challenge and complicate representations of young women', in A. Harris (ed.), *All About the Girl: Culture, power, and identity* (New York: Routledge).

Davidson, J., Bondi, L. and Smith, M. (2005), *Emotional Geographies* (Ashgate: Aldershot).

Ferguson, G. (2001), 'Too Scared to be a Parent?', *The Scotsman*, 21 August.

Freely, M. and Bright, M. (2001), 'Stop being Paranoid, Britain's Parents Told', *The Observer*, 11 March.

Furedi, F. (2001), *Paranoid Parenting: Abandon your anxieties and be a good parent* (London: Penguin).

Furedi, F. (2002), *Culture of Fear: Risk taking and the morality of low expectation* (London: Cassell).

Gregory, D. and Pred, A. (2007), 'Introduction', in D. Gregory and A. Pred (eds). *Violent Geographies: Fear, terror, and political violence* (New York: Routledge).

Hartless, J.M., Ditton, J. Nair, G. and Phillips, P. (1995), 'More Sinned Against than Sinning: A study of young teenagers' experiences of crime', *British Journal of Criminology* 35:1, 114–33.

Hillman, M., Adams, J. and Whitelegg, J. (1990), *One False Move: A study of children's independent mobility* (London: Policy Studies Institute).

Loader, I., Girling, E. and Sparks, R. (1998), 'Narratives of Decline: Youth, dis/order and community in an English 'Middletown'', *British Journal of Criminology* 38:3, 388–403.

Maguire, S. and Shirlow, P. (2004), 'Shaping Childhood Risk in Post-Conflict Rural Northern Ireland', *Children's Geographies* 2:1, 69–82.

Matthews, H., Limb, M. and Percy-Smith, B. (1998), 'Changing Worlds: The micro-geographies of young teenagers', *Tijdschrift voor Economische en Sociale Geografie* 89:2, 193–202.

Morgan, J. and Zedner, L. (1992), *Child Victims: Crime, impact and criminal justice* (Oxford: Clarendon).

Mori (2001), *Youth Survey 2001* (London: Youth Justice Board).

Muncie, J. (2003), 'Youth, Risk and Victimization', in P. Davies, P. Francis and V. Jupp (eds), *Understanding Victimization* (Basingstoke: Macmillan).

Pain, R. (1997), 'Social Geographies of Women's Fear of Crime', *Transactions of the Institute of British Geographers* 22:2, 231–44.

Pain, R. (2006), 'Paranoid Parenting? Rematerialising Risk and Fear for Children', *Social and Cultural Geography* 7:2, 221–43.

Pain, R. (2007), 'Globalised Fear? Towards an Emotional Geopolitics', unpublished paper.

Pain, R. and Francis, P. (2004), 'Living with Crime: Spaces of risk for homeless young people', *Children's Geographies* 2:1, 95–110.

Pain, R., Grundy, S. and Gill, S. (2005), '"So Long as I Take my Mobile ...": Mobile phones, urban life and geographies of children's safety', *International Journal of Urban and Regional Research* 29:4, 814–30.

Pain, R., Panelli, R., Kindon, S and Little, J. (2007), 'Moments in Everyday/Distant Geopolitics: Young people's fears and hopes', unpublished paper.

Percy-Smith, B. and Matthews, H. (2001), 'Tyrannical Spaces: Young people, bullying and urban neighbourhoods', *Local Environment* 6:1, 49–63.

Roberts, H., Smith, S. and Bryce, C. (1995), *Children at Risk? Safety as a Social Value* (Buckingham: Open University Press).

Robin, C. (2004), *Fear: The history of a political idea* (Oxford: Oxford University Press)

Scott, S., Jackson, S. and Backet-Milburn, K. (1998), 'Swings and Roundabouts: Risk anxiety and the everyday worlds of children', *Sociology* 32:4, 689–705.

Skelton, T. (2001), '"Nothing to Do, Nowhere to Go?": Teenage girls and "public" space in the Rhondda Valleys, South Wales', in S.L. Holloway and G. Valentine (eds), *Children's Geographies: Playing, living, learning* (London: Routledge).

Sparke, M. (2007), 'Geopolitical Fears, Geoeconomic Hopes, and the Responsibilities of Geography', *Annals of the Association of American Geographers* 97:2, 338–49.

Stanko, E. (1990), *Everyday Violence: Women's and men's experience of personal danger* (London: Pandora).

Tucker, F. (2003), 'Sameness or Difference? Exploring Girls' Use of Recreational Spaces', *Children's Geographies* 1:1, 111–24.

Valentine, G. (1996), 'Angels and Devils: Moral landscapes of childhood', *Environment and Planning D: Society and Space* 14, 581–99.

Valentine, G. (1997), '"Oh Yes You Can" "Oh No You Can't": Children and parents' understanding of kids competence to negotiate public space safely', *Urban Geography* 17:3, 205–20.

Walklate, S. (1989), *Victimology* (London: Unwin Hyman).

Chapter 16

Practising Hope: Learning from Social Movement Strategies in the Philippines

Sarah Wright

Introduction

Hope and resilience are found in surprising places. Our world resounds with practices of possibility that persist in tenacious defiance of the oppressions that characterise so much of existence. It is to such defiant practices of hope that I turn in this chapter. In doing so, I draw inspiration not from the question of why and how people are manipulated and paralysed by fear but from the more elusive and possibly more important question, particularly for those involved in the work of social change, of why and how they are not. Why is it that in some situations of threat, poverty and violence there is evidence of an active and empowered response? The work of social movements throughout the world, and particularly in the Global South where stakes are high, reveals an attempt to meet fear with action and in doing so generate that most radical of responses: hope.

I discuss here the experiences of one such social movement from the Philippines called MASIPAG. MASIPAG, a network of small, mostly subsistence farmers, promotes discourses of empowerment and hope as a strategy for engaging farming families in sustainable agriculture. Network participants are encouraged to redefine themselves as active and hopeful (rather than passive and fearful) subjects. In doing so, these farmers bring hope into being through action.

Resisting fear cannot be associated only with meeting fear head-on. It also needs to be recast as the generation of hope, of creating empowered subjects and of generating alternative realities that make fear, if not redundant, no longer central to the way that people live their lives. Subsistence farmers in the Philippines face hunger, military and paramilitary violence and landlessness. While fear is a very real part of their lives, there is considerable room for transgression in the imagination of alternatives. In this case, farmers create alternative networks of farmer-bred seed and organic agriculture that stress the subjectivity of farmers in ways that reconstruct them not as victims, or rather not *only* as victims, but build upon the creativity and resilience of farmers.

What emerges is a politics of hope. Hope is bound up with action and is generated through practice. As small farmers reinvent themselves as fully formed, active agents able to imagine and bring into being new futures, they are working with a hope that exists in the present with its roots in empowerment and the articulation of alternatives. It is not premised on the absence of fear and does not exist in reaction against fear. Rather, hope draws on connection and on the work of creating and recreating solidarities through the very act of living.

In this chapter, I parallel the practice of MASIPAG and focus on hope rather than fear. As I write, it is my aim to allow hope to push fear aside, to displace and marginalise it. It is, admittedly, a rather cheeky move in a volume that has fear as its focus. Yet, by sapping the shibboleth of fear, watching it fade (though not disappear), it *is* possible to shed light on its nature. The inspiration that can come from a study of social movements is precisely that fear need not be central to life, that it can be superseded by hopeful practices that can, in turn, bring hope.

What is this thing called hope?

> Hope can be what sustains us in the face of despair, and yet it is not simply the desire for things to come, or the betterment of life. It is the drive or energy that embeds us in the world – in the ecology of life, ethics and politics. (Zournazi 2002, 14–15)

Hope and fear are part of an emotional complex that weaves through our lives and mediates our experience. The generation and manipulation of these emotions are strongly bound up with political and economic life. While motifs of fear abound in the political landscape, influencing everything from immigration policies (Green 2004; Hage 2003; Lloyd et al. 2006) to planning and infrastructure (Day 2006; Siebel and Wehrheim 2006), those associated with hope are less prevalent. Hope, as a lure or unfulfillable (in the present at least) fantasy has tended to be mobilised in support of consumption and religion. The endless search for glossy hair, translucent skin and eternal life has provided ample grist for both secular and religious outreach. For this reason, some philosophers have tended to be sceptical of concepts of hope (Fromm 1968; Zournazi and Hage 2002). They see hope as associated with a suspension of action in which attention to the joys and trials of everyday life are subsumed in favour of a distant goal either in this life (in terms of social mobility in a capitalist sense) or beyond (in ideas of the afterlife in a religious one). Hope then, comes to be associated with stasis, deferred joy, and the status quo. Yet the activities of social movements and the tenacious existence of hope amid despair belies moves to dismiss hope in its entirety.

In response to this dilemma, Ghassan Hage introduces a concept of 'hope on the side of life' (Hage 2003; see also Pontamianou 1997; Wise 2005). Hage stresses the distance between 'hope on the side of life' and capitalist aspirations that collapse hope and consumption. For Hage, hope on the side of life is found in the present, in being. Based on what he calls an 'ethics of joy,' it is drawn from an appreciation of positive changes in existence, 'the capacity to experience life as a transition and movement in one's own state of being' (Zournazi and Hage 2002, 153). Here, hope is dynamic and embodied. It is drawn from the appreciation of a capacity to act and relate to others.

The association of hope with movement is supported by work in psychology. Research by Snyder (1994; 2000) and Feldman and Snyder (2005) has linked hope to two interrelated concepts: agency and pathways. Feldman and Snyder use a study of 139 college students to interrogate the meaning of hope and to understand where and why it occurs. They call this a theory of hope and find that hope – made up of the perception of pathways and the sense of an ability to move along them – lies at the center of the meaning construct itself.

For Feldman and Snyder, a pathway is the perceived capacity of a person to produce a route that they can follow to realise their aspirations. This doesn't mean that such pathways need to be concrete and immediately realisable. Indeed, it is the perception that pathways exist rather than their actual existence that lies at the crux of the concept. There needs to be a 'perception that effective pathways could be charted if needed and so desired' (Feldman and Snyder 2005, 406).

The second component of hope theory is the notion of agency or 'agentic thinking' which is defined as 'the thoughts that people have regarding their ability to begin and continue on selected pathways toward those goals' (Snyder et al. 1999, 407). It is through a sense that people can or could move along a pathway, through the sense of potential agency, that they become motivated to instigate and maintain such movement. The two components are, of course interrelated. Hope, then, is the sense of having a pathway and feeling that one could move along it if one so chose.

In late capitalism, the existence and the very meaning of both agency and pathways are often manipulated. As Mary Zournazi (2002) points out, our sense of agency is funneled into consumption while our sense of humanity is often based on aspirations of security tied to economic success. In turn, the existence of credible alternative pathways is denied. The theory of hope provides a way of looking at life meaning that has the potential to illuminate the emptiness of the capitalist chimera in providing pathways and a sense of agency built on consumption.

I will now turn to the experiences of the MASIPAG network in the Philippines and use the dual lens of agency and pathways to illuminate their activities as they build an alternative politics of hope. In doing so, I aim to add depth to a theory of hope moving beyond understanding hope in terms of apolitical goal-setting and drawing out the ways that social movements bring hope into being through practice. I draw on insights based on a period of 18 months participant observation that I undertook with the network and a series of 60 interviews with farmers in two farming communities, one in Southern Luzon and one on Panay in the Philippines.

Introducing MASIPAG

MASIPAG is a network involving 30,000 farmers, organisations and scientists based in the Philippines. The network originated in the early days of the green revolution when the negative aspects of the so-called 'miracle varieties' of high-yielding seeds (known as HYVs or high-yielding varieties) and the accompanying packages of pesticides, fertilisers and credit were first coming to light. A gathering of farmers and scientists in Los Baños in the Philippines was convened to study the impacts of the green revolution. The gathering found problems of indebtedness, health and environmental pollution, soil depletion and increased pests and diseases that often wiped out any gains associated with high yields. It also found that the green revolution's approach to knowledge had crucially shifted agency away from small farmers to external 'experts'. Farmers were recast as passive receivers of the knowledge, expertise and 'solutions' generated by scientists in research institutes and corporations. MASIPAG emerged in response to these problems with a central focus on promoting farmers as active agents and experts in their own right.

MASIPAG is an acronym for *Magsasaka at Siyemtipiko para ang Pagunlad ng Agrikultura* or Farmer-Scientist Partnership for Development. The word *masipag* means industrious in Tagalog. The acronym is meant to conjure a sense of labour and of creativity reflecting the stress the organisation puts on farmers as productive, innovative and hardworking. The central work of the organisation is the promotion and development of locally adapted, sustainable farming systems using farmer-bred and farmer-selected seeds. It does this through a decentralised structure based on farmer groups and farmer-to-farmer outreach supported by three regional offices, one for each of the major regions of the Philippines (Luzon, Visayas and Mindanao), with a national secretariat in Los Baños. Each region has its own board, secretariat and internal structure.

Creating Active Subjects (Agency)

As a central part of the network's focus, the concept of 'farmer empowerment' has multiple aspects. In an economic sense, farmer empowerment means increasing the control of farmers over their economic circumstances by 'breaking the chains of economic dependence'. Dependence here refers to the cycle of indebtedness that many farmers face as they borrow money to buy farm inputs and then need to sell rice to recoup costs, effectively tying them to a capitalist, corporatised agriculture. For the network, though, while economic independence is about escaping indebtedness and, in turn, potential landlessness, it is also, crucially, about autonomy. If farmers are limited to purchasing the seeds and inputs on offer from corporations and government agencies, using 'approved' methods of production, and are then compelled to sell rice in the market at prices set by intermediaries, their possibility of having some sense of control and direction over their lives is severely compromised.

Control and direction are also associated with the question of knowledge and expertise. The network promotes farmer to farmer knowledge exchange as a way to support them in developing their own skills. In terms of seed varieties, MASIPAG farmers are encouraged to breed and select locally adapted varieties and to recover traditional seed varieties that they may then use as a basis for further breeding. No easy 'solution' is offered. One MASIPAG farmer explains: 'MASIPAG is an open laboratory without walls. It is why I am in MASIPAG. I love to experiment, to improve.'

Trial farms are set up in rural communities and managed by local farmers who thereby become the leaders of the recovery and conservation programme. Through this mechanism, the most promising varieties for a particular location are selected and subsequently bred in order to obtain new rice varieties that will be suitable for local mass production. This is in contrast to the approach of most government and company-based extension workers in which the experimentation is done offsite and farmers are presented with a *fait accompli*.

The spirit of experimentation has contributed to the ongoing enthusiasm about MASIPAG. The need for validation builds a more meaningful partnership and empowers farmers. It also helps ward off problems associated with farmers that may have only partially implemented the system, and/or do it without a full understanding of the process. If concepts of the green revolution, technocentric and capitalist oriented farming practices draw knowledge producing power away from farmers and communities, the work of MASIPAG and other organisers tries to draw it back by emphasising farmer capability. As one woman farmer from a small village in the mountains behind Iloilo in the Visayas says:

> We would be nothing without it. It makes us feel informed and empowered. Before, I felt .. I felt that I couldn't do anything. We just had to do what we were told [laughs]. We have had access to new information, met different people and learned so much.

The sense that farmers can take control of their own lives is achieved through hard work. There is no immediate and easy state of hopefulness and agency. Rather, it is generated through practice, the practice of planning, of working long hours in the hot sun, of harvest, of subsistence and of hard decisions. In this sense, the choice of MASIPAG as an acronym meaning industrious is no accident. It is in and through action that hope is generated (Unger 2001). In focusing on farmer empowerment, the network is crucially trying to recognise and create farmers as active subjects on multiple scales, in the field, in the home, the village and beyond. Through practice, farmers in the network engage in what Snyder would call agentic thinking – a sense that the fear, despair and problems that they face in their daily life can be met – and most importantly, that the farming families themselves hold solutions to these problems.

Pathways

A second important element here is the generation of alternatives and the sense that there are other ways that farmers can relate to their labour, their communities and knowledge. This speaks to the issue of pathways. The construction or imagination of pathways is associated with the idea that there are different routes that can be taken and that the farmers themselves can be part of imagining them. Breeding new varieties in ways that empower and respect farmers and developing locally adapted farming systems that encourage economic, social and ecological sustainability is central to the creation of new imaginaries and new futures. The world is not changed for them, but by them.

MASIPAG's focus is clearly on the articulation of alternatives, on building pathways that diverge from those associated with a top-down, corporatised and exploitative agriculture. The network talks of *in-situ* conservation, for example, where the genetic resources are bred and maintained on the farms of the peasants themselves in contrast to centralised, *ex-situ* seed banks (like that of the International Rice Research Institute or IRRI based in Los Baños). Indeed the network itself is ambivalent about the term 'alternatives' pointing out that they are not 'alternative' but original, with a lineage of thousands of years of successful diversified practice, and of continual improvement and experimentation.

In articulating these pathways, and in asserting themselves as 'central,' rather than 'alternative,' MASIPAG farmers are not going back to a traditional or somehow authentic agriculture of the past. Rather, they have the sense they are forging new pathways, albeit ones that have deep historical roots. Their approach is thought of as new, advanced and scientific by its advocates who relegate IRRI and the green revolution to the 'bad old days.' Farmers will talk of how some others in the community are 'yet' to adopt the new (i.e. the organic) techniques or how they themselves have 'yet' to trial the MASIPAG and 'new' traditional seeds such as Red Burong to check their performance. In fact, most farmers see their contribution to the development of the community as moving beyond the chemically dependent ways of their parents to an innovative agriculture that is healthier and more sustainable both environmentally and financially for them and the village as a whole.

And these are viable systems. In the community of Puno, for example, one village within which the MASIPAG network is active, 24 of 78 families have adopted this approach. People see themselves as more healthy and food secure than in the past with more control over their lives and a brighter future. It is not that the farmer-bred varieties are necessarily more high-yielding than the HYVs but that they are more hardy and perform better without inputs. Throughout the Philippines, the 30,000 farming families involved in the network have similar experiences.

One farmer from the Puno area, Demy Alipao, explained his experiences:

My life used to be full of worry and despair. We had problems with health. With chemicals I noticed the effect on my health. Especially during the spraying. If I inhaled the chemicals, I felt dizzy. The problem was also that we felt trapped. If there would be a sickness in the family we would have no money to buy medicines. We would have to go into debt. But we couldn't see any other way. MASIPAG is very good for my family. Our expenses are less because we do not have to buy fertilizer or chemicals to grow the plants. The money that would have gone to chemicals is used on my allowance going to college. Plus we have been able to save money for things that are needed in the house. Also, the health of our whole family has improved since we started using MASIPAG. We feel more hopeful. We work hard but we do not feel so trapped. Being industrious and being helpful to each member of the family makes the work easier. In order to overcome our problems, we need a strengthened heart, patience, and to face the trials in our life and struggle to overcome them.

The despair that Demy felt was associated not only with the direct problems of health and poverty but significantly with the feeling of being trapped, of the perceived lack of pathways outside the future offered by industrial agriculture (understood as one of ill-health and indebtedness). Although the family's pesticide use had yet to create a health emergency or overwhelming indebtedness, he saw these as inevitable outcomes of the path they were on. The future comprised just one road, homogenous and threatening. Through the family's involvement in the network, however, the possibility of multiple pathways was suggested. The family could imagine the future within which education and health were realisable, and gained a sense that with a strengthened heart, patience and hard work they would be able to reach it. The threats associated with poverty were diminished and decentred. Hope was generated. The previously foreclosed future burst open.

An Emerging Politics of Hope

The experience of social movements in the Philippines reveals some important insights that add depth to the theory of hope as elucidated by Snyder and his colleagues. In particular, refocusing on the MASIPAG experience highlights the importance of the power relations and politics associated with the generation of hope, and suggest the need for a collective, rather than purely individual, understanding of agency and pathways.

In Snyder's theory of hope, hope is understood through a lens of individuality. This is unsurprising given that his work comes from psychology, a tradition that has tended to emphasise the individual. The experience of MASIPAG shows, however, that relationships and connections are of crucial importance in building hope. Indeed, both 'agentic thinking' and pathways can usefully be understood in a collective or at least a connected sense. In many ways, what nourishes farmers, what allows them to see these alternative pathways as viable, is a sense of collective effort. While some members of the group are able to create a pathway seemingly out of thin air, the sustainability of the effort and its applicability to the broader community is associated with joint effort – with connection.

This is illustrated by the sentiment expressed by many farmers that being involved with the organisation has allowed them to move away from the alienating individualistic approach associated with capitalist agriculture. One farmer, Lazaro Serag, gives an example:

> *Bayanihan* or as we call it *dagyaw* in Karay'a is the name of a Filipino tradition. It is when people help each other without expecting money or anything in return. For example, we would get together to harvest someone's farm and then another time move on to someone else's. It is a joint effort. This tradition began not to be practised in the time of IRRI because people began asking what they could get from their neighbour. The attitudes changed. But now it is coming back again. When using MASIPAG, it makes the communication closer and we share more as a community. When we discover a problem we share it together and when we find something good we share this with others also.

The sense of connection, then, of mutual effort and of sharing, is important. Of course, the connection is not something that can be forced and does not imply an homogeneity of desire. Rather, it is associated with a sense of overlapping visions and the building of solidarities. The network stresses diversity, within agricultural systems, for seeds, cultures and possibilities. This is a diversity understood always in the context of connection whether these be the connections between diverse species in ecological communities, the connections between on-farm diversity and families' food needs, the connections within and between communities, or throughout the movement. Hope itself is found in the creation and sustenance of bridges, of relationships and belongings associated with multiple convergences across, but not negating, difference.

The importance of looking beyond hope as an individual effort is also underpinned by the role of organisations in supporting farming families and encouraging them to imagine different pathways. MASIPAG itself is a network made up of smaller farmers' organisations, collectives and associations. In fact, farmers must organise themselves into a group before they can become official members of MASIPAG. This means all farmers that undertake the shift to farmer-bred seeds and organic agriculture – a huge leap given the vulnerabilities within which these farmers live – have some kind of connection and support at the village level. In many instances, organisations are created to facilitate the villagers coming together and deciding upon priorities for action (examples of outcomes include a cooperative store, an income generation project, a collective work day and a mini-hydro). Organisations are also ways that communication and training can be managed and resources distributed. Whether formal or informal, the organisations are a coming together within which individuals' efforts can be supported and their goals situated within a broader landscape of connection and change.

As the network members imagine pathways and generate a sense of diverse possibilities, individuals are able to associate with a social and political project that takes them beyond themselves. Situating themselves within a set of dilemmas and alternatives allows the members of the network to place themselves in an extended tapestry of connection and belonging (Zournazi 2002). Crucially, this belonging is not imagined out of a fear of others and does not have exclusion as its basis. Instead it is drawn from the hard work of negotiated solutions. It is the villagers themselves who come together to analyse the issues they face in their lives and envisage, plan for and implement solutions.

The second point raised by the MASIPAG experience relates to the political nature of hope. Hope is both generated by and generates action. While psychologists tend to divorce this from politics, it is clear that the absence or presence of pathways can be suggested or manipulated for political ends. Hage (2003) points out that the distribution of hope and the form that hope takes within a society is unequal. The success of right-wing political movements such as associated with Thatcher in Britain and Howard in Australia is due in part, according to Hage, to their ability to deploy hope in ways that leave voters unwilling to share the shreds of hope they hold and unable to look elsewhere for its generation. In the west, societal hope is sparse and it is in part the 'deficit of hope' that leads citizens to be less likely to extend hope to asylum seekers and (more) marginalised peoples. This is a hope associated with fear with the promise of progress based on the exclusion of others.

It becomes clear that the pathways offered by a hope based on fear are no pathways at all. The absence of agency, or the channelling of agency into choice in the marketplace, economic definitions of the self or the stasis of delayed action, is hidden beneath the lure of an easy, if disempowered, sense of movement generated by the oppression of others. Yet MASIPAG shows a different kind of hope, associated with different kinds of pathways. This is hope augmented, rather than diminished, through sharing and connection. In the case of MASIPAG, the insistence that farmers can and do have the solutions and the means to sustain themselves and their families, that they don't need to rely on external scientists or salespeople associated with chemical companies who hawk the questionable offerings of capitalism, is a fundamental and radical move.

Hope then is both an act of living and an act of politics. It is also a call to action. Joining with other Asian social movements to protest the World Trade Organisation at the 6th Ministerial in Hong Kong in December 2005, MASIPAG stood with a broad cross-sectoral coalition under the banner of 'Globalise struggle, globalise hope!' (see Plate 16.1). In doing so, they were asserting the presence of diverse futures, insisting upon the agency of the marginalised in the form of struggle, on the possibility of connections through globalisation and on the existence of hope as the promise and inspirer of change.

Plate 16.1   Social movements protest the WTO at the 6th Ministerial meeting in Hong Kong, 2005

Source: Asian Peasants Coalition.

The call to globalise hope in no way negates the realities of threat and oppression or indeed the existence of fear. Increased militarisation has seen an estimated 57 farmer leaders murdered in the Philippines in extra-judicial killings since the current president took power in 2001 (Visaya and Rivera 2006), while poverty, landlessness and marginalisation all permeate every day life for small farmers. It is clear that this coalition of farmers has more than a cursory familiarity with violence of many kinds. Yet they choose to unite under a banner of globalised hope. In doing so they insist that in any and every moment hope, rather than fear, should be fore-grounded. Each moment contains within it multiple pathways with multiple pasts and futures, connected to the pasts and futures of others. Fear is allowed to recede, its power diminished simply because it is not fed. Through a politics of hope such hopeful moments run together to create a state of open-ended becoming.

It is this lead that I have followed as I have refocused my exploration of fear onto practices of hope. Certainly, I could have discussed in detail the ways in which hope and a politics of possibility have not been achieved, where farmers have not joined the network, where they live in fear of poverty and violence, or chronicled the ways that the network has failed to live up to its democratic and radically anti-oppressive goals. But this has not been my intention. Rather in recognition of the hope that *is* generated, the social transforations that *are* practised and the anti-oppressive politics that *are* enacted I have stubbornly and joyfully tried to cultivate myself as a 'theorist of possibility' (Gibson-Graham 2006, xxviii) engaged in writing and living hope.

Understood as an act of living it becomes less surprising that hope may be found in surprising places. This is because hope has nothing to do with an absence of fear or an absence of threat. Neither does, or can, hope replace fear. Rather, there is a complexity associated with the relationship between hope and fear, a dynamic relationship within which hope and fear exist together in tension. Hope is an ongoing project, a journey. The generation of hope – meeting fear with action – is an effort of will, a political strategy and an important step in imagining and realising new futures.

Bibliography

Day, K. (2006), 'Being Feared: Masculinity and race in public space', *Environment and Planning A* 38:3, 569–86.

Feldman, D. and Snyder, C.R. (2005), 'Hope and the Meaningful Life: Theoretical and empirical associations between goal-directed thinking and life meaning', *Journal of Social and Clinical Psychology* 24:3, 401–21.

Fromm, E. (1968), *The Revolution of Hope: Towards a humanized technology* (New York: Harper and Row).

Gibson-Graham, J.K. (2006), *A Postcapitalist Politics* (Minneapolis, MN: University of Minnesota Press).

Green, L. (2004), 'Bordering on the Inconceivable: The Pacific solution, the migration zone, and "Australia's 9/11"', *Australian Journal of Communication* 31:1, 19–36.

Hage, G. (2003), *Against Paranoid Nationalism: Searching for hope in a shrinking society* (Annandale, NSW: Pluto Press).

Lloyd, K., Suchet-Pearson, S. and Wright, S. (2007), 'Decentring Fortress Australia: Borderland geographies as relational spaces', in B. Mitchell, S. Baum, P. O'Neill, and P. McGuirk (eds), *Proceedings of the ARCRNSISS Methodology, Tools and Techniques and Spatial Theory Paradigm Forums Workshop*, University of Newcastle, Australia, 15–17 June 2005 (Melbourne, Vic.: RMIT Publishing) Available at http://search.informit.com.au/documentSummary;dn=774646553835911;res=E-LIBRARY.

Pontamianou, A. (1997), Hope: A shield in the economy of borderline states (London: Routledge).

Siebel, W. and Wehrheim, J. (2006), 'Security and the Urban Public Sphere', *German Policy Studies* 3:2, 19–46.

Snyder, C.R. (1994), *The Psychology of Hope: You can get there from here* (New York: Free Press).

Snyder, C.R. (2000), 'Hypothesis: There is hope', in C. R. Snyder (ed.), *Handbook of Hope: Theory, research and applications* (Orlando, FLA: Academic Press).

Snyder, C.R., Michael, S.T., and Cheavens, J.S. (1999), 'Hope as a Psychotherapeutic Foundation of Nonspeciific Factors, Placebos and Expectancies', in M.A. Huble, B. Duncan and S. Miller (eds), *Heart and Soul of Change* (Washington, DC: APA).

Unger, R. and Muralidharan, S. (2001), 'Some Heresies of Development: An interview with Roberto Unger', *Frontline: India's National Magazine* 18, 18.

Visaya, V. and Rivera, B. (2006), 'Another Farmer-Leader Killed', *Philippine Daily Inquirer*, 28 November, A1.

Wise, A. (2005), 'Hope and Belonging in a Multicultural Suburb', *Journal of Intercultural Studies* 26:1–2, 171–86.

Zournazi, M. (2002), *Hope: New philosophies for change* (New York: Routledge).

Zournazi, M. and Hage, G. (2002), '"On the Side of Life" – Joy and the Capacity of Being: A conversation with Ghassan Hage', in M. Zournazi (ed.), *Hope: New Philosophies for change* (New York: Routledge).

Chapter 17

(Re)negotiations:
Towards a Transformative Geopolitics
of Fear and Otherness

Kye Askins

While I do want to underscore that I do embrace colour-blindness as a legitimate hope for the future, I worry that we tend to enshrine the notion with a kind of utopianism whose naivety will assure its elusiveness.

(Williams 1997, 2)

… and while no one can argue that black self-help is not a fine thing, I wonder about its meaning when it is used as an injunction that black concerns be severed from the ethical question of how we as a society operate.

(Williams 1997, 66)

Let me start with some explanation, the story behind this chapter, if you will. I am drawing here on the theoretical and empirical work undertaken for my PhD thesis, which explored perceptions and use of the English national parks amongst people from Asian and African Caribbean backgrounds. As such, my narrative is situated: the empirical research was undertaken in the cities of Sheffield and Middlesbrough (in the north of England), and the Peak District and North York Moors national parks, between 2001 and 2004. (And I am indebted to the hundreds of individuals who gave me their time and shared their experiences and thoughts.) However, the issues discussed here may be useful more widely when considering the geopolitics of fear in everyday lives. I should also explain that, as part of the funding of the research, I was required to write policy recommendations for the national park authorities. I want to speak to both theoretical and policy concerns because I believe there is an ethical duty to address research to intervention – very carefully. Specific policy is not detailed here,[1] rather I touch on an overarching ideology for policy direction.

And let me be upfront – my focus is on exploring how negotiating between and across bodily and spatial difference can move us towards a transformative politics of place and identity. I am arguing that we need honest engagements with the complex ways in which otherness and fear play out in the everyday

---

1   The policy document that came out of the research is available at http://www.visitnorthyourkshiremoors.uk/content.php?nID=675.

– alongside an understanding that encounters between different groups draw upon, reiterate but also have *the potential to shift* how we see and how we feel about our others. I want to emphasise that these encounters occur *in place*, and are embedded in histories of encounters re-produced through local, national and international discourses. But also that it is through a candid reckoning with fear, exclusion, and all those negative constructions that have very real material consequences, that we may move to a more radical openness offering possibilities for other emotions – empathy, care, even love – to become major players in our encounters with difference. However, I would warn that any 'pronouncements' are likely to be highly contested, fragile arrangements. That is, the content of this chapter surrounds the evolution of an inclusive, progressive version of visible communities in the English countryside (and England more broadly), and how we may encapsulate such fluid understandings of fear, identity and spatial in/ exclusion within policy-making – while the tone is one of ongoing (re)visioning rather than a definitive account.

I also need to explain my use of the term 'visible communities' (after Alibhai-Brown 2001) to describe people of Asian, African and Caribbean backgrounds. Terminology around ethnicity is highly problematic, and after a great deal of reflection during and since the research, I'm opting for this term to avoid both the homogenising tendencies of the term 'black' (as critiqued by Modood 1992) and the power-laden term 'minority'. 'Visible communities' is *not* intended to reify visible difference from a white 'norm', but I use it as a *political signifier* to highlight that there are power inequalities endemic in English society, which are commonly grounded in perceptions of inferiority and threat attached to visible difference from a white 'norm' – especially in the English countryside.

And let me offer an overview. There is an important body of work around the social exclusion of visible communities and racism in the countryside (see Milbourne 1997; Cloke and Little 1997; Neal 2002; Agyeman and Neal 2006), which in terms of fear/anxiety tends to focus on the fear experienced by visible communities through both emotional and physical exclusion. However, I want to concentrate on the role of fear among white society in processes of social and spatial exclusion, and how we might progressively theorise and practically address this fear. Visible ethnic difference *is* recognised and reacted to, and non-white bodies continue to be marginalised as other in English society within everyday perceptions of difference caught up in global discourses around fear and 'terror' (see also Haldrup et al.; Hopkins and Smith; Hörschelmann; Noble and Poynting in this volume). Given this, my narrative opens by examining debates regarding 'positive action', multiculturalism and equality, and how they remain trapped in/by the paradox of essentialising visible communities as always already and only different. Next, working through the construction of 'strangers' in dominant identifications of this other, I suggest that the concept of 'monsters' offers a more honest engagement with otherness. It first demands effacing the ambivalence accorded difference (awe as well as fear), and also offers a strategy for acknowledging, appreciating, holding on to the impossibility and possibility *of sameness between self and other*.

While most of my discussion surrounds issues regarding identity construction in place, the chapter moves on towards the end to focus on place and space itself. I argue that we need to understand the rural as positioned within a web of spaces, local, national and international, and call for a serious commitment to conceiving space relationally in order to shift exclusive constructions of ethnic difference and *who* can be *where* in contemporary England. Across the research, space as *different and similar* appeared interdependent within people's everyday geopolitics around fear and belonging: dualistic constructions of very fixed 'rural versus urban' rubbing alongside understandings of these spaces as porous, mobile and plural. I suggest that progressive theorising around multiculturalism/inter-ethnic encounters, which predominantly remains trapped in the 'only urban' realm, needs to critically engage with rurality; while thinking about the rural needs to engage with notions of multi-ethnic citizenship – that the rural sees itself and is thought through as a multicultural space.

(Re)viewing Rural Others

Positive Action: Multiculturalism, Difference and Equality

Throughout the research, visible community participants reiterated a desire to 'be together', to sustain mutual support and a sense of security, as well as emphasising that they should be encouraged and actively enabled to visit national parks. People described this need for positive action as necessary to redress imbalances endemic in English society, drawing on a discourse of 'strategic essentialism' (after Hall 2000). Such calls for specific attention can be argued to stem from an 'affirmative politics of recognition' (Fraser 1995), wherein visible communities challenge lived experiences of exclusion using the same fixed, essentialised identities through which they are marginalised. Rattansi (1999) links such 'affirmative politics' to an 'additive' model of representation central to the multiculturalism of liberal cultural pluralism pursued in England over the last two decades – a model based on minority-driven demand for 'recognition' and social advancement for racialised groups, with each 'minority' group 'added on' as/when it claims to be recognised.

The intention of a 'politics of recognition' and positive action projects is to achieve equality of opportunity, through emphasising ethnic and cultural rights *based on difference*, and promoting the celebration of cultural pluralism. As Parekh (2000, 240) states:

> Equal rights do not mean identical rights, for individuals with different cultural backgrounds and needs might require different rights to enjoy equality in respect of whatever happens to be the content of their rights. Equality involves ... full recognition of legitimate and relevant [differences].

The research engaged with positive action initiatives, in particular the work of the Black Environment Network (BEN) and a three year project jointly

Plate 17.1   Affirmative politics of recognition

Source: The Mosaic Partnership.

managed by BEN and the Council for National Parks called the Mosaic Project. Both Mosaic and BEN foreground the excluded status of people from 'ethnic' backgrounds,[2] campaigning for positive action to enable 'ethnic minority' participation in the mainstream environmental field, raising awareness of ethnic and cultural difference and highlighting the responsibilities of public bodies to be inclusive of diverse communities. Despite the positive aspects of this 'additive model' approach, however, within the research it seemed that countryside managers continued to see visible communities as rural others, as *only* different *and fixed*. Thus visible communities remained racialised. There is a need, then, to unsettle any 'celebration' of 'other' cultural practices that refuses the possibility of fluidity, pluralism or intercultural similarity – to avoid essentialising groups through emphasis on *difference as spectacle*. As Bennett (1998, 4) writes:

> ... state-managed multiculturalisms reify and exoticise alterity; addressing ethnic and racial difference as a question of 'identity' rather than of history and politics, they

2   BEN 'uses the word "black" symbolically' and states that it works 'with black, white and other ethnic communities' (BEN, 2003). In real terms, BEN predominantly engages with ethnic *minority communities*, who come from Asian, African Caribbean, Middle Eastern and Eastern European backgrounds.

translate alterity as cultural diversity, treating difference (a relation) as an intrinsic property of 'cultures' and as a *value* (a socially 'enriching' one), to be presented as such. [Emphasis in original]

Exactly this kind of emphasis, albeit well-intended, was exemplified by an event held in the Peak District. Attended by national park staff, other relevant countryside management actors and visible community groups who had participated in the Mosaic Project, the day included lunch prepared by the visible community groups (each group contributed 'traditional' dishes to a buffet), followed by an afternoon devoted to 'ethnic minority activities': a tai chi workshop led by the Chinese group; henna tattooing by Indian women; Asian silk screen painting run by 'an Asian group'; a display of 'urban black street dancing' by 'urban black dancers', etc. While it was an enjoyable and 'successful' day, it was an invitation-only event (out of sight of visitors and residents), in which people performed to specific stereotypes. Undoubtedly, some intercultural exchange occurred between the visible community groups present, but for the national park staff/countryside managers it was a one-way 'see and learn' experience reiterating visible community difference.

This pluralist approach is applauded/demanded by many as part of the liberal multicultural agenda, as enthusiasm for African Caribbean carnivals, Asian Melas and the popularity of the Mosaic Project attest. Yet there has also been an increase in recent years of a 'politics of resentment' (Wells and Watson 2005) among white (often but not only working class) groups to such 'affirmative politics of recognition', fuelling ethnic tensions in society. Bhattacharyya (1998, 259) critiques the 'feel-good multiculturalism' of cultural relativity as increasingly at odds with contemporary British society in which, given the widespread vilification of Muslims, pluralism seems a 'concept out of time', and sees the possibility of a multiculturalism based on 'getting by in cheerful diversity' decreasing. Thinking about events across the world since, her analysis rings even more acutely. 'Cheerful diversity' in the everyday has arguably been replaced by a geopolitics of fear fuelled by a dominant western international discourse placing Muslims as feared and dangerous Others, which is then elided with people of Asian appearance, slipping further to (re)attach fear/ danger to any/all non-white others (see Hopkins and Smith in this volume).

Indeed, political concern that cultural pluralism hasn't worked, especially apprehension surrounding the sense that society is increasingly segregated (for example, see Bunting 2007) has led to a shift towards the ideology and rhetoric of 'community cohesion'. The cultural/ethnic other is no longer allowed free rein to be different – they may be different only as long as they adhere to a set of shared ideals and values (Cantle 2001). These ideals and values, though, are non-negotiable and inevitably determined by dominant (white) society. From commitment to an 'English' sense of 'fair play', to oaths of allegiance, to the requirement to pass a 'Citizenship Test', there appears an inherent understanding of community cohesion that closely echoes the common (lay) understanding of 'integration' as a process in which minorities adopt majority values and practices: a one-way process. And this narrow understanding of cohesion was evident in countryside organisations' approaches to positive action initiatives. Events targeting visible communities aimed to 'bring them' into the countryside, to 'introduce them' to 'our' wildlife, 'our' traditions and 'our' values and practices, with the expectation that 'they' will adopt/conform to these traditions, values and practices. A key example is the construction of 'acceptable behaviour' in the rural. Alongside a Countryside Code outlining 'dos and don'ts' regarding wildlife and habitat conservation, the research found unwritten rules of behaviour that are culturally circulated. These include being quiet, undertaking passive activities, and maintaining a sense of 'decorum': 'being unobtrusive and respectful' and 'keeping standards up', with an (often implicit) understanding that large group visits, parties/celebrations, or playing (loud or indeed any) music, are not appropriate activities/behaviour in national parks.

Examined more closely, though, these dominant values are context- and identity- dependent. Large group visits often take place, with coach loads of older retired people in particular welcomed at market towns and visitor centres. Open air concerts are acceptable – promoted! – when 'properly' organised and with specific, 'appropriate' musical genres. And scenic rural settings remain popular with wedding parties. However, visible community groups visiting the countryside with the Mosaic project turned heads that a similar size group of white ramblers wouldn't. And in one interview, a visitor centre member of staff talked about a situation where a 'large group of Asians' had been spotted by residents and visitors in the Peak District, who had contacted national park rangers concerned that these might be terrorists, and the park staff had actually deliberated whether to contact the police. Instead, a ranger went to talk to the group (actually a dozen strong), who, it transpired, were celebrating a religious occasion. Positive action within a community cohesion agenda does nothing to derail racism if it ignores/denies dominant social constructions of others, or fails to question whose cultural practices are legitimate by (re)acting hypocritically towards practices common across groups.

So, neither cultural pluralism nor community cohesion address the need to combat continuing essentialism and ethnic stereotyping in rural areas. While the research clearly showed that positive action is an important catalyst to including visible communities in the countryside, and that cultural sensitivity is critical to social equality, it also suggested a need for a new approach incorporating both the positive aspects of cultural relativity alongside a recognition/acceptance of universal behaviours. Crucially, people are at the same time:

> ... both natural and cultural beings, sharing a common human identity but in a culturally mediated manner. They are *similar and different*, their similarities and difference do not passively coexist but interpenetrate, and neither is ontologically prior or morally more important. (Parekh 2000, 239 [emphasis added])

This emphasis on *difference and similarity as interconnecting* requires a fundamental shift in outlook. To enable progressive positive action, visible communities (and white ethnic groups), cannot be automatically construed as 'having' fixed cultural values based on their (visible) ethnic background – while at the same time being open to cultural specificity. At this point, then, I want to consider a more provocative engagement with otherness that complicates binaristic or reductive tendencies.

Plate 17.2   How different, how similar?

Source: The Mosaic Partnership.

Monsters not Strangers: Visible Communities and the English Countryside

I have drawn elsewhere on Sara Ahmed's conceptualisation of 'the stranger' to unpack the ways in which the non-white body is constructed as other or threat in the English countryside (Askins 2006). I want to work through and beyond such always already othering here to explore the potential for a more transformative politics of encounter. Ahmed (2000) writes that 'the stranger' is recognised not as someone unknown to us, but constructed already *as different*. Productions of 'the stranger', then, are tied up with the history of previous meetings and experiences between 'us' and 'them' attached to this recognition – and with socialised understandings of previous encounters between 'our' group and that of 'the stranger'. Significantly, stranger stereotypes incorporate ideas of potential threat, and this works both ways: 'they' fear 'us' as 'we' fear 'them' – thus, visible communities' anxiety about their reception in a dominant white countryside mirrors and is reflected by white fears around their presence. But it is through *unequal power structures* and notions of territorial ownership that these constructions lead to social exclusion based on visible difference. To accept the figure of the stranger as simply present conceals the antagonistic social relations that produce the stranger as a figure in the first place, and the materiality of these relations. As such, Ahmed questions the ontological possibility of strangers in the sense of the 'unknown', because strangers *are presumed known*, and argues that such productions of difference should be theorised through:

> ... thinking about the role of everyday encounters in the forming of social space ... Such differences are not then to be found *on the bodies of others*, but are determined through encounters between others; they are impossible to grasp in the present. (Ahmed 2000, 9 [emphasis in original])

But if this is the case, then how do shifts in perceptions of the other ever occur? At some point, in some present, change can happen – I believe the research evidenced such change, but catching hold of it and describing it has been and remains a tricky task!

I want to suggest that the concept of 'monsters' and 'the monstrous' may offer a way towards grasping shifts in the production of the other, drawing on the work of Sue Ruddick (2004). She writes that the idea of monsters is useful because, unlike strangers, the monstrous directly engages with issues of *recognised difference*, and as such enables a more honest, open connection with how we act towards/act upon our others. Monsters have been imagined and produced in response to anxiety about difference across human societies and throughout histories: the monster is different from 'us' and we acknowledge 'it' already as such. Moreover, the concept allows us to – demands that we – capture the *ambivalence* accorded difference: monsters are held *in fear* but also *in awe*. What makes working with this ambivalence valuable in the context of (re)viewing rural others is that it forces us to engage with difference that *simultaneously* evokes awe/interest even as it threatens, and it is this which facilitates the potential for a radical openness – an alternative engagement with an other (see also Haraway's (1992) 'promise of monsters').

Ruddick, drawing on Derrida, explains that the fear response leads not only to revulsion and exclusion, but also to an attempt by majority society to 'domesticate' the monster, to get 'it' to assume the habits of dominant society. This resonates with community cohesion discourses, and the ways in which countryside organisations attempt to introduce visible communities to the English countryside, via the 'correct' cultural practices and values. The awe response, on the other hand, leads to a celebration of ethnic difference – the positive pluralism of African Caribbean carnivals, Asian Melas, etc. Ruddick's project goes further than examining fetishism, though, invoking the radical openness of 'that uncomfortable and disquieting moment' to suggest that monsters themselves are *capable of 'domesticating' majority society* – the popularity of chicken tikka masala or the impact of 'black' music on the mainstream are two often cited examples of shifts in English culture that perhaps illuminate this point. What is so important about conceptualising this reverse influence is that it allows for and highlights an agency and subjectivity of the monster that is denied the stranger. And this is important because the research clearly showed that visible communities not only resist being positioned as 'outsiders' in the English countryside, but claim the countryside and country as multicultural and multi-ethnic (Askins 2006). Thinking about visible communities provocatively as monsters in the rural entails effacing the fear caught up in dominant constructions – the threat to 'traditional white' English identity occurs in *the fact* of multi-ethnic England, hence the anxiety around the presence of this new/different Englishness in the nation's perceived 'traditional white' space – and, crucially, how this is bound up in material exclusions … while at the same time acknowledging the awe of the other, *and* how both aspects play with and against each other. The transformative potential of the concept lies in the possibility that visible communities may domesticate dominant society – in any/all of its spaces.

However, monsters as feared and fetishised are still and only caught up with *difference*, and thus fall short of Parekh's contention that people's similarity and difference interpenetrate. What I believe the monstrous offers is the *technique* of thinking radically, a strategy to think inclusively beyond notions of a singular way of being, or singular reactions to an other being. This alternative engagement:

> … requires that we be able to hold onto that uncomfortable and disquieting moment before we collapse the other into someone 'just like us' (the pitfalls of certain forms of class and gender politics) or damn them into an irreconcilable 'them'. It begs the question: 'how are we to handle what is other without robbing it of its otherness?' (Mason 1990 cited in Ruddick 2004, 26)

A strategy of radical openness – retaining that disquieting/uncomfortable moment of unknowingness where and when *difference and similarity are ambiguous* – enables an engagement with the im/possibility of the other, a way to grapple with the interconnectivity of difference and similarity. Mindful of Ahmed's writing about ontology and strangers, I do, however, think that new, transformative engagements may potentially occur in the moment of encounter … or/and *in the moments that follow*. That is, during situations where/when we encounter otherness we may find our stereotypes challenged and shift our perceptions accordingly; or this can occur on reflection, after such encounters. The role of encounter may be important, the openness is critical.

I'm arguing, then, that the positive action and targeted outreach programs suggested through the research need to emanate from an ideology based on radical openness. What might such thinking look like in terms of policy, though? At the very least, positive action must be open to the range of possibilities of ethnic difference: celebrating cultural difference must be accompanied by *also* accepting other values and traditions regarding countryside practices – if you have henna tattooing at the countryside fair then you should also appreciate different cultural behaviours, perhaps large groups or picnics with music, in rural areas. More progressively, national parks need to hold the interconnectivities between difference and sameness at the core of positive action – targeting visible communities within programmes that also reach out to other groups identified as largely excluded from the countryside, working with visible communities separately where that need is identified, but also basing positive action on cross-cultural themes that enable people to come together. A key example identified in the research was a 'healthy living' focus – walking and food growing and cooking initiatives. Such progressive action is vital if national parks are to grasp the reality of a multiethnic England and move beyond fear. And critical within this project of rethinking identities is rethinking the spaces in which they play out.

(Re)placing the Countryside: Engagement across Rural-Urban Englishness

Towards an Emancipatory Countryside

There is an ever-developing and rich literature around multi-ethnicity, social inclusion, hybrid identities and transformative intercultural interaction in Britain (and more widely). Multi-ethnic encounters in places of work, school, consumption, leisure – 'spaces of everydayness' – are discussed as sites where people contest fixed identities, traverse cultures and negotiate difference, with the very local, the 'micropublic', imperative in reconciling ethnic and cultural differences (Back 2002; Houston et al. 2005). These are spaces where 'prosaic negotiations' are mandatory, and as such enable often imperceptible yet on-going cultural investigations and transruptions (Hesse 2000; Amin 2002). They are spaces of 'emergence', with the potential for cultural displacement and shift, where identities, values and practices can meet, dis/agree, merge and disentangle in such processes of negotiation. If we consider these sites closely, however, we are returned to the *everyday urban* as equated with such daily arbitration in encounters with ethnic difference. Cities as the spaces of inter-cultural and inter-ethnic potential, where monsters may be domesticated and may domesticate majority society. A new Englishness may be struggling into existence, but it appears to be restricted to a 'cosmopolitan urbanity' and isolated from a 'rural idyll', enabling the latter to retain its hegemonic whiteness that fears the visible community other.

In the research, however, while space was essentialised (with dualistic constructions of rural versus urban), it was *also* perceived as porous, mobile and plural. Senses of belonging in the English countryside were constructed by visible communities in complicated and contested ways that drew upon other ruralities across the world through diasporic and cultural memories, and people recognised themselves as English in multiple, hybrid and fluid ways that positioned the countryside within a web of national spaces (Askins 2006). Space as both *different and similar* appeared interdependent within people's everyday geopolitics around fear and belonging – indeed, the impact of a range of spatialities on identity and social relations is difficult to over-estimate, in particular the more subtle shades to identity that are influenced by movement (physical and emotional) across, through and between many spaces (for example see Lewis and Neal 2005; Yuval-Davis et al. 2005). These multiple identifications demand that the rural engages with notions of multi-ethnic citizenship and claims to nationality: that the rural *sees itself and is seen as a multicultural space*. And this in turn will entail de-privileging the urban as the only site of multi-ethnicity and multiculturalism in England.

Now, I can't suggest that the countryside be considered as everyday space for people from Asian and African Caribbean backgrounds living in England (or for the majority of English society, for that matter). But I think there is a need to re-envisage national parks and the rural more widely as *potential* sites of prosaic inter-ethnic and inter-cultural negotiation, as spaces of emergence, where visible communities can be and are present. Importantly, the countryside can no longer be viewed as a place that 'accommodates' or 'welcomes' other (than white) ethnic groups, which substantiates a fantasy of white supremacy that, even at its most 'benign', patronisingly speaks of 'tolerance' and 'welcome' while mistakenly believing that such tolerance or welcome is majority white society's to give (see Hage 1998). Instead, there is a need to decentre the position held by Anglo-Saxon history in national park narratives – rurality must be re-placed in the national imaginary as a space that *may compose* and *is composed of* multiple, hybrid and shifting ethnic identifications. The obvious flipside to this is that thinking about ethnicity, citizenship, multiculturalism and national identity *must engage with the rural*, in order to avoid the tendency to always already re-site multi-ethnicity only in the city. Reconstructing the rural as mobile or incorporating mobility, as a space of multi-ethnicity, will require being open to plural values and claims to national identity and belonging. A 'politics of propinquity and flow' (Amin and Thrift 2002) need to be brought to bear in the rural as much as in the urban – or, rather, across these spaces. We need, then, in theory, policy and practice, a serious commitment to the relativity of space (Massey 2004).

Plate 17.3   National parks as sites of negotiation

Source: The Mosaic Partnership.

So, I am arguing for a transformative geopolitics that not only attempts to juggle with simultaneous difference and similarity within identities, but also encapsulates the ways in which space as different and similar is interwoven through identity production. In the policy recommendations arising from the research, I suggest that positive action needs to focus on two main factors: facilitating encounters to unpack difference/similarity between and across groups (as mentioned in the previous section); and mediating such meetings *across rural/ urban space*. Importantly, and mostly lacking in initiatives aiming to increase visible communities' access to the countryside, encounters need to be *two-way exchanges*. Work needs to be done across the rural/urban divide commonly invoked in social imaginaries, to highlight links and explore differences in terms of perceptions of place. The onus shouldn't always be on urban visible communities to visit the countryside: rural white communities, and countryside managers especially, should experience an encounter in the city if cultural exchange rather than voyeurism is to occur, meeting visible communities in the neighbourhoods where they live or places where they work, rather than only meeting them in the national park and 'showing them' around.

And let me finish on an encouraging note. While the Mosaic project focused on enabling trips to the countryside, much was learned through its experiences and, about the time I finished my research, the CNP were successful in securing a further three years funding to take the initiative forward. Renamed the Mosaic Partnership to reflect changes in emphasis, it aims to 'broaden the range of people involved in caring for and influencing the future of National Parks'[3]. It encourages and supports 'community champions' from within visible communities to act as links between national parks/countryside managers and urban residents, as well as working with the national parks to effect meaningful organisational change. And the Community Champions Annual Event 2007, where national park staff and visible communities come together, took place in the city of Bradford ... with trips out to nearby countryside, of course.

Acknowledgements

To all involved with Mosaic, and everyone who participated in the research (funded through ESRC CASE studentship award no. S42200034003, with the North York Moors national park as CASE partners) – for so many (almost imperceptible!) moments of transformative encounter ... To Rachel for encouraging me to write against my stubborn instinct!

Bibliography

Agyeman, J. and Neal, S. (eds) (2006), *The New Countryside?: Ethnicity, nation and exclusion in contemporary rural Britain* (London: Policy Press).

---

3   See http://www.mosaicpartnership.org.

Ahmed, S. (2000), *Strange Encounters: Embodied others in post-coloniality* (London: Routledge).

Alibhai-Brown, Y. (2001), *Mixed Feelings: The Complex LIVES OF MIXED-RACe Britons* (London: The Women's Press).

Amin, A. (2002), 'Ethnicity and the Multicultural City: Living with diversity', *Environment and Planning A* 34, 959–80.

Amin, A. and Thrift, N. (2002), *Cities: Reimagining the urban* (London: Polity Press).

Askins, K. (2006), 'New Countryside? New Country: Visible communities in the English national parks', in J. Agyeman and S. Neal (eds), *The New Countryside?: Ethnicity, nation and exclusion in contemporary rural Britain* (London: The Policy Press).

Back, L. (2002), 'Guess Who's Coming to Dinner? The Political Morality of Investigating Whiteness in the Gray Zone', in V. Ware and L. Back (eds), *Out of Whiteness: Color, politics and culture* (London: University of Chicago Press).

BEN (2003), *Ethnic Environmental Participation*, vol. 4 (Llanberis: BEN Sharing Good Practice Series).

Bennett, D. (ed.) (1998), *Multicultural States: Rethinking difference and identity* (London: Routledge).

Bhattacharyya, G. (1998), 'Riding Multiculturalism', in D. Bennett (ed.), *Multicultural States: Rethinking difference and identity* (London: Routledge).

Bunting, M. (2007), 'United stand', *The Guardian*, June 13th.

Cantle, T. (2001), *Community Cohesion. A Report of the Independent Review Team* (The Cantle Report) (London: Home Office).

Cloke, P. and Little, J. (1997), *Contested Countryside Cultures* (London: Routledge).

Fraser, N. (1995), 'From Redistribution to Recognition? Dilemmas of Justice in a "Post-Socialist" Age', *New Left Review* 212, 68–93.

Hall, S. (2000), 'Conclusion: The multi-cultural question' in B. Hesse (ed.), *Un/settled Multiculturalisms: Diasporas, entanglements, transruptions* (London: Zed Books).

Hage, G. (1998), *White Nation* (Annandale, NSW: Pluto Press).

Haraway, D.J. (1992), 'The Promise of Monsters: A regenerative politics for inappropriate/d Others', in L. Grossberg, C. Nelson and B. Treichler (eds), *Cultural Studies* (New York: Routledge).

Hesse, B. (ed.) (2000), *Un/settled Multiculturalisms: Diasporas, entanglements, transruptions* (London: Zed Books).

Houston, S., Wright, R., Ellis, M., Holloway, S. and Hudson, M. (2005), 'Places of Possibility: Where mixed-race partners meet', *Progress in Human Geography* 29:6, 700–17.

Lewis, G. and Neal, S. (2005), 'Introduction: Contemporary political contexts, changing terrains and revisited discourses', *Journal of Ethnic and Racial Studies* 28:3, 423–44.

Massey, D. (2004), 'Geographies of Responsibility', *Geografiska Annaler* 86 B:1, 5–18.

Milbourne, P. (ed.) (1997), *Revealing Rural Others: Representation, power and identity in the British countryside* (London: Pinter).

Modood, T. (1992), *Not Easy Being British: Colour, culture and citizenship* (Stoke-on-Trent: Runnymede Trust and Trentham Books).

Neal, S. (2002), 'Rural Landscapes, Representations and Racism: Examining multicultural citizenship and policy-making in the English countryside', *Ethnic and Racial Studies*, 25:3, 442–61.

Parekh, B. (2000), *Rethinking Multiculturalism: Cultural diversity and political theory* (London: Palgrave).

Rattansi, A. (1999), 'Changing the Subject? Racism, Culture and Education', in J. Donald and A. Rattensi (eds), *'Race', Culture and Difference* (London: Sage).

Ruddick, S. (2004), 'Domesticating Monsters: Cartographies of difference and the emancipatory city', in L. Lees (ed.), *The Emancipatory City: Paradoxes and possibilities* (London: Sage).

Wells, K. and Watson, S. (2005), 'A Politics of Resentment: Shopkeepers in a London neighbourhood', *Journal of Ethnic and Racial Studies* 28:2, 261–77.

Williams, P. (1997), *Seeing a Colour-Blind Future: The paradox of race* (London: Virago).

Yuval-Davis, N., Anthias, F. and Kofman, E. (2005), 'Secure Borders and Safe Haven and the Gendered Politics of Belonging: Beyond social cohesion', *Journal of Ethnic and Racial Studies* 28:3, 513–35.

Afterword:
Fear/Hope and Reconnection

As far as fear is concerned geopolitics are local; everyday life is geopolitical. Documenting this, the aim of this book has been not just to shift the emphasis from authoritative, remote, top-down models of fear to more nuanced and grounded approaches, but to recognise and challenge the politics embedded in this scalar view of the fear assemblage. The chapters have not only underlined the complementarity and relationality of everyday and geopolitical fears, but have emphasised the extent to which the everyday always and already speaks back, resists, and changes seemingly immutable forces. So our aim has been not simply to reimagine what fear is, but to set out a new way of knowing what it is and how it works. We have worked, then, with the facticity of fear, its materiality and its emotional qualities, to challenge political attempts to manipulate fear and to find a space for – to enable – other ways of human being.

As many individual authors have shown, this is not merely an academic exercise. The issues covered have immediate and urgent relevance. Speaking from, through and back to fear, wherever it comes from and however it manifests itself in people and places, is a vital task. Not to confront the creeping materialisation of global fear in the landscapes around us is to let broader unjust political acts go unchallenged. At a time when the young urban poor and the homeless are vilified, during a wave of Islamophobia and caught in a tide of vitriolic hatred towards refugees and asylum seekers, paying attention to the fears of feared groups has never been more urgent. But this is not 'our' task as critical scholars. People have done and are doing this for themselves. In recent years, for example, refugees and asylum seekers in the west have self-organised and created positive innovative projects to tackle these issues. 'Our' role is not to determine people's futures for them but to think about how best to support these enterprises. Many of the authors in this collection have lent their resources to work which actively addresses the local fallout of global fears, as well as more longstanding issues; collaborating with communities and activist groups in their academic research, in an effort to harness and represent emotional geographies for more positive and empowering social change.

Such social movements are themselves emotionally charged. Emotions do not simply reflect, like a blank canvas, what happens in international or local politics; they actively drive political actions and events. Fear is often seen as a negative and disempowering emotion – and a monolithic one at that – but it has always been a powerful force that galvanizes new forms of political action. These actions are sometimes large scale, public, spectacular resistances; sometimes personal, quieter transformations. Loud politics might grab the headlines, but soft, small stories also make a difference.

Moreover, 'fear' is not a singular emotion, cut off in a separate category from the range of other affective states. Hope is threaded through the chapters in this book, coming out especially powerfully in the last section. How hope lies in relation to fear – as a response, an alternative, against it, or as simultaneous – is open to a debate we are not primarily concerned with here. For the moment it is enough to reflect on the extent to which every chapter signals a degree of hope that is always and already there, wherever fear raises its head. Accounts of resistance, resilience and positive action in the face of risk, danger and harm have made this clear, from feminists' earliest accounts of domestic abuse in the 1970s to recent restatements of Muslim identities in the west. Hope, like fear, holds tight the connective strands between geopolitical and everyday events and actions (see Figure 1.1b): emotions move between the two, interweaving these assemblages.

Like fear, too, hope is materialised and embodied in everyday environments and encounters. But hope is not new, poking its head out nervously in the face of threatening times. It has been practiced in age-old struggles, and paradoxically, as Sarah Wright suggests, it is most finely-tuned and enabling in some of the most desperate situations. And it can be borrowed and shared. Just as globalisation appears to proliferate risk and fear into a more oppressive biosphere around the world, so common political struggles in places which are far apart are rapidly shared and joined through new enabling technologies.

To hear the powerful/authoritative talk about fear is to envision it only as an oppressive, hopeless prison that fixes everyday lives in introversion and acquiescence. To listen to other accounts of real lives is to recognise robust rebuttals, resistances and struggles. We end on a hopeful note, already being written.

Index